Congratulations on finishing a great 2018 MGBL season. We aim to inspire deep Torah and Jewish values while also providing a forum for great sportsmanship and fun.

ArtScroll® Series

Rabbi Nosson Scherman / Rabbi Meir Zlotowitz

General Editors

TO BE A

Published by

ARTSCROLL®
Mesorah Publications, ltd

MENTCH

The Torah path
in interpersonal relationships

by Yitzchak Shkop

FIRST EDITION
First Impression ... August 2016

Published and Distributed by
MESORAH PUBLICATIONS, LTD.
4401 Second Avenue / Brooklyn, N.Y 11232

Distributed in Europe by
LEHMANNS
Unit E, Viking Business Park
Rolling Mill Road
Jarow, Tyne & Wear, NE32 3DP
England

*Distributed in Australia and New Zealand
by* **GOLDS WORLDS OF JUDAICA**
3-13 William Street
Balaclava, Melbourne 3183
Victoria, Australia

Distributed in Israel by
SIFRIATI / A. GITLER — BOOKS
Moshav Magshimim
Israel

Distributed in South Africa by
KOLLEL BOOKSHOP
Northfield Centre, 17 Northfield Avenue
Glenhazel 2192, Johannesburg, South Africa

ARTSCROLL® SERIES
TO BE A MENTCH
© *Copyright 2016, by* MESORAH PUBLICATIONS, Ltd.
4401 Second Avenue / Brooklyn, N.Y. 11232 / (718) 921-9000 / www.artscroll.com

*The author can be contacted via e-mail at: yshkop@ProspectResources.com,
and via phone at: 847-673-1959*

ISBN 10: 1-4226-1755-6 / ISBN 13: 978-1-4226-1755-7

Typography by CompuScribe at ArtScroll Studios, Ltd.

Printed in the United States of America by Noble Book Press Corp.
Bound by Sefercraft, Quality Bookbinders, Ltd., Brooklyn N.Y. 11232

The English edition is dedicated
to the memory of

Sara Chana (Anna) Lev-Toaff ע"ה

נלב"ע י"ד ניסן תשע"ה

Whose brilliance as a physician,
and devotion to her patients
was matched by the dedication to her parents
and her love for her sisters and children.

With gratitude to

Rabbi Shmuel Kurtz שליט"א

For painstaking and devoted work
in the initial translation of
מאיש לרעהו

לעילוי נשמות

אבי מורי הרה"ח ר' ישראל זאב שקופף ז"ל
בן הרה"ח ר' יצחק שמואל ז"ל
נלב"ע י"ג תשרי תשנ"ז

אמי מורתי מרת בלומה ע"ה
בת הרה"ח ר' יחיאל מיכל סטרובינסקי ז"ל
נפטרה בדמי ימיה בכ"ב שבט תשכ"ט

חמי הרה"ח הרב יהודה יוסף לב ז"ל
בן הרה"ח ר' אהרן ז"ל
נלב"ע י"ז ניסן תש"ע

חמותי מרת הינדה ע"ה
בת הר"ר הלל כהן ז"ל
הלכה לעולמה ביום א' דר"ח חשון תשס"ה

אשת אבי, אמי חורגתי
מרת מרים יקיר־שקופף ע"ה
בת הרה"ח הרב משה גוטליב ז"ל
הלכה לעולמה ביום א' דראש השנה תשע"ד

הרב אהרן פלדמן
RABBI AHARON FELDMAN
421 YESHIVA LANE, APT 3A, BALTIMORE, MD 21208
TEL.: 410-6539433 FAX: 410-6534694
STUDY: 410-4847200 EXT. 114
E-MAIL: RAF@NIRC.EDU

ROSH HAYESHIVA
NER ISRAEL RABBINICAL COLLEGE

ראש הישיבה
ישיבת נר ישראל

בס"ד יום ה' תשרי שנת פ"ק ולמאורי אב.

לכ' ידידי הרב ר' בלב שמח אל"ס

הנני אסיר תודה לו שזרי בספר החדש "מאיר נתיבו"
שעיינתי בו בספר תמות רבים דינים
שהשכיל לבאר (אבל) להריא לחזורו ט ת מוקדת והם
ושגובר מעיינותו תורה חזק חיים בחתם ופתח מה,
חפרתא דדינא להלכה דא מאשה יכיים כולה.

וערן שלומם,

ותפן פלומן

בע"ה

RABBI ARYEH MALKIEL KOTLER
BETH MEDRASH GOVOHA
LAKEWOOD, N.J. 08701

ארי' מלכיאל קוטלר
בית מדרש גבוה
לייקוואוד, נ. דז.

יום ועש"ק פ' משפ'

מע"כ מוהר"ר יצחק מינל שליט"א
אחדשה"ט באהבה

רב יקר

רא"ה הסכם הר"ר מאיר לידיהן וזעמ"ג יקר של כמ"ר,
כחמיות וחלט' דש"ם נחאתם וקימם לדידו בייני רבן ולם
לתמויו, ומסתפ' לפני יצ"ים הר רש של שועי ונ"צ פ',
לעבר לחם סכר פב, ויהי' להתקבלו דש"ו וצבו, לחמ" זו
ספ"ם פעונא , היחוא הרוסת בל לב שלי, כי'יקית וקומר

אוהב נא"ב גדול
כמחא' הא

Rabbi BARUCH M. EZRACHI
Yeshivat "ATERET ISRAEL" Jerusalem
DEAN

הרב ברוך מרדכי אזרחי
ישיבת "עטרת ישראל" ירושלים
ראש הישיבה

בס"ד [illegible] התשנ"ד

כבוד
הרה"ג רבי יצחק שרגא [illegible] הי"ו נ"י [illegible]
אחדשה"ט בהוקרה.

אומרים בשם מרן הגר"ש [illegible] זצוקללה"ה. כי "הגשמיות של זולתך היא הרוחניות שלך". ואולי יש להוסיף לאמרה זו, גם, כך: "הבין אדם לחבירו" של זולתך הוא "הבין אדם למקום" שלך.

הנני מלא התפעלות מספרך, כי זהו יסודו ומהותו של ספרך המעולה "מאיש לרעהו" [illegible] [illegible] של "בין אדם למקומו של עולם" [illegible] "בין איש לרעהו" [illegible] [illegible] [illegible] [illegible] [illegible].

ראיתי את [illegible] "מכתבים" [illegible] [illegible] [illegible] [illegible] "מאיש לרעהו" [illegible] [illegible] [illegible] [illegible] [illegible] [illegible] [illegible] [illegible] [illegible] [illegible] [illegible] [illegible] "מאיש לרעהו" חלק ב.

[illegible] [illegible] [illegible] [illegible] [illegible] [illegible] ברוחניות וגשמיות [illegible] [illegible] [illegible].

[illegible] [illegible] [illegible] [illegible]

ב. [signature]

רח' קסוטו 22, ירושלים 91051, טל. 421337, ת.ד. 5227
22, Kassuto St., Jerusalem 91051, Tel: 421337, P.O.B. 5227

Rabbi Dovid Zucker
6630 N. Mozart
Chicago, Ill. 60645
(773) 761-0212

דוד צוקער
ראש כולל
כולל זכרון שניאור
שיקאגו

בס"ד

עש"ק פ' וארא כ"ד שבט תשע"ד

לכבוד ידידי הרב ר' יצחק מיכל שקופ שליט"א

נהנתי מאד לראות פרי עמלך מעשה ידי אומן ס' "מאיש לרעהו" על עניני מצוות שבין אדם לחברו, שאתה מתכונן להוציא לאור העולם. והנה דבריו ערוכים ומסודרים בטוב טעם ודעת, וניכר שנכתבו ברוב עמל ויגיעה. ובודאי יהא לתועלת גדולה לכל מי שיעיין בו.

והנה כבר כתב המשך חכמה (ויקרא ט"ז ל') דחטא של מכירת יוסף הוא השורש לכל חטאים שבין אדם לחברו, ומטעם זה איתא בחז"ל (מדרש משלי, שוחר טוב סי' א') בשם ר' אבין "בכל דור עדיין חטא של מכירת יוסף קיים" עכ"ד. והנה הרמב"ם בשמונה פרקים (פ"ו) כתב דכל עבירות שבין אדם לחבירו, שהם מצוות שכליות, מעלת הנפש היא כשאינו מתאווה להם כלל. ובעו"ה מחמת אורך הגלות מצוות אלו צריכות חיזוק. וזכות גדולה נפלה בחלקו של מע"כ לעורר על ענינים אלו כדי לתקן אותו עון חמור שעדיין מרקד בינינו.

ונסיים בברכה להרב המחבר שליט"א שיזכה שיפוצו ממעינותיו חוצה ויזכה לאורך ימים ושנות חיים ולשמחות וכל טוב.

הכו"ח לכבוד התורה

דוד צוקער

דוד צוקער

RABBI Yitzchok M.Weinberg
Tolner Rebby
10 David Chazan st.
Jerusalem . Israel

יצחק מנחם וינברג
נכד אדמו"ר מטאלנא זצללה"ה
רחוב דוד חזן 10
בעיה"ק ירושלים תובב"א

Tel. 02-5825543 :טלפון

ב"ה, יום מוצש"ק ב' ויגש תשע"ג

כבוד הרה"ח בעל נפש יקרה עוסק בצ"צ באמונה
ומגדל את ילדיו בדרך התורה והמסורה עשה
ולהגדיל ולהאדיר מוה"ר יצחק סקאבל נ"י
אחדשה"ט

עברתי [illegible] על רשימת דבריך המחוכמים
בענין המצוה שאין אנו לחוגירו דברים שנאמרו
כשיעורים קבועים ברוב עם בעיר שאנחנו וכו'
ובעצה טובה הרבנו הדברים לפני ב' ספרים נכבדים.
והנה ענין זה של אין אנו לחוגירו הוא
דברים העומדים ברומו של עולם [illegible] חז"ל
מקלקלים בהם [illegible] מה נכבד היום [illegible]
[illegible] ובני אדם (שכמותם)
[illegible] על איפניו [illegible] בני מקומם
על אמירת השיעורים ועל [illegible] נכון וכו' של ה
[illegible] עולם [illegible] האמרים [illegible]
[illegible] והנני בברכתי לעם ישראל בכלל
[illegible] ולחזק את בני ישראל [illegible]
[illegible]

ISRAEL MEIR LAU
CHIEF RABBI
TEL-AVIV-JAFFA, ISRAEL

ישראל מאיר לאו
הרב הראשי
תל-אביב-יפו, ישראל

בס"ד, ח' בטבת תשע"ד
8 בדצמבר 2013

מכתב ברכה

היה לפני הרב יצחק מיכל שקופ שליט"א משיקגו ובידו עליס מספרו "מאיש לרעהו" הליכות
והנהגות במצוות שבין אדם לחבירו.

ספר זה תורתנו ולידתו משיעור שנמסר ע"י הרב המחבר שליט"א, לבעלי עסקים, במרכז העסקי
של שיקגו, המבקשים לדעת מהי חדרך הישרה שיבור לו האדם העסוק למחייתו. על חובתו
לשאת ולתת באמונה, לקבוע עיתים לתורה, להתרחק מחשיער וחרמיה, ושאר מצוות שבין אדם
לחבירו.

מהמעט המעיד על המרובה שערכתי, ראיתי את חשיבות החיבור, ואת ראיית המחבר מש"ס
ופוסקים על ענייניס אלו אשר הם עומדים ברומו של עולם ובני אדם מולעלים בהם. וחיא
השאלה חראשונה שנשאל האדם בבואו לפני בית דין של מעלה, "נשאת ונתת באמונה", כמבואר
בגמ' שבת לא.

ב"ה אכשר דרא, וספרים רבים בכל מקצועות התורה יוצאים מידי יום ביומו, אך בנושאים שבין
אדם לחבירו הענין העיקר חסר מן הספר. אמנם חס"ק רבינו חחפץ חיים זצ"ל, חיבר ספרים
בנושאים אלו, "חפץ חיים", "שמירת חלשון", "אהבת חסד", ועוד, וזעק את חומרת עוונות
שבין אדם לחבירו ובפרט חטא לשון הרע שנעשה אבל רבים כהיתר גמור, ודבריו עשר פירות, אך
עדיין יש חרבה לתקן בזה. וידוע מה שאמרו בזה בשם רבי ישראל מסלנט זצ"ל שאדם נזהר
ונשמר ממה שהוא מכניס לפיו, אבל אינו נזהר במה שהוא מוציא מפיו.

הרב חיד"א בספריו כותב פעמים רבות שאותו שטן שהחריב את ביתנו על חטא שנאת חינם
הכולל בתוכו את איסור לשה"ר, רכילות ומחלוקת, עדיין הוא מרקד ביניני. על כן בואו ונחזיק
טובה לרב המחבר שליט"א על אשר קבץ אל פונדק אחד את חלכות אלו.

והנני לברך את הרב המחבר שליט"א אשר כל כוונתו לשם שמים לזכות את חרבים, שיעשו
דבריו רושם בלב הקוראים, ויעלה בידו לחרבות אהבה ואחוה בין איש לרעהו, ובזכות החיזוק
במצוות שבין אדם לחבירו נזכה לראות את בית הבחירה עומד על תילו.

ביקרא דאורייתא,

הרב ישראל מאיר לאו

לשכה: רח' אורי 1, ת.ד. 9, תל-אביב-יפו 61000 - טל' 03-6938911 - פקס: 03-6938912
OFFICE: 1, URI ST., P.O.B. 9, TEL-AVIV-JAFFA, 61000, ISRAEL - TEL: +972-3-6938911, FAX: +972-3-6938912
e-mail: lau@rabanut.co.il :דוא"ל

רבי מאיר חדש זצ״ל Rav Meir Chadash זצ״ל
רבי שמחה וסרמן זצ״ל Rav Simcha Wasserman זצ״ל

ישיבת אור אלחנן
YESHIVA OHR ELCHANAN

הרב משה מ. חדש
ראש הישיבה

ע״ש הגאון הקדוש
רבי אלחנן וסרמן הי״ד

Rav Elchanan Wasserman זצוק״ל

ט׳ טבת תשע״ב פעיה״ק ירושלים ת״ו

בס״ד

אבואה בכמה שורות לשבח מפעלו של ידיד נפשי הרה״ג ר׳ יצחק שקלים שליט״א ספר „ואהבת לרעהו" אסופת מאמרים-שיעורים שנאמרו בציבור לפני שומרי תורה ודעת בעניני מוסר ומצות שבין אדם לחברו ובדיני של נשא ונתן באמונה.

הנה אני מכיר את בית-המדרש בשיקאגו. בית שמקיימין בכל שנים כבוד התורה וכבוד הבריות. מקיימים בהידור מצות ואהבת את ה׳ אלקיך וגו׳ שיהא שם שמים מתאהב על ידיך. שיהא אדם קורא ושונה ומשא ומתנו באמונה ודיבורו בנחת עם הבריות, מה הבריות אומרות עליו, אשרי אביו שלימדו תורה אשרי אביו אשרי רבו וכו׳ ומעשיו מתוקנים ועליו אומר בך אתפאר.

והנה אנו מתפעלים מהשפעה בימינו, אשר משמיעים להרבות דברי תורה של תורה בשיעורים קבועים לפני הציבור, שיעורים שנאמרים בטעם ודעת ובהבנה נעימה ומושכת כיד ה׳ הטובה עליו ונותן להם להשפיע רבה לגדולים וקטנים.

„ואהבת לרעהו" נוסף כותרת לציבור להגדיר את ההרגש במצוות שבין אדם לחברו, ויהי שימלאו משאלות לבם להשפיע להעלות קרנה של תורה, ובמיוחד תורת המוסר לחזק התורה ואהבת הבריות. ויהא רב נחת ממפעליהם היקרים.

הכו״ח לכבוד התורה
באהבה משה מרדכי חדש

27 Oholiav St., P.O.B. 36200, Jerusalem, Fax. 537-5002 .פקס Tel. 538-3666 .טל ,36200 .רחוב אהליאב 27 ירושלים ת.ד

RABBI NAFTALI JAEGER
ROSH HAYESHIVA

בס"ד אור לא' תמוז תשנ"ג

כבוד ידידי מוקירי רבנן שלהו גוליה
ולרבא מבחרן הרב כ' יתתן נ"י יאיר וזרח

[טקסט בכתב יד בלתי ברור]

"אמר לדודי על לבי והלכות רב אחם
אמרתי. ודאי על עניני... (ואמה על הדין
הכי... הלון מאד נתבלאבל... איך לברכם
חולה מן המעלות דהכי... רבותינו
הראשונים והאחרונים... הרבה דעות והלה הלון
כאה... על... לברן אחר סוג א רבה כ
ואחרונתו (ודאי כי לו ענאותינו... העון ואם
אין מ"ס... אמרו... יהבו... אחר היין ולו
א כן דעת משפט... ולזון... נם דעת... כך
אריכות כן אחם אמרתי... לא לך אריכות לבלתי
ויריך מהב... לא נם על ולרואים... פולין דין
את אחיו ולאראתי... רפתיך יטע ולאחד
אל אום דניאות והנה דאלא בא רואלם האו
ענ... לאבכן ספכו דר... אלא... לבכ... גנה
לבאל... רב אמול אאה... כל ה... לב... ל ...
גא לכלו דאו... אל אות... כל היך... הלם לי...
עשבון... כ א הוך כ' אהרן...

...לברכה נהכב הלל

[חתימה ושורות נוספות בכתב יד]

שער ישוב
SH'OR YOSHUV
INSTITUTE

ONE CEDARLAWN AVENUE • LAWRENCE, NY 11559 • (516) 239-9002 • FAX: (516) 239-9003

שאול אלתר
ראש ישיבת שפת אמת
ת.ד. 41160
עיה"ק ירושלים

בס"ד, ה' אדר תש..ה לפ"ק

.9.9. נ... ונו... הרב .לנתק אבכ... אקפם ש',
אשר אירה.ל מונה קא.לוחת חשבן כספין, ואאוד לקה..ז. ד.בם ש..צ.אף לאור
לקבוע זאת את הנהיג, ומם בהויה ..ורח ..ה.ה.ת, ..כ ..דור 6 אולפו,
..ולב ל.נ.ע בן .וסורות ..ואונ. וא.אה ו.ן ..ל.ל.ע ..הן אפא לא..ע,
ו...וא.. .ל.א.... ..חד ...ל.או ..ל.בם, ..ורד ..ה.ל.. ..הה ..א.ל..ורות
..ל.ק ..ד.נ..ת ..חו.ק.ו.ות ..ל.א.א..א ..ן ד.ל.ע אל.ק.ם ו.א.בם, ..ה.. ..ק.ק
..ה.מ.א ..ה.ל.א ..א.נ.ע .ל.ע ..ד.כ.ד ..ע.ק ד.ל.ע ..ל.א ..ל.ב.א .ק.נ.א.

כ.נ.ע ..ד.ו

Shlomo Moshe Amar
Rishon Lezion Chief Rabbi Of Israel
President of the Great Rabbinical Court

שלמה משה עמאר
הראשון לציון הרב הראשי לישראל
נשיא בית הדין הרבני הגדול

בס"ד - לפנים שיקרא, הטוב בשבת חמשה ימים בשבט התשע"ד.

לאגרת ברכה והצלחה

הנביא ישעיהו ע"ה אמר ואמר, ובא לציון גואל ולשבי פשע ביעקב נאום ה'. ואני זאת בריתי אותם אמר ה', רוחי אשר עליך ודברי אשר שמתי בפיך, לא ימושו מפיך ומפי זרעך ומפי זרע זרעך אמר ה', מעתה ועד עולם. והן הם דברי הקדוש ה' הגואל הגואל...

[המשך הטקסט בכתב יד]

באמצע שורות...

... ויהי רצון שיתקיים בו ובכל שהתקיים בו ואנשי ביתו כל שנאמר, ואמרת שבת... ונאמר נחמות...

כאשר בישרת... ברחמים, ה' צבאות... נ"א א"ר... אמן סלה.

Table of Contents

Dedication

Words are inadequate to express thanks and praise to the Almighty Who bestowed upon me the blessing of a "woman of valor." I acknowledge my gratitude to my wife, Esther Malka *amv"s*, daughter of Rabbi Yehuda Yosef Lev *zt"l*, who exemplifies many of the principles promulgated in this book. She has devoted her entire life to the education and edification of Jewish women, and the fruits of her labor make their mark across the globe, where her students enrich and enlighten their families and communities. Her concern and sacrifice for so many of her students — past and present — know no boundaries, as she relates to each one as her own daughter. Her willingness to help friends and strangers — hosting so many in our home with genuine warmth and empathy — model the behaviors and attitudes which are the focus of this book.

There was never an iota of doubt that Torah learning is the supreme value which motivates her life's work. Throughout our marriage, she has encouraged my learning, and was willing to make untold sacrifices to enable it. I cannot recall a single instance in which she interrupted my learning to ask for my help with the household chores or childrearing — though there must have been many such occasions when she needed that help. Aside from supporting my learning during all these years, she invested untold time and effort in assuring that this book would accurately express my intentions. How apt are Rabbi Akiva's words, "Mine and yours are hers."

May Hashem grant us many years of good health and spiritual enlightenment, and may we both continue to enjoy much nachas from our children and grandchildren, as He fulfills our hearts' desires for the good.

I dedicate this book to Yishai and Bluma, Ephraim and Chana, Elie and Adina, Yisroel Menachem (Srulik) and Racheli, Ahuva, Binyamin and Fraidy, Aharon Ephraim (Archik) and Miriam (Mimi) — with heartfelt gratitude and joy for your love and support. We are so proud of your accomplishments and your devotion, particularly in the manner in which you exemplify loving-kindness to others, near and far. You demonstrate concern for others through multiple acts of chesed fulfilled with humble sensitivity — and in so doing you have earned the esteem and affection of all who know you.

Preface

I *will thank Hashem exceedingly with my mouth, and amid the multitude I will praise Him (Tehillim 109:30) — for He has kept us alive, sustained us, and enabled us to reach this day —* upon which I merited to publish the English edition of my book, *Me'Ish L'Re'eihu*, written in Hebrew on the basis of my *shiurim* on the topic of interpersonal mitzvos.

Due to my upbringing and the exemplary role models I saw in my parents' home, this topic has always been close to my heart. The preparation of *shiurim* on interpersonal mitzvos enhanced my awareness of their profound importance and motivated me to disseminate this knowledge with the hope that *study will bring to action*.

I am fortunate to have my office in a very unique office building — owned and populated by members of the observant Jewish community in Chicago — in proximity to the Jewish neighborhoods. It is home to a large synagogue — Binyan Olam — that also serves as a *beis medrash* (study hall) that is a hub of continuous learning throughout the day. My monthly *shiurim* are delivered in the middle of the day to those who work in the building, as well as to others who come from around the city.

Many of the participants in the *shiur* (study group) are acquaintances and neighbors, who meet each other before, during, and after work. The frequency of their encounters and the matrix of their business and neighborly associations increase the chance of misunderstandings and flawed relationships. These realities catalyzed my efforts to expand the listeners' knowledge, while emphasizing practical applications for everyday living. Indeed, the synthesis of the many sources cited in each lesson with "real-life" conclusions has generated the most positive feedback from regular participants.

Addressing an audience of diverse backgrounds, men and women of various levels of erudition, requires a special teaching style. Similarly, in writing this book, I was determined that its style and language should be comprehensible to a broad spectrum of readers. Entire treatises could be written (indeed, many have) on numerous topics contained in this book. However, my purpose in writing this *sefer* was not to anthologize the scholarly sources on each mitzvah. Rather, I wanted to awaken interest and attention to the subject of interpersonal mitzvos in general, and particularly to the issues selected for this book. I endeavored to collect and sift through a tremendous amount of material and to present it in a way that would facilitate easy and pleasurable reading, while at the same time generating fluency with the sources.

This book follows the content of the Hebrew version, but it is by no means a literal translation. I wish to express my deep gratitude to Rabbi Shmuel Kurtz, who undertook the vast majority of high quality literal translation of the Hebrew book, and to Rabbi Shlomo Cook who translated a few chapters. Their work provided the raw material which then required a great deal of editing, as well as adding and subtracting of content. Words cannot express the gratitude I owe to my dear wife, Esther *amv"s*, who spent hundreds of hours polishing the material to its final format, and assured the reliability of translation and contemporary style for the book.

I wish to thank the *Mara D'Asra* of Binyan Olam, Rabbi Tzvi Feiner, who encouraged me to start these lectures, and to the *gabbai*, Rabbi Shlomo Cherrick, who announces and records every *shiur*, and sends a copy to anyone who requests. It goes without saying that I am grateful to all of the participants who "abandon" their work in the middle of the day to attend and actively participate in the lessons. The feedback and the encouragement that I receive from the participants give me the strength and the motivation to continue. My gratitude is extended to Azriel (Azi) Feifel and the entire staff of Prospect Resources Inc. for their dedication and commitment, enabling me to devote the time for learning and writing required to produce this book.

Likewise, I wish to express my appreciation and gratitude to my *mechutan*, Rabbi Tzvi Ryzman, who personifies the dictum, *"Make your Torah learning primary and your occupation secondary,"* for inadvertently motivating me to write this *sefer*. His own works entitled *Ratz KaTzvi*, triggered my קִנְאַת סוֹפְרִים, the jealousy of authors to imitate the achievements of others, in order to increase wisdom. I am not sure that without his personal example, I would have even considered the possibility of writing my own *sefer*.

Without elaborating upon the importance of the interpersonal mitzvos, it is sufficient to note that our Sages attributed many of our national calamities and tragedies to the indifference and demeaning attitudes of one Jew to another. To our great chagrin, our own generation does not excel in its meticulous observance of these mitzvos, though it may exceed previous generations in the quantity of charity and acts of kindness. It is my hope that this *sefer* will contribute to a greater understanding of the importance of interpersonal mitzvos and will motivate an improvement in their observance in our daily conduct. By doing so, may it hasten the coming of *Moshiach* in our days, *Amen*.

Yitzchak M. Shkop

1

Stringency in Mitzvos Between Man and G-d in Contrast to Leniency in Interpersonal Mitzvos

---

◆§ An Exquisite Esrog or Clothes for the Wife and Children?

The sights and sounds in Jerusalem on the eve of Succos heralded the arrival of the joyous festival. As a young kollel student, I headed toward the home of R' Shalom Eisen, of the *Beis Din Tzedek* of the *Eidah Chareidis,* for his assessment of an *esrog* I considered buying. Upon entering the courtyard of Batei Neitin, I saw a long line of men on the exterior staircase leading to R' Eisen's apartment on the third floor. As I reached the apartment, Reb Shalom asked me to stand at his side to observe and listen.

Among those in line was a young kollel scholar who was literally shaking with joy. The *esrog* in his hand was beautiful, and he was confident that Reb Shalom would praise its splendor and beauty. He handed over the *esrog* and watched as Reb Shalom turned it around and around, checking for any possible imperfections.

Abruptly, Reb Shalom lifted his head and with a penetrating look, said to the young man in a quiet yet forceful tone, "For you, this *esrog* is disqualified!" Stunned, the young man tremulously asked, "What flaw did the Rav find in my *esrog*?" Reb Shalom answered him with a question: "How much did you pay for this *esrog*?" The young man nervously responded, "One hundred *lirot*."

Reb Shalom sighed deeply and said, "Just as I thought. Indeed this *esrog* is exceptional in its beauty and has no imperfection whatsoever; therefore it is so expensive." Before the young man grasped his intentions, Reb Shalom turned to him and inquired, "Did you buy new clothes for your wife for *Yom Tov* yet?" He responded, "No, I am a kollel student and do not have the means to buy new clothes for my wife for every *Yom Tov*." Reb Shalom pressed his line of questioning, "Have you bought new clothes for your children for *Yom Tov*?" He hesitantly replied, "I already told the Rav that I am a kollel student and my income is very small. How should I have the money to buy new clothes for my family for *Yom Tov*?"

Then Reb Shalom stated emphatically, "For you, this *esrog* is disqualified! Go and return the *esrog* to the store and buy a regular *esrog* for fifteen *lirot*. With the remaining eighty-five *lirot*, go buy new clothes for your wife and children, in order to enhance their joy of *Yom Tov*, just as prescribed in *Shulchan Aruch*" (*Orach Chaim* 529:2).

I left Reb Shalom's home perplexed. I could not comprehend why some people are so extremely meticulous in performing the mitzvos between man and G-d, yet very lenient with regard to interpersonal mitzvos. Why did this G-d-fearing young man prefer to go all the way to buy an *esrog*, while ignoring an explicit Jewish law requiring him to enhance the festival joy and happiness to those who are closest to him — his wife and children?

৺§ Stringent for One, Lenient for Another

The phenomenon of neglecting interpersonal mitzvos is not limited to the uneducated or inexperienced, and — unfortunately

— can be found even among those who are otherwise very particular in their observance of mitzvos. Very often, the very same people who always consult a rabbi — even on the smallest detail regarding observance of mitzvos between man and G-d — will feel perfectly competent to decide on their own what is right or wrong in interpersonal behaviors. A prominent Rabbi in Israel succinctly defined the duality often observed in attitudes toward these two realms: "Behaviors between man and G-d that are not one hundred percent permissible are categorically prohibited; whereas, interpersonal behaviors that are not one hundred percent prohibited, are deemed permissible ...."

The lenient attitude toward interpersonal mitzvos, and the multitude of justifications people find for inappropriate behavior, are found in both premeditated and spontaneous behavior. A lack of consideration and respect for others finds expression in everyday, routine interactions. Indeed, on occasion a person tramples upon the dignity of another because he believes that he is actually fulfilling a mitzvah and gratifying his Creator. The following incident illustrates this point:

It was late Friday afternoon and the synagogue was quickly filling with men who had just shed their weekday clothes and donned their finest Shabbos garb. The last of the congregants had finally arrived and the *chazzan* began *Kabbalas Shabbos*. Suddenly, shrill shouting erupted, "*Muktzeh, muktzeh, muktzeh!*" interrupting the service, as all cast their gaze in the direction of the noise. I noticed one man yelling at another, "*Muktzeh!*" — pointing to some object in the other's hand, which in the eyes of his detractor was *muktzeh*. The sun was about to set and the Sabbath was just arriving, so he protested loudly until the alleged wrongdoer left the synagogue, deeply embarrassed. Only then did the disturbance subside and the *davening* continued.

Once again I found myself in a state of tremendous consternation. I did not understand which was more severe: the prohibition of *muktzeh* at dusk, when the sun has not yet set, and there is doubt if

Shabbos has begun, or the certain violation of shaming another Jew in public?! Couldn't the detractor voice his complaint in private? What was this person thinking when he disgraced his fellow man? How could he forget the saying of our Sages, ... הַמַּלְבִּין פְּנֵי חֲבֵרוֹ בָּרַבִּים אֵין לוֹ חֵלֶק לָעוֹלָם הַבָּא, *One who embarrasses his friend in public ... has no portion in the World to Come (Avos 3:15).*

✍§ A Worm and Not a Man

Such divergence in attitudes displayed toward mitzvos between man and G-d and the interpersonal mitzvos are not exclusive to our generation. An analysis of diverse sources indicates that this profound dichotomy has existed from time immemorial.

The *Pardes Yosef*, expounding on the verse, זֶה קֵלִי וְאַנְוֵהוּ, *This is my G-d and I will glorify Him (Shemos 15:2)*, refers to the Gemara in *Maseches Shabbos (133b)*:

> This teaches us that an individual should beautify oneself before G-d with mitzvos: make a beautiful *succah, lulav, shofar, tzitzis,* and *sefer Torah* — which should be written with the highest quality ink and quill, by the most expert scribe, and wrapped in the finest material. Abba Shaul says, "*V'anveihu*" — one should emulate G-d: just as He is gracious and compassionate, so too, you should be gracious and compassionate.
>
> I have seen many who are meticulous in this regard, and will spare no money to purchase a magnificent *esrog.* Yet, when it comes to charity, they are like a stone. This is what *Abba Shaul* intended — even though it is appropriate for a person to have a beautiful *succah*, this is not enough! The main thing is, "one should emulate G-d: just as He is gracious and compassionate ...."

The *Pardes Yosef* continues by elaborating on the verse in *Tehillim* (22:7) in which the Psalmist bemoans, וְאָנֹכִי תוֹלַעַת וְלֹא אִישׁ, *I am like a worm and not a man ....*

Many of the enemies of David HaMelech were very particular in their fulfillment of mitzvos between man and G-d: Before they would consume any food, they would check to ensure there were no worms … those same people treated interpersonal mitzvos with disdain and never ceased persecuting David and embittering his life. David chided them, "Why don't you, at least, treat me *like a worm and not a man ….*"

David recognized and understood that some of his adversaries displayed fear of Heaven and were scrupulous in their performance of the mitzvos. However, they considered it permissible (perhaps even a mitzvah) to malign and persecute David HaMelech. From the depths of his being arose an anguished plea that his enemies should be no less conscientious in their treatment of him than their diligent effort to avoid even the slightest possibility of eating a worm.

≈§ Hatred Equated with the Consumption of Pork

Often we witness internecine quarrels that drag down the entire family, tearing apart children and parents from one another. I knew a family of scholarly and observant Jews, in which three brothers suspected that their fourth brother had illicitly taken money from their parents, thereby depriving them of part of their future inheritance. The home setting became a virtual battlefield. Siblings did not speak to each other, and forbade their spouses and children any interaction with the children of the suspect brother.

The dispute exacted a heavy toll upon the parents, who were Holocaust survivors. They passionately begged their children to end the strife, disavowing the claim that the fourth brother had misappropriated any money. They further argued that even if he did, the money belongs to them and they totally forgive his alleged indiscretion, demanding that the siblings and their spouses cease their mounting and divisive argument. Their pleas fell upon deaf ears and the fires of conflict continued to rage. As mentioned, all of the brothers were scholars, devoting many hours to Torah study each day. Apparently they approached this controversy with the same enthusiasm, as if it were a mitzvah mandated by the Torah itself!

One day, after hearing the plight of the parents, I approached one of the brothers and told him that his behavior is worse than eating non-kosher food. Startled, he inquired, "How did you reach such a conclusion — to compare me to a person who eats non-kosher food?" I responded by quoting the *Chofetz Chaim* (*Kuntrus Ahavas Yisrael, Perek* 4):

> The verse proclaims, לֹא תִשְׂנָא אֶת אָחִיךָ בִּלְבָבֶךָ, *Do not hate your brother in your heart* (*Vayikra* 19:17). In what way is an individual who hates another any better than a person who eats non-kosher food? Just as one defiles his mouth by eating non-kosher food, so too, one defiles his heart with hatred!
>
> When the evil inclination tempts a person to hate his friend, he must respond, "Evil inclination, what are you thinking? Why do you constantly seduce me to loathe my friend? Every moment that you instill animosity in my heart, it is as if you are forcing pork down my throat!"

I then asked, "And, what about honoring your parents? They pleaded with you more than once to end the quarrel, yet you violate their wishes every second by not doing so!" I pointed out the precarious health of the elderly parents and my concern that the lingering quarrel will further deteriorate their well-being. I told him:

"This is potentially a trespass of לֹא תַעֲמֹד עַל דַּם רֵעֶךָ, *you shall not stand aside while your brother's blood is shed* (ibid. v. 16)! What about *lashon hara*? What about the prohibition of "*Not hating your brother in your heart* .... Furthermore, the Torah explicitly states, לֹא תֵלֵךְ רָכִיל בְּעַמֶּיךָ, *You shall not be a gossipmonger among your people* (ibid.). How much gossip have you spread about your brother and his family? Is it not 'easier' just to eat non-kosher food and violate fewer prohibitions?"

This man stared at me with anger, and I knew that I had failed in bringing peace to that family.

Once again I found myself at a loss: How is it possible that people who are so meticulous in the detail of every mitzvah and distance themselves from even the slightest prohibition, nonetheless go awry, do not consult with esteemed and experienced rabbis, and do whatever is right in their own eyes? They do not allow even the simplest doubt to enter their mind that perhaps their actions are not pleasing in the eyes of their Creator! On the contrary, it seems they are confident that their deeds are a delight to G-d. As I pondered the causes underlying such a horrific mistake, I found a few possible explanations.

🕉 The Self-Centered Human

The first explanation is the simple bias inherent in every interaction with others. A person can't be objective in judging his own behaviors. The Torah prohibits a man to preside as a judge if he is a relative of any of the parties, or is prejudiced in any way — under such circumstances he could not possibly render a fair decision. Yet, we all judge our own behaviors, and think we are making "objective" decisions about how we treat others, oblivious to our own blind-spots.

A story is told of the butcher of Brisk, who asked the Rabbi of the city about the *kashrus* of an animal that had just been slaughtered by the local *shochet*. The Rabbi investigated the issue, and ruled that the animal was not kosher. The butcher then sold the meat as "not kosher" at a substantial loss. A few days later the butcher had a monetary dispute with one of his suppliers. Both came before the Rabbi of Brisk to litigate their case. The rabbi heard the arguments of each party and ruled in favor of the supplier. As soon as the butcher walked out of the Rabbi's house, he spoke disparagingly of the Rabbi and his ruling.

The bailiff of the Rabbi's court, who was present during both of the butcher's cases, was shocked at this disgraceful behavior. He turned to the Rabbi and asked, "Why is it that when the Rabbi ruled that an animal is not kosher, the butcher did not even think of disparaging the Rav's decision, and lovingly and respectfully accepted it despite the financial loss. Yet, when he lost the case brought by his supplier and suffered a much smaller loss, he commenced defaming the Rav?" The Rabbi smiled and answered, "When the animal was declared not kosher, no one attacked the butcher's honor or self-esteem. However, when I decided in favor of the supplier the butcher felt humiliated and disrespected. He could not tolerate his honor being disgraced!"

An amazing passage in Tractate *Sanhedrin* (18b) illustrates the extent of the influence of self-interest, and its corruptive impact on a person's judgment. The *Gemara* considers disqualifying a high priest to adjudicate the question of establishing a leap year in the calendar. *Rashi* explains: A high priest would not want an additional month of Adar added, since this would advance the *Yamim Noraim* further into the chill of autumn, making his numerous immersions in the *mikveh* during the Yom Kippur service quite uncomfortable. This judicial process takes place in Adar, a full six months before Yom Kippur; nonetheless, a high priest is suspect that he will oppose this decision, due to his concern that he may suffer a little bit more from the increased cold at a much later date. Such is the power of self-interest!

The simple reality is that we serve as judges and bailiffs in our relationships with others. These biases have an impact on our actions and feelings toward the other, and it is extremely difficult to maintain any level of objectivity. We always need to question whether the choice to relate to someone harshly or pleasantly is the result of a prejudiced mind. Such choices require thoughtful analysis, and possible consultation with an astute Torah sage.

ᵉᔆ Rational Mitzvos

There is another possible explanation for the variant attitudes toward interpersonal mitzvos and those between man and G-d: The latter we obey to fulfill the will of G-d, even when we do not understand the reason for the mitzvah. No one would ever consider painting *tefillin* green or placing a *mezuzah* at the bottom of the door frame! We fulfill these mitzvos as we were told — whether or not they make sense to us.

That is not the case regarding interpersonal mitzvos. Most of these mitzvos are ostensibly understood, and are considered humanistic and rational. People do not view the commandments against theft or murder as religious in nature, and consider these imperatives binding on all people — regardless of their creed. These mitzvos prevent social chaos resulting from wanton theft and killing. It is clear that in order to have a functional society there must be an established system of justice. Furthermore, many actions of kindness and charity, visiting the sick, and the love of others are perceived as universal ideals befitting every society and nation.

Given that we comprehend so well the need for interpersonal mitzvos, we tend to fulfill them according to our own understanding. As G-d-fearing people, with some understanding of ethics and Halachah, we deem ourselves worthy of making our own decisions in these matters. It is self-evident that this perspective on interpersonal mitzvos is fundamentally flawed.

All mitzvos are Divine directives, and their fulfillment is mandated by the Torah, not by our understanding and intuition. History provides an endless list of appalling actions that have been done, and are being done, in "accord" with human intellect and best judgment. Enlightened nations have legitimized and rationalized genocide and horrific atrocities. On a smaller scale, we witness "decent" people justifying non-payment of debts, and rationalizing shady practices and even outright theft. Woe unto us if we allow human intellect alone to define what is permissible and proper in interpersonal relationships! Only the Torah, with its Halachah and ethical guidelines, can teach us what is the most appropriate and desirable conduct, as evident in the following vignette.

The Gemara in *Succah* (53a) records: "They said about Hillel the Elder, that when he rejoiced at the *Simchas Beis HaShoeivah* he declared, 'If I am here, then everything is here! If I am not here, who is here?'" This statement seems to display bravado and self-aggrandizement, two qualities that belie Hillel's fame as the epitome of humility. To explain this uncharacteristic statement by Hillel, *Rashi* insists that the "I" of this declaration does not refer to Hillel, but to G-d. G-d is saying, "If I am here, then everything is here!"

The interpretation of the *Tzitz Eliezer* (*Chelek* 13) on this matter is striking:

> The Sages (*Shabbos* 31a) relate about Hillel the Elder an incident in which a non-Jew came before him, demanding, "Convert me to Judaism, on condition that you teach me all of the Torah while I stand on one foot ...." Hillel the Elder converted him after teaching him, "Do not do unto others that which you despise! This is the entire Torah! The rest is commentary. Go and learn!"

Some mistakenly concluded — upon hearing of Hillel's words — that a Jew can fulfill his entire religious obligations by observing the interpersonal mitzvos, excluding mitzvos between man and G-d! In response to this mistaken interpretation of his words, Hillel referred to the verse (*Vayikra* 19:18) in the Torah that commands us to love another Jew, which opens with the phrase, וְאָהַבְתָּ לְרֵעֲךָ כָּמוֹךָ, *you shall love your fellow as yourself,* and concludes with the phrase, אֲנִי ה', *I am Hashem.*

> Our obligation is to know that it is only the word of G-d, as communicated to us in the Torah, which determines how the mitzvah of "*you shall love your fellow as yourself*" shall

be performed. This mitzvah is not given to the discretion of every individual to decide its content and means of fulfillment.

Accordingly, the *Tzitz Eliezer* concludes that what Hillel meant by saying, "If I am here ..." is:

> If the last phrase of the verse — *I am G-d* — is integral to the manner in which one expresses empathy and love for another, then "everything is here." But, if "I am not here," meaning, if the "*I am G-d*" is not central to the mitzvah, then "Who is here?" Such love of another person is not valued at all because it is neither permanent nor authentic. Whenever a personal interest interferes, the bond is destroyed and can degenerate into the worst ... even into hatred and war.

The proper performance of interpersonal mitzvos is conditional on the understanding that these mitzvos were given at Sinai, and the manner of their fulfillment is not dependent upon our understanding alone.

⇜§ Of Secondary Importance

Many people think that the mitzvos between man and G-d are just more important than interpersonal mitzvos, which are universal and logical. In their mind, since the mitzvos between man and G-d differentiate Judaism from other religions, they should be given higher priority. Unquestionably, this is fallacious thought, and has no basis whatsoever! *Rashi* already alluded to this misconception, and rejects it at the beginning of *Parashas Mishpatim*:

> וְאֵלֶּה הַמִּשְׁפָּטִים אֲשֶׁר תָּשִׂים לִפְנֵיהֶם, *And these are the ordinances that you shall place before them (Shemos* 21:1). Wherever it says *And these,* the verse is coming to add on to the previous verses; just as earlier verses are from Sinai, so too, are these from Sinai.

Just as the Ten Commandments and the building of the *Beis HaMikdash*, which are in the preceding *Parashas Yisro*, were said at Sinai, so too, all of the civil and monetary laws — which are interpersonal mitzvos, concentrated in *Parashas Mishpatim* and scattered throughout the Torah — were given at Sinai, and comprise one organic whole.

◄§ Perceived Permission

A fourth reason for the dismissive attitude toward interpersonal mitzvos is habitual violation on a daily basis. Habits — howsoever onerous — are hard to break and easy to rationalize. The Gemara (*Yoma* 86b) cites the words of Rav Huna on the proverb, כְּכֶלֶב שָׁב עַל קֵאוֹ כְּסִיל שׁוֹנֶה בְאִוַּלְתּוֹ, *Just as a dog revisits his vomit, so does a fool repeat his folly* (*Mishlei* 26:11):

> Once a man commits a wrongdoing and then repeats it …
> it is now considered by the wrongdoer a permissible act.

Metzudas David presents an analogy to explain this verse:

> Just as a dog goes back to eat the food which he had vomited, and does not understand that because of its contamination he vomited it in the first place, so too the fool repeats his folly upon which he stumbled, and does not understand the absurdity of his actions!

The *Malbim*, in his commentary on this verse, concludes that it would be foolish to try to convince such a person to change his ways. Habitual wrongdoing dulls a person's sensitivity to the severity of his actions. Furthermore, he convinces himself that it is not an offense at all. In many instances he even considers his hatred of another individual a positive action and mitzvah! The longer he perpetuates this behavior, the more he convinces himself that his actions are correct and justified. This person will refuse to see the truth, for to do so entails self-condemnation.

According to the *Chofetz Chaim* in his letters (*Siman 35*), this nonchalant and demeaning attitude toward interpersonal mitzvos is widespread, even among those who are otherwise punctilious in their religious observance.

> I have come to awaken only the wise of our nation, those who possess knowledge of the Torah, yet do not equate in their mind this prohibition with the consumption of non-kosher soup .... The reason for this is because this transgression has become permissible in the eyes of most people, who do not take notice of it at all. Consequently, this prohibition is treated frivolously even by the wise men of our nation, who do not afford it much attention.

In the forthcoming chapters we will amplify on the immense importance of the interpersonal mitzvos, the tremendous virtue of meticulous observance of these mitzvos, the outstanding reward that awaits an individual who is strict in their performance, and the severe punishment for those who treat them with disdain.

2

Interpersonal Mitzvos Are Also from Sinai

As mentioned in the previous chapter, one reason that people are very meticulous in their observance of mitzvos between man and G-d, yet are lenient regarding interpersonal mitzvos, is the notion that the essence of Torah and Judaism is concentrated in the mitzvos between man and G-d. In this chapter we will discuss sources that assert that the opposite is true! Not only are the interpersonal mitzvos of no lesser significance, but they are either of the same or greater import.

❧ You Shall Not Ascend My Altar on Steps

In *Parashas Yisro*, the Torah prescribed the construction of a ramp, rather than a staircase, upon which a *Kohen* would ascend to the Altar: וְלֹא תַעֲלֶה בְמַעֲלֹת עַל מִזְבְּחִי, *You shall not ascend My Altar on steps* (*Shemos* 20:23). In explaining this verse, *Rashi* cites the words of the Sages:

> To [ascend] on steps you need to widen your stride .... Doing so is a display of irreverence. These stones do not possess the intelligence to care about such treatment, yet the Torah said that since they provide a needed function, do

not treat them disrespectfully. All the more so, your friend, who is fashioned in the image of your Creator and does care about his shame, one must be careful not to mistreat him.

Why is the Torah so concerned about the preservation of the "honor" of stones — inanimate objects that neither feel nor understand anything? Perhaps, the Torah is teaching us a fundamental principle about the essence of interpersonal mitzvos.

Unquestionably, the ultimate aim of these mitzvos is the respectful treatment of another human being, who has inherent value as each is created in the image of the Creator. However, there is yet another purpose beyond this: to develop inner sensitivity and refined character, regardless of their impact on another person. *Rashi* writes that the reason one must be mindful of the stones is because they are needed and useful, and one must not disgrace something that he needs, even if it is inanimate. Such misconduct would reveal that this individual is lacking in the quintessential attribute of gratitude. (See the chapter on gratitude.)

There is an additional point alluded to in *Rashi's* words. Though the interpersonal mitzvos seem rational, the Torah teaches us here that it is incumbent upon us to fulfill these mitzvos according to the dictates of the Torah, and not based on our own understanding. Consequently, there are four key points that are important to emphasize regarding interpersonal mitzvos:

1) Interpersonal mitzvos were given at Sinai as an organic part of the whole Torah and there is no excuse for leniency in their fulfillment.

2) The Torah went out of its way to impress upon us that we need to conduct ourselves with extra caution and regard for the honor of another human being because he is created in the image of his Maker.

3) Often the purpose of an interpersonal mitzvah is not just to help another human being, but to cultivate good character traits.

4) In spite of the ostensive logic inherent in interpersonal mitzvos, nonetheless one is required to fulfill them because they are Divinely prescribed and not because of our endorsement of them. Furthermore, the manner of their performance must be in accord with the Torah and Halachah. Consequently, a person must confirm that he is doing these mitzvos in the halachically prescribed fashion, even if at times it may contradict his own reasoning.

The understanding and internalization of these points are unconditional prerequisites for the proper fulfillment of interpersonal mitzvos.

ᴥᔕ The Jewish Slave as a Paradigm for Interpersonal Mitzvos

Parashas Mishpatim is one of the primary sources for monetary laws in the Torah, yet opens with the laws pertaining to a Jewish slave. At first blush this demands some explanation: This *parashah* details significant legal doctrines, such as justice, the laws of torts and loans, the prohibition of taking bribes, etc. — issues that affect every person on an ongoing basis. Why, then, did the Torah choose to open it with the laws of a Jewish slave, which are not very common and apply only in certain times (they apply only when the entire Jewish people is living in the Land of Israel)?

One might suggest that the Torah chose this subject in order to emphasize a fundamental tenet underlying the laws of interpersonal mitzvos. The Torah demands of a slave owner to treat his Jewish slave with respect and sensitivity beyond that accorded to the average person. This is despite the fact that the owner spent money to purchase a slave, who in many cases was a person of dubious character, convicted of stealing! (A Jewish court could sell a person as a slave for having committed a theft and not having the means to repay.)

The *Mechilta* clarifies the enormous responsibility to preserve the dignity of the Jewish slave. Contrary to our own "human" common sense, the Torah's requirement to guard the dignity of a slave is more stringent than the one of guarding the dignity of an employee (*Shemos* 21:2):

> ... The Torah tells us, כִּי יָמוּךְ אָחִיךְ עִמָּךְ וְנִמְכַּר לָךְ לֹא תַעֲבֹד בּוֹ עֲבֹדַת עָבֶד, *If your brother becomes impoverished with you and is sold to you; you shall not work him with slave labor* (*Vayikra* 25:39) .... even though he is impoverished, afford him the same treatment as a brother. [The phrase] "... *with you*" teaches us that you should not treat him with condescension; "... *and is sold to you*" — his sins have caused him to be sold; nonetheless, "... *you shall not work him with slave labor*" — he must not [perform demeaning labor such as] carry your clothes to the bathhouse ... but you may hire a free man [an employee] for slave [demeaning] labor!

Demeaning work that can be given to a regular employee cannot be given to a slave. A person who was sold into slavery has "touched bottom" and has already been humiliated, and thus the Torah commands us to be sensitive to his feelings.

Beyond the obligation to safeguard the dignity of a slave, the Torah demands that his master provide him with food, drink, and accommodations in the same manner that he affords himself. The *Pesikta* explains the verse, כְּשָׂכִיר כְּתוֹשָׁב יִהְיֶה עִמָּךְ, *Like a laborer or a resident shall he [the Jewish slave] be with you* (*Vayikra* 25:40):

> Just as with a laborer there is an obligation to pay his wages on time, so too, you must treat him [the slave] ... he shall be like you regarding food, drink, and clean clothing. You should not eat fine bread, while he eats coarse bread; you should not drink old wine, while he drinks fresh wine; you should not sleep on soft cushions, while he sleeps on straw.

The Torah obligates the master to equate the food and living conditions of a Jewish slave to his own. He should give the slave the same prime beef, fine wine, and comfortable bed as his own. It is worthy of note that such an obligation does not exist toward any other members of his family, household, or workforce.

The master's obligations to the Jewish slave go even further. The *Pesikta* referenced earlier concludes:

> …. you should not live in a city, whereas he lives in a village, nor should you live in a village, whereas he lives in a city …. Just as the master is obligated to provide food for his Jewish slave, so too, he is obligated to provide food for the slave's wife and children.

The Gemara in *Kiddushin* (20a) succinctly describes the situation of the master of a Jewish slave, and the enormous responsibilities that it entails, by saying, "From here we coined the adage, 'buying a slave is tantamount to acquiring a master.'" *Sefer HaChinuch* (*Mitzvah* 42) explains why the Torah was so particular about preserving the dignity of a Jewish slave, as follows:

> One of the basic reasons for this mitzvah is that G-d wants the nation of Israel, whom He chose, to be a holy nation, adorned with virtuous and exceptional attributes — for this will be the source of blessing upon them. Kindness and compassion are among the most outstanding attributes in the world. Therefore, G-d admonished us to have compassion upon those who are under our power and to bestow goodness upon them.

Given these explanations, we may have a new perspective on why the Torah began *Parashas Mishpatim* with the laws of a Jewish slave. The Torah teaches that a person should not rely upon his intellect and intuitive moral compass when deciding what is permitted or prohibited in the laws of interpersonal mitzvos. Instead, his behavior should be guided by Halachah and *mussar*, and *Da'as Torah*.

◆§ The Two Tablets of the Covenant

The Ten Commandments, given to the Jewish people at Mount Sinai, encapsulate the essence of all 613 commandments, as *Rashi* writes (*Shemos* 24:12). Moreover, the structure and division of the Ten Commandments upon the two tablets of stone teach us how to approach mitzvos. *Ramban* addresses this division into two tablets as follows:

> The Ten Commandments — five of them relate to the honor of the Creator and the other five to the benefit of humankind. Honoring one's parents is considered a commandment between man and G-d — for He instructed us to honor parents, who are His partners in our creation. The remaining five are directed at the needs and benefits of people.

The *Beis Yisrael* asks why the word לחת, *tablets*, is written without a second letter *vav* (since the word is ostensibly plural). He answers that the *vav* is missing to teach us that the two tablets were inextricably bound to each other: The commandments that were on the right tablet (which pertain to the relation of man to his G-d) and the commandments that were on the left tablet (which pertain to interpersonal relations) are one organic unit. Whoever does not embrace both tablets simultaneously — as if they are one — is lacking in his service of G-d.

The *Bartenura*, in his commentary on *Maseches Avos*, also notes the incredible emphasis that the Torah places on interpersonal mitzvos. This tractate focuses primarily on matters of character and ethical behavior, yet opens with the detailed chain of transmission of the Torah from one generation to the next. To explain the need for the preamble, the *Bartenura* suggests:

> Since this tractate is not based on a specific mitzvah of the Torah, unlike other tractates, but is principally a study of ethics and character, and the wise men of the nations

of the world also crafted tomes of morals and proper conduct; therefore the *Tanna* [R' Yehudah HaNasi] began this work with the chain of Torah transmission to teach us that the Sages of the Mishnah did not invent these ethical principles, but they too were given at Sinai.

It is clear from the words of the *Bartenura* that the manner in which these mitzvos are to be fulfilled was also given at Sinai.

The *Kli Chemdah* (*Parashas Ki Seitzei*) highlights the unity of the tablets and both sets of commandments through their common purpose.

It appears that all of the mitzvos between man and G-d, as well as the interpersonal mitzvos, have one purpose: to unite all of the Jewish people so that they will all be connected to G-d, such that G-d, His Torah, and the Jewish people will be one!

These words leave no doubt that interpersonal mitzvos are a precondition to the attainment of oneness with G-d.

⋖§ Tefillin of the Head and Tefillin of the Arm

R' Aaron Lewin *zt"l*, in his seminal commentary *HaDrash V'HaIyun* (*Parashas Va'eschanan*), presented an apt allusion to clarify the connection between interpersonal mitzvos and those between man and G-d:

One could suggest that the mitzvah of *tefillin* contains a thoughtful hint to awaken an individual to two kinds of obligations: Those which are between man and G-d and those relating to interpersonal obligations. *Tefillin* of the arm awaken us to fulfill our responsibilities to one another, since these duties are met primarily through action ... [where] even if the action was done without proper intention, it remains significant. This is due to the fact that the action in and of itself results in a net benefit to society.

As such, even if he did not intend to perform a mitzvah, he has generated some good. *Tefillin* of the head awaken us to fulfill our responsibilities toward G-d, since the critical factors in their performance is desirable intent and appropriate thought. What would be the possible value of the mitzvos between man and G-d if they are lacking in correct intent? The medieval sages described this condition as: "A mitzvah without intent is like a body without a soul."

Furthermore, he reinforces his position that priority is given to an interpersonal mitzvah in a situation when it conflicts with a mitzvah between man and G-d:

Interpersonal mitzvos take precedence over mitzvos between man and G-d .... When it is impossible to fulfill a mitzvah between man and G-d without violating an interpersonal mitzvah, it is better not to do the [former] mitzvah at all. A classic example is the unacceptability of using a stolen *lulav*.

Therefore, one should first don the *tefillin* of the arm, which represents the interpersonal mitzvos, and only afterwards the *tefillin* of the head, which represents the mitzvos between man and G-d. Likewise, the order of removing the *tefillin* is first the *tefillin* of the head and only afterwards the *tefillin* of the arm .... This also teaches us that it is impossible to fulfill the mitzvos between man and G-d unless they are performed together and in harmony with the interpersonal mitzvos. Therefore, without the *tefillin* of the arm — i.e., the performance of interpersonal mitzvos — there cannot possibly be the *tefillin* of the head, i.e., the implementation of the mitzvos between man and G-d.

It is possible that this is the meaning of what our Sages said, "G-d showed Moshe the knot of the *tefillin*." This means that G-d showed Moshe that the two parts of the *tefillin* are organically connected and cannot be separated one from the other.

These eloquent and penetrating words were spoken by HaRav Aaron Lewin, among the greatest rabbis and leaders of Polish Jewry before the Holocaust.

◄§ The Borrower and the Guarantor

The following vignette is an illustration of the divergent attitudes of many people toward interpersonal mitzvos and the mitzvos between man and G-d. The story was related by a dear friend, who is the director of a free-loan fund that lends significant sums of money with no interest to individuals who are in need.

A respected man signed as a guarantor for his friend who borrowed money from the fund. Though the time of repayment arrived, the loan was not repaid. After repeated yet unsuccessful entreaties, the fund director turned to the guarantor and requested that he pay the debt. The guarantor nodded and promised that before day's end he would speak to the borrower and everything would be set right.

Days and weeks passed, yet nothing was heard from either. At the monthly meeting of the board of the free-loan fund, a respected Rabbi, and a member of its board of directors, expressed his desire to contact the guarantor immediately and "set him straight."

In the conversation that ensued, the Rabbi asked the guarantor, "Why have you not paid the debt which you secured with your signature?" The guarantor responded, "I do not have the money to pay for the debt." The Rabbi retorted, "I know that you have magnificent *Rabbeinu Tam tefillin*, because I commissioned the scribe and *batim* maker who made your *tefillin*! I am telling you that you must sell your *Rabbeinu Tam tefillin* and with the proceeds repay the loan."

The shocked guarantor asked how the rabbi had reached such a dramatic decision. The Rabbi responded, "There is no obligation in the Torah to own a pair of *tefillin*, let alone a second pair of *Rabbeinu Tam tefillin*. I am prepared to lend you my *Rabbeinu Tam tefillin* every day. However, the Torah does demand of you to pay back the loan on which you are signed as a guarantor. As long as you have not fulfilled this obligation, you are violating a grave prohibition!"

The Rabbi continued and said: "The laws that are written in the *Shulchan Aruch's* section of *Choshen Mishpat* are no less important than the laws that appear in *Yoreh Deah* or *Orach Chaim*. The prohibition to steal is no less severe than wearing *kilayim* (a garment containing woven wool and flax). Both of them were given to us by G-d, and neither of them is subject to the whimsical judgment of an individual."

◄§ Bankruptcy in the Fulfillment of Mitzvos

It is appropriate to quote the stirring words of *HaDrash V'HaIyun* about people who treat interpersonal mitzvos indifferently:

> There are people who are meticulous in their performance of the mitzvos between man and G-d, yet act carelessly toward interpersonal mitzvos — speaking *lashon hara* and gossiping, acting corruptly to deceive others and to gain wealth by malfeasance .... On the contrary, the interpersonal mitzvos are even more stringent than the mitzvos between man and G-d: If one violates a mitzvah between man and G-d, Yom Kippur will atone for his wrongdoing. However, Yom Kippur will not atone for one who violates an interpersonal mitzvah until he has pacified his victim.
>
> Such people are comparable to one who owes a certain amount of money. He goes bankrupt and negotiates with his creditor to pay only a portion of his debt. Such are people who do not want to perform all of the mitzvos of the Torah with the utmost care and precision, and make the

following compromise: We will keep the mitzvos between man and G-d, but we will disregard the interpersonal mitzvos. Such a compromise is an abomination. The Torah has no association with people who are bankrupt — there is no room for compromise when it comes to fulfilling its commandments and abiding by its admonitions.

The comparison between one who acts dismissively toward interpersonal mitzvos and someone who has gone bankrupt should shock any G-d-fearing individual. Any person who has a bit of self-esteem would never want to declare bankruptcy. If, Heaven forbid, he was forced into such a situation, it would be a result of circumstances beyond one's control and not an act of volition. Any disregard for interpersonal mitzvos or leniency that we allow ourselves in these mitzvos implies that not all mitzvos are equal. This is tantamount to an announcement of bankruptcy in our faith!

3

Interpersonal Mitzvos:
A Precondition for the
Attainment of Holiness

⚜ "You Shall Be Holy"

Parashas Kedoshim (Vayikra 19:1-2) opens with G-d's command: וַיְדַבֵּר ה' אֶל־מֹשֶׁה לֵּאמֹר: דַּבֵּר אֶל כָּל עֲדַת בְּנֵי יִשְׂרָאֵל וְאָמַרְתָּ אֲלֵהֶם קְדֹשִׁים תִּהְיוּ כִּי קָדוֹשׁ אֲנִי ה' אֱלֹקֵיכֶם, *Speak to the entire assembly of the Children of Israel and say to them: You shall be holy, for holy am I, Hashem, your G-d.* The Torah's requirement of holiness begs explanation since the epithet "holy" is reserved for a select few — saintly people who dedicate their entire lives to G-d's service with minimal interest in the material world! If so, how can the Torah expect every member of the Jewish nation to be *holy*?

According to many commentators, the command "to be holy" is not meant to be understood in its colloquial sense. *Rashi* understands this directive as "one must avoid the prohibited relationships" proscribed in the previous *parashah*. *Ramban* explains that while the Torah permitted marriage between a man and woman, and the consumption of kosher meat and wine, it did not grant *carte blanche* to indulge without limits in drunkenness, gluttony, or profanity.

A person could behave abominably without actually violating the letter of the Law by presuming that whatever the Torah permits is acceptable without restrictions. *Ramban* sharply censures one who gives free rein to his desires, as a "repugnant person who acts within the confines of Torah." He concludes, "Therefore, after detailing those things which are absolutely forbidden, the Torah mandated a general rule that we should refrain from excesses." Accordingly, the primary command of "being holy" is to sanctify one's life by limiting indulgence in permitted physical behaviors.

According to the *Rambam* (*Sefer HaMitzvos, Shoresh* 4), the directive of "being holy" serves as a general admonition to keep all the commandments of the Torah:

> Others have already made a mistake in regards to this hermeneutical principle to the extent that they have counted *"You shall be holy ..."* as one of the positive commandments. They did not comprehend that *"You shall be holy ..."* and *"... you are to sanctify yourselves and you shall become holy ..."* are directives to fulfill all of the Torah. It is as if the Torah said, "You will be holy by doing all the mitzvos that I commanded you and by refraining from all the things that I prohibited to you."

According to all of these commentators, this verse does not require us to aspire to those levels of holiness and purity attainable by a select few.

The *Alshich HaKadosh* disagrees with the aforementioned commentaries. In his opinion, the directive to be holy is to be understood in its conventional sense, and indeed, the Torah teaches us that every person is able to reach sublime sanctity. In order to emphasize this, the *parashah* was said in the presence of the entire assembly.

> G-d is inspiring each person in regard to piety and holiness so that he might emulate his Creator ... there are people who [erroneously believe] that not every person is capable or can achieve this, except perhaps for one or two people

in a generation. This attitude causes them to abandon any attempt to climb the ladder of perfection through Torah, mitzvos, and pious conduct. However, it is not so! There is no Jew who is incapable of achieving these things, if he but decides to ascend the ladder of Torah and piety until he reaches the level of holiness. Therefore, to impress this all-inclusive potential upon the nation, He assembled them all together ... for to each one of them it was said, *"You shall be holy."*

❧ Holiness Exists Only in the Context of a Community

The directive to be holy was given *to the entire assembly of the Children of Israel* .... G-d commanded Moshe to gather all of the Jewish people — men, women, and children — and direct them to be holy. *Rashi* explains: "This teaches us that this *parashah* was said before the entire assembly because the majority of the Torah's fundamental principles are contingent upon it." One needs to understand the unique nature of this general admonition.

The *Meor VaShemesh* writes that the reason this *parashah* was said to all of the Jews when they were assembled together was to illustrate that holiness can be attained only when one is part of a community, and not in isolation.

> A person could mistakenly think that holiness means isolating oneself from society, and this is the only way to attain personal sanctity. Therefore *Rashi* proactively explained that this *parashah* was said to the entire assembly of the Jewish people — [to indicate] that a person cannot achieve holiness without connecting himself to a congregation who seeks G-d.

R' Yonason Eibeschutz, in *Tiferes Yonason (Parashas Kedoshim)*, concurs that this directive was said to the entire Jewish assembly to emphasize that the only way to achieve holiness is through being part of a community and treating all people with respect and genuine fraternity:

> Josephus ben Gurion wrote in his book to the Romans that during the Second Temple era there were Jews who lived reclusively in the forests. They ate nothing but the fruits of trees, and practiced asceticism in all other areas of their lives. The Pharisees did not approve of their conduct at all! This is because a person, who is a paradigmatic servant of G-d, needs to conduct all of his spiritual and civic interactions in a way of pleasantness. He should not violate conventional civility, societal norms, and political etiquette. If everyone would become ascetics like these men, the natural order would be frustrated, the world would cease to exist, and the nation would be disbanded …. This is the intent of the *Midrash: "This parashah was said before the entire assembly of the Jewish people"* — sanctifying oneself in those things that are permissible should only be done in those things that the entire assembly can withstand and maintain.

In light of these words it is possible to answer a different perplexing question: In scanning this *parashah* one finds a total of fifty-one mitzvos — the majority of which are interpersonal, such as fearing one's mother and father, loving every Jew, honoring the Sages, the prohibition to curse parents, etc. Given the intuitive understanding of the concept of holiness, it would make more sense for this *parashah* to command the fear and love of G-d, the study of Torah day and night, the preservation of personal and spiritual purity, etc. — as the pathway to come closer to one's Creator! As such, why does this *parashah* busy itself with interpersonal mitzvos? Based on R' Eibeschutz, one can suggest that the Torah's intent is to emphasize that the pathway to a pristine level of holiness is paved with meticulous observance of interpersonal mitzvos.

⌘ Emulating G-d

The Gemara in *Sotah* (14a) explains the phrase (*Devarim* 28:9), וְהָלַכְתָּ בִּדְרָכָיו, *go in His ways*, as follows:

> R' Chama b'R' Chanina asked: What could be the possible
> meaning of the verse (*Devarim* 13:5), אַחֲרֵי ה' אֱלֹקֵיכֶם תֵּלֵכוּ,
> *Hashem, your G-d, shall you follow* .... Is it possible for a
> human being to follow the Divine Presence about which is
> written (*Devarim* 4:24), אֵשׁ אֹכְלָה הוּא, *He is a consuming fire!?*
> Rather, the verse means to tell us to emulate the attributes
> of G-d: Just as He clothes the naked ... so should you; just
> as He visits the sick ... so should you; just as He consoles
> mourners ... so should you; just as He buries the dead ...
> so should you.

What emerges from this Gemara is that appropriate interpersonal
behavior is a fundamental expectation from every human being by
which he emulates his Creator.

⌘ The Creator of Man

R' Moshe Cordovero (*Tomer Devorah, Perek* 1) highlights the
importance of emulating the ways of G-d:

> It is proper for a person to emulate G-d, for then he will
> enter into the secret of the supernal structure: image and
> form. If only a person's body reflects this likeness, but not
> his actions, then he betrays the image. They will say of
> him, "A beautiful shape, but ugly actions."

Later, he explains that recognizing that others are also created
in the image of G-d is fundamental to ethical reasoning and living:

> A person should habituate himself in two things:
> One thing is to honor all human beings, based on the
> recognition of the greatness of G-d, Who created them all
> .... If a person shames them, Heaven forbid, then he has
> tainted the honor of their Creator. This can be compared

to a brilliant silversmith, who displayed an artifact he had fashioned with tremendous wisdom. One observer denigrated and belittled the artist's handiwork. Imagine how angry this craftsman was, for this individual had denigrated his wisdom by belittling his workmanship!

The second thing is to internalize the love of every human being in one's heart, even wicked men, as if they were his brothers .... He should say to himself, "Let's wish that they become righteous men, who have repented from their evil ways and become outstanding individuals, cherished by G-d."

These words of R' Moshe Cordovero, one of the greatest Kabbalists of all generations, are a charge: It is incumbent upon a person to respect all others, inasmuch as they are the creation of G-d's handiwork, and love every person, even the sinful.

Furthermore, R' Cordovero offers advice on how to internalize the love of another in one's heart:

"How will one come to love another?" He must review in his mind all of the favors this person did for him and disregard all of his imperfections. One should overlook shortcomings, but concentrate on the positive character traits. He should say in his heart, "If this disgusting beggar was extremely rich, how happy would I be to share his company ...!

R' Moshe Cordovero wants to exploit a human weakness for a positive purpose. His advice is composed of two steps. First: An individual is to think about the virtues of another person and not his flaws, as the Rebbe R' Elimelech from Lizhensk penned in his prayer for one to say before *Shacharis* each day: "Place in our hearts that we should see the virtues of our friends and not their flaws." Second: We should imagine the other individual is a wealthy and respected man, for people are willing to ignore his imperfections, since everyone desires his closeness.

To illustrate how germane is this advice in our own generation, I would like to share an anecdote that took place when one of our community members married off a son. The wedding took place in the bride's hometown. The father of the groom, an exceedingly affluent and very kind-hearted person, decided to take one of the poor people of our city as a member of his entourage to the wedding. He chose an unfortunate individual, whose conduct was rather bizarre. Understandably, the destitute man jumped at the chance to celebrate at this most illustrious wedding, along with the esteemed and posh members of both cities.

The affluent man took up residence in a luxurious hotel and housed the poor man on the same floor, as an indistinguishable part of the groom's family. On the night of the wedding, he entered the banquet hall with the family. After the *chuppah*, he was seated at the table reserved for family members who had flown in for the wedding.

One of the groom's entourage played a joke and told a guest of the bride's family, "Do you see the man with slightly tattered clothing sitting next to the groom's family? While he looks a bit eccentric, I can share his secret: he is one of the wealthiest men of our city, whose fortune is estimated at hundreds of millions of dollars." The listener, one of the well-respected members of the bride's city, ran to tell his friends about the "fabulously rich guest." Shortly thereafter a large circle of prominent people of the host city gathered around this poor man, trying to befriend him and converse with him. This poor man had absolutely no clue why all these affluent individuals were attending to him!

There was great joy and mirth at the tables of the groom's friends and family — not just from the joke they had played on the unsuspecting bride's friends and relatives, but also from the pleasure of seeing the radiant face of the downtrodden, poor man!

This incident helped illuminate the words of R' Cordovero about the extent that judgment of another can be altered if one thinks that there is advantage or profit to be gained from that person. It is wrong to judge a person based on externalities; rather, one should respect every person as a creation of the Master of the universe. Moreover, one who honors his friend is considered like one who honors the Creator, Who designed every living thing. The opposite is also true: If one behaves improperly toward G-d's creatures, it is like he shamed their Creator.

To summarize:

1) Every Jew can and is expected to attain holiness — it is not intended only for the select few.

2) Holiness is not attained through isolation and asceticism. On the contrary, to attain holiness, one must be an integral part of the community and display a pleasant demeanor to all people.

3) A person who considers himself a servant of G-d must ensure that all of his words and actions are pleasing to both G-d and people.

4) The way to honor G-d is by emulating His conduct through extreme caution in carrying out the interpersonal mitzvos.

5) Belittling another person is likened to discrediting G-d, for all humans are His creations.

Those who are very punctilious in fulfillment of mitzvos between man and G-d, without maintaining the same level of vigilance in their performance of interpersonal mitzvos, deny themselves the possibility of ever reaching holiness.

4

Interpersonal Mitzvos: A Precondition for Cleaving to G-d

M oshe Rabbeinu's departing words to the Jewish people as they were about to enter the Promised Land included the imperative (*Devarim* 11:22): שָׁמֹר תִּשְׁמְרוּן אֶת כָּל הַמִּצְוָה הַזֹּאת אֲשֶׁר אָנֹכִי מְצַוֶּה אֶתְכֶם לַעֲשֹׂתָהּ לְאַהֲבָה אֶת ה׳ אֱלֹקֵיכֶם לָלֶכֶת בְּכָל דְּרָכָיו וּלְדָבְקָה בוֹ, *... observe this entire commandment that I command you, to perform it, to love Hashem, your G-d, to walk in all His ways and to cleave to Him.* Aside from the command to "walk in all His ways" (discussed in the previous chapter), this verse presents two additional provisions: to love G-d and to cleave to Him.

►§ Fearing, Loving, and Cleaving to G-d

In his explanation of the mitzvah of cleaving to G-d, *Ramban* writes:

> ... a person should remember and love G-d always. One's thoughts should not be separated from Him when one walks on the road, when one lies down, and when one wakes — to the degree that even when he is engaged by other people, his heart will not be with them, but rather with G-d.

The *Chofetz Chaim*, in the introduction to his work *Ahavas Chesed*, elaborates on these words of the *Ramban*:

> It appears that there are three levels in the service of G-d: One — awe; above this — love; and above this — cleaving to G-d. The difference between love and cleaving is that for love of G-d it is sufficient if it is only felt from time to time, whereas cleaving to G-d requires that one's love of G-d be always affixed in his heart, resulting in the bonding of his soul to G-d.

According to the *Chofetz Chaim*, cleaving to G-d implies an endless love that brooks no interruption. The *Chofetz Chaim* then cites the three places in *Parashas Eikev* in which the command to walk in the ways of G-d are mentioned:

1) וְשָׁמַרְתָּ אֶת מִצְוֹת ה' אֱלֹקֶיךָ לָלֶכֶת בִּדְרָכָיו וּלְיִרְאָה אֹתוֹ, *You shall observe the commandments of Hashem, your G-d, **to go in His ways and to fear Him*** (Devarim 8:6).

2) וְעַתָּה יִשְׂרָאֵל מָה ה' אֱלֹקֶיךָ שֹׁאֵל מֵעִמָּךְ כִּי אִם לְיִרְאָה אֶת ה' אֱלֹקֶיךָ לָלֶכֶת בְּכָל דְּרָכָיו וּלְאַהֲבָה אֹתוֹ וְלַעֲבֹד אֶת ה' אֱלֹקֶיךָ בְּכָל לְבָבְךָ וּבְכָל נַפְשֶׁךָ, *Now, O Israel, what does Hashem, your G-d, ask of you? Only to **fear Hashem**, your G-d, **to go in all His ways, and to love Him**, and to serve Hashem, your G-d, with all your heart and with all your soul* (Devarim 10:12).

3) כִּי אִם שָׁמֹר תִּשְׁמְרוּן אֶת כָּל הַמִּצְוָה הַזֹּאת אֲשֶׁר אָנֹכִי מְצַוֶּה אֶתְכֶם לַעֲשֹׂתָהּ לְאַהֲבָה אֶת ה' אֱלֹקֵיכֶם לָלֶכֶת בְּכָל דְּרָכָיו וּלְדָבְקָה בוֹ, *For if you will observe this entire commandment that I command you, to perform it, **to love Hashem**, your G-d, **to walk in all His ways**, and **to cleave to Him** ...* (Devarim 11:22).

The *Chofetz Chaim* notes the variances among these verses in their sequential structure, and explains the change in the order of the attributes.

The Torah comes to teach us an important principle: It is impossible to obtain any level of worshiping G-d without paying attention to *going in His ways* by fulfilling interpersonal mitzvos, and being kind and gracious to others. In the first verse, לָלֶכֶת בִּדְרָכָיו וּלְיִרְאָה אֹתוֹ, *to go in His ways and to fear Him*, the Torah stresses that going in His ways precedes, and is a precondition to, attaining the lowest level of worshiping G-d: to fear (or be in awe of) Him.

In the second verse, לְיִרְאָה אֶת ה׳ אֱלֹקֶיךָ לָלֶכֶת בְּכָל דְּרָכָיו וּלְאַהֲבָה אֹתוֹ, *to fear Hashem, your G-d, to go in all His ways, and to love Him*, the Torah addresses one who has already attained the level of fearing G-d and wants to ascend to the next level, of loving G-d. That person may mistakenly think that to rise to the next level he should meditate on the sublime nature of G-d, study His holy Torah, and not be concerned at all about worldly matters in which he may benefit others. Therefore, the Torah stresses that the only way to ascend from fear of G-d to the love of G-d is by *going in His ways* — i.e., paying attention to interpersonal mitzvos.

Finally, in the third verse, לְאַהֲבָה אֶת ה׳ אֱלֹקֵיכֶם לָלֶכֶת בְּכָל דְּרָכָיו וּלְדָבְקָה בוֹ, *to love Hashem, your G-d, to walk in all His ways, and to cleave to Him*, the Torah addresses one who has attained the level of loving G-d and now wants to ascend to the highest level, of cleaving to Him. That person should not imagine that it is proper for him now to only concentrate upon Torah study and reflect on the greatness of G-d without paying attention to matters pertaining to the benefit of others. On the contrary, the Torah declares that to attain the status of cleaving to G-d, a person must galvanize himself further in *going in G-d's ways*; i.e., to be compassionate and magnanimous. In the merit of this conduct, G-d benevolently allows one to be close to Him constantly.

⋖§ Cleaving to G-d

Rashi questions the possibility of fulfilling this imperative, וּלְדָבְקָה בוֹ, *to cleave to Him (Devarim* 11:22):

Is it possible for a person to cleave to Him? Is not G-d a consuming fire? Rather, one should bond with Torah scholars and the Torah will consider it as if this individual is closer to the Divine Presence.

Closeness to G-d is achievable through intimate association with Torah scholars. The Gemara (*Kesubos* 111b) illustrates this by recommending that one marry one's daughter to a Torah scholar, create business opportunities for a Torah scholar, and provide benefit to a Torah scholar from one's material wealth; the Torah considers these as cleaving to the Divine Presence.

Yet, *Rashi* in a different place seems to contradict this explanation! In *Devarim* 13:5, it is written, אַחֲרֵי ה' אֱלֹקֵיכֶם תֵּלֵכוּ וְאֹתוֹ תִירָאוּ וְאֶת מִצְוֹתָיו תִּשְׁמֹרוּ וּבְקֹלוֹ תִשְׁמָעוּ וְאֹתוֹ תַעֲבֹדוּ וּבוֹ תִדְבָּקוּן, *Hashem, your G-d, shall you follow and Him shall you fear; His commandments shall you observe and to His voice shall you hearken; Him shall you serve and to Him shall you cleave.* In explaining the words *and to Him shall you cleave*, *Rashi* writes, "Cleave unto His ways: perform acts of kindness, bury the dead, and visit the sick, just as G-d did."

Sifsei Chachamim reconciles the apparent contradiction by stating that the essential meaning of *to Him shall you cleave* is to emulate His ways through acts of kindness, etc. However, since in *Parashas Eikev* the words *to Him shall you cleave* are preceded by the words *going in His ways*, in that context "cleaving" must have an additional connotation, namely attaching oneself to Torah scholars. Accordingly, one might conclude that fulfillment of interpersonal mitzvos is not just a means to reach the highest level of closeness to G-d, but these actions — in and of themselves — inhere the experience of closeness to G-d.

R' Aharon Kotler *zt"l* poses the question: How can the fulfillment of interpersonal mitzvos culminate in the experience of cleaving to G-d?

This intimacy seems much more related to the mitzvos between man and G-d wherein one's heart is directed to

Heaven, and even more so, through prayer with contrition and reflection on G-d's transcendent nature! However, when one is busy in an effort to help his friend, on the streets and in the marketplace, involved with all kinds of people, and speaking about things that are mundane and ostensibly meaningless, how can this activity provide a closeness to G-d greater than sitting wrapped in a *tallis* and *tefillin* …? (*Mishnas R' Aharon*, I, 144)

R' Kotler's answer is based on the writings of R' Moshe Cordovero:

The ultimate purpose of Creation is absolute benevolence — this is the intent of all of G-d's actions … a person is also required to act accordingly, especially since he was endowed at Creation with faculties of generosity and munificence. The objective of a person's existence is not to take from this world, but to give and provide to others. This is the "likeness" in which he was created. **Therefore, the quintessential way of cleaving to G-d is emulating His ways of kindness and compassion. By this, one actualizes and perfects his own creation in the Divine image.**

Accordingly, a person who does not bestow goodness upon others has diminished the Divine image within himself, and consequently he cannot bond with his Creator.

There is an additional approach to explain why closeness to G-d is possible only through attentive adherence to the interpersonal mitzvos. In the previous chapter we quoted the words of the *Meor VaShemesh*, "… it is impossible for a person to achieve holiness unless he is a part of a community actively engaged in the service of G-d." Likewise, we cited the words of R' Yonason Eibeschutz, "This is because a person, who is a paradigmatic servant of G-d, needs to conduct all of his spiritual and civic interactions in a way of pleasantness. He should not violate conventional civility, societal norms, and political etiquette." The conclusion that emerges from a synthesis of these comments is that in order to achieve the level of holiness, it is necessary for a person to be socially integrated and to conduct himself with G-d and men in a congenial manner.

Accordingly, every moment of the day in which a person is in the presence of other people, he is required to be mindful of his actions, and to think how he should behave toward and relate to other individuals, including his wife, children, neighbors, acquaintances, partners, etc. When he walks down the street, he should greet every person, be careful not to ignore or appear to ignore someone he knows, and show people a pleasant and radiant disposition. Without enumerating the myriad situations that a person confronts in the course of a day, it is evident that a person's Torah obligations vis-à-vis his surroundings encompass him from the moment he wakes up until the moment he goes to sleep.

In contrast, the majority of the action mitzvos between man and G-d are limited in time and place. Moreover, we are guided in great detail how to perform them by the halachic masters. This is not so in regard to the interpersonal mitzvos. While the obligation to observe the interpersonal mitzvos extends to every moment of the waking day, in many instances there are no precise and comprehensive guidelines for how they should be performed.

Actually, there can be no standardized guidelines because each interaction is contingent upon the specific people and circumstances. This is very similar to what *Ramban* wrote on the verse, וְעָשִׂיתָ הַיָּשָׁר וְהַטּוֹב, *You shall do what is fair and good…* (*Devarim* 6:18):

> Since it is impossible for the Torah to mention all possible interactions between a person and his neighbors and associates, the entire array of business transactions, and all social and civil mores … the Torah codified a general directive that a person should do that which is good and fair in all matters. This includes compromise in civil proceedings, and going beyond the letter of the law … to the degree that one would be deemed a wholesome and just person.

According to *Ramban*, the Torah needed to write one overarching ethic — *You shall do what is fair and good* — to encompass all the countless situations for which it is impossible to detail specific instructions. The Torah apparently relies on the good judgment of the individual to decipher what behavior would render one "a wholesome and just person."

Just as people's external looks are different, so too, their ways of thinking are different, and people vary considerably in their decision-making. This is further complicated by the decision-making process regarding interpersonal relationships, which is inevitably tainted with subjectivity. If so, what can one do to securely reach an appropriate decision — one that meets the criteria of *fair and good* in the eyes of G-d and man?

It appears that proper observance of the entire spectrum of interpersonal mitzvos requires that whenever one encounters another person, he should ask himself two questions:

1) Is G-d pleased with my treatment of this other person?

   If a person has even the slightest doubt, he must refrain from taking any action. The same degree of caution one exercises to refrain from the consumption of any non-kosher food applies equally to one's avoidance of committing any wrong to another human being.

2) Even in those instances where a person finds an allowance to treat another person with callousness and severity, a person must ask himself another question: It is known that G-d evaluates a person according to how he treats others and judges a person measure for measure. If so, would I want G-d to treat me with the same severity and lack of forgiveness as I am treating others?

One needs to ask himself these two questions throughout the course of the day. For example: How should he react if his wife did not prepare a proper meal? How should he respond to her request for help in the house? How should he treat his neighbor who had raised such a commotion last night? How should he react to his business associate who insulted him? How should he divide his time among the various *chesed* opportunities that come his way? Should he greet every stranger in the street?

In these daily occurrences, and in hundreds of others, a person must ask himself these same two questions: Is G-d pleased with my actions and do I provide Him with *nachas*? And, do I want G-d to judge and treat me in the same way that I judge and treat others? When one performs interpersonal mitzvos consciously with these questions in mind, closeness to G-d becomes an ongoing and constant state of being, and that is the essence of cleaving to Him.

5

Punishment for Transgressing Interpersonal Mitzvos

Throughout its history, the Jewish people endured destruction, exile, pogroms, and genocide. According to our Sages, the primary cause for the majority of these tragedies is the lack of proper respect for the interpersonal mitzvos, whether in regard to another's person or property.

❧ The Generation of the Flood vs. the Generation of the Tower

Our Sages in *Sanhedrin* (88a) discuss the iniquities of the generation of the Flood, which included idolatry and immorality, yet they were not punished until they had violated common civil law:

> R' Yochanan said, "... Behold, the generation of the Flood violated everything, yet their judgment was not sealed until they engaged in robbery, as it is written (*Bereishis* 6:13), כִּי מָלְאָה הָאָרֶץ חָמָס מִפְּנֵיהֶם וְהִנְנִי מַשְׁחִיתָם אֶת הָאָרֶץ, *... for the earth is filled with robbery through them; and behold, I am about to eradicate them from the earth.*"

The *Talmud Yerushalmi* (*Bava Metzia* 15a) quotes the words of R' Acha:

It is written, כִּי מָלְאָה הָאָרֶץ חָמָס מִפְּנֵיהֶם, *for the earth is filled with robbery through them.* What kind of robbers were they? A person would carry a basket full of legumes on his way to the market and they would grab an amount of legumes valued at less than a *prutah,* which could not be recovered in court.

The generation of the Flood was destroyed because they were thieves. They did not commit armed and violent robbery; they engaged in petty theft that could not be adjudicated in a court of law. Since this became a widespread and socially acceptable practice, the generation was subject to obliteration.

In contrast, the generation of the Tower of Bavel committed serious transgressions by building a tower to ascend to the heavens to rebel against G-d. Seemingly, their punishment should have been much harsher than that of the generation of the Flood. *Rashi* explains the phrase, וּמִשָּׁם הֱפִיצָם ה', *and from there Hashem scattered them (Bereishis* 11:9):

> Who committed a greater sin: the generation of the Flood or the generation of the Tower? The former did not rebel against G-d, whereas the latter did! Yet, the former were swept away by water, whereas the latter were not obliterated from the world. The difference is that the generation of the Flood were thieves and there was discord among them, whereas the generation of the Tower treated each other with love and affection, as it is written (*Bereishis* 11:1), וַיְהִי כָל הָאָרֶץ שָׂפָה אֶחָת וּדְבָרִים אֲחָדִים, *The whole earth was of one language and of common purpose.* This teaches us that quarrelling is despised [by G-d] and peace is praised!

A comparison between the punishments of these two genera-tions teaches us two fundamental principles:

1) When a person violates severe prohibitions in the realm of mitzvos between man and G-d, and at the

same time commits interpersonal sins, his punishment and its severity are determined by the nature of the interpersonal sins.

2) Unity, even among incorrigible wrongdoers, has tremendous power to safeguard even the most rebellious from harsh punishments.

During *Sefiras HaOmer*, we practice certain laws of mourning to commemorate the death of the students of R' Akiva. The Gemara in *Yevamos* (62b) describes the reason for their death:

> R' Akiva had twelve thousand pairs of students, who resided from Gevas until Antiparis [the length and breadth of Israel]. All of them died during the same period because they did not treat each other with respect.

R' Akiva's students did not violate any explicit Torah prohibition, yet, their behavior precipitated an awful destruction! After the tragedy, R' Akiva tried to salvage whatever was left and to launch a new generation of students by giving them a compelling charge:

> My sons, those who came before you died only because they treated each other with miserliness. Make sure that you do not mimic their actions! (*Bereishis Rabbah* 61:3).

ৼৢ The Destruction of Temples

The Gemara in *Yoma* (9b) discusses the causes of the destruction of the two Temples:

> Why was the First Temple destroyed? It was destroyed because of three things: idolatry, adultery, and murder. However, the Second Temple, in which the Jews were engaged in Torah study, mitzvos, and acts of kindness, why was it destroyed? It was destroyed because of baseless hatred. This teaches you that causeless hatred is tantamount to idolatry, adultery, and murder put together!

The concept of "causeless hatred" needs some clarification. A sane person does not wake up one day and suddenly decide to hate someone without "justifiable" cause. There is always a reason for animosity, and in the eyes of the hater, it is always justified. There are times when a person may develop a conviction that it is a halachic obligation to hate a specific individual. Nonetheless, the Gemara refers to the vast majority of reasoned hatred as "causeless hatred."

Such "causeless hatred" was committed even by people who engaged in Torah study, mitzvos, and acts of kindness. The *Netziv* of Volozhin aptly described this phenomenon in his introduction to *Ha'amek Davar* on *Bereishis*. His words are a glaring indictment of many of the things that we witness today:

> We explained that they [the scholars in the era of the Second Temple] were righteous and pious people, who toiled in their Torah study. However, they were not upright in matters of the world. **Therefore, due to their causeless hatred, they suspected someone who did not exhibit fear of Heaven, according to their understanding, of being a Sadducee or a heretic. Through this they came to commit ... every evil in the world, until the Temple was destroyed.**
>
> It was regarding this situation that Moshe Rabbeinu [in his prophetic epic, *Ha'azinu*] justified the Divine decree: [הַצּוּר תָּמִים פָּעֳלוֹ ... צַדִּיק וְיָשָׁר הוּא], *The Rock! [G-d]— perfect is His work ... righteous and fair is He (Devarim 32:4)*] for G-d is upright and cannot tolerate such "righteous" people, unless they also walk in the path of uprightness, without any deceitfulness — even for the sake of Heaven — in matters of the world. Such crookedness causes the ruination of Creation and the collapse of social order.
>
> This was the accolade of the forefathers: In addition to their being righteous and pious men, who were consummate lovers of G-d, they were also upright individuals — meaning they treated the nations of the world, even

unbecoming idolaters, with love and benevolence, as a way of promoting the continued existence of Creation. We saw how much Avraham Avinu pleaded on behalf of the inhabitants of Sodom, even though he abhorred them and their king on account of their wickedness. Nonetheless, he pleaded on behalf of their survival.

The learned and kindly people in the Second Temple era saw fit to hate others whom they deemed heretics because they worshiped G-d in a different — though halachically appropriate — style. Their hatred was "for the sake of Heaven," and they were confident that not only was there nothing wrong with what they were doing, but that they were actually fulfilling the will of G-d. Nonetheless, the Gemara calls this hatred "causeless."

> R' Yonason Eibeschutz comments that the First Temple was rebuilt because the sins that caused its destruction (idolatry, adultery, and murder) were corrected within a short span of time. However, the cause of the destruction of the Second Temple — causeless hatred — has not yet been rectified. Therefore, the Temple has not yet been rebuilt.

๔ The Essence of the Punishment for Interpersonal Sins

R' Chaim Shmulevitz *zt"l* (*Sichos Mussar, Ma'amar* 105) elaborates on the severity of interpersonal sins and the essence of retribution for them. These are his main points:

1. **Causing another person pain even if it is for "the sake of Heaven" will result in a heavy punishment.**

    Our Sages (*Bava Basra* 16a) discuss the fate of Penina, who needled Chana to motivate her to increase her prayer and plead for children from G-d (*I Shmuel* 1:6): וְכִעֲסַתָּה צָרָתָהּ גַּם כַּעַס בַּעֲבוּר הַרְּעִמָהּ, *she sorely angered her sister in order to make her "complain."* Rashi explains, "She should complain that she is barren and pray for children." Penina was a righteous woman who would not readily pain another person. She so empathized with Chana's barrenness that she overrode her natural tenderness in order to goad Chana to plead with Hashem to change her plight. Despite her laudable intentions, Penina was later severely punished with the death of some of her own children.

2. **Even unintentional causation of pain results in punishment.**

The Gemara in *Kesubos* (62b) tells the following story:

Rav Rachumi stayed with Rava in Mechuza, and was accustomed to return home every Yom Kippur Eve. One Yom Kippur Eve, Rav Rachumi became engrossed in his learning. His wife anticipated his imminent arrival and kept saying to herself, "Now he must be coming. Now he must be coming," but he did not come home. She was distraught and a tear fell from her eye. As Rav Rachumi was sitting on a porch, it collapsed and he died.

Rav Rachumi did not intend to cause his wife any grief. Yet her tear caused his death. This proves that punishment for inflicting pain or sorrow on someone is not a function of the intent to harm, but a result of the actual suffering caused.

3. **A person who harms his friend is likened to one who places his hand into a fiery oven.**

Another salient principle can be derived from the story of Rav Rachumi: The punishment for interpersonal sins is not aimed at pacifying the victim. Clearly, Rav Rachumi's wife, who had been waiting so eagerly for her husband, did not want him to die. Reb Chaim writes:

This is because a person who hurts his friend, whatever his intentions may be, is like someone who puts his hand into a fiery oven. His good intentions cannot change the outcome in the slightest way (his hand will be severely burned). The punishment for interpersonal sins is a natural phenomenon, just as fire inevitably burns whatever is placed into it.

◄§ Honoring Others as a Condition for Acquisition of Torah

Furthermore, inflicting harm or pain to another person prevents one from genuine acquisition of Torah. At the beginning of *Parashas Vayeira*, it is written, וַיֵּרָא אֵלָיו ה' בְּאֵלֹנֵי מַמְרֵא וְהוּא יֹשֵׁב פֶּתַח הָאֹהֶל כְּחֹם הַיּוֹם. וַיִּשָּׂא עֵינָיו וַיַּרְא וְהִנֵּה שְׁלֹשָׁה אֲנָשִׁים נִצָּבִים עָלָיו, *Hashem appeared to him in the plains of Mamre, while he was sitting at the entrance of the tent in the heat of the day. He lifted his eyes and saw: And behold! Three men were standing over him (Bereishis 18:1-2).* On this verse, the *Yalkut Shimoni* writes:

> Avraham said, "If I see that the Divine Presence waits for them, I know they are righteous men. If I see that they treat each other with respect, I know they are righteous men." Since he saw the Divine Presence waiting for them and that they treated each other with respect, he surely knew that they were righteous men.

R' Simcha Zissel Broide *zt"l* (*Sam Derech*) finds this *Midrash* mystifying: "After all, they appeared to Avraham as simple Arabs, idol worshippers, who bow down to the dust of their feet — for this reason he washed their feet so they would not bring it into his house." Apparently, Avraham Avinu was willing to bring idolaters into his home. If so, what was his great fear of bringing people who were not righteous into this same space?

Furthermore, why did he seek two criteria to confirm that

they were righteous: the Divine Presence was waiting for them, and they treated each other respectfully? Is not the fact that the Divine Presence was waiting for them sufficient proof of their righteousness?!

Reb Simcha Zissel clarifies that uprightness and decency displayed toward another person are not just good character traits; rather, they comprise a basic prerequisite for the acquisition of Torah. Avraham Avinu was very hospitable, but at the same time, had a sublime mission: to transform his guests into his students so that he can bring them under the wings of the Divine Presence. He accomplished this by giving them food and drink and then asking them to express their thanks to the Master of the World.

When a Torah scholar selects his students, he must make certain that they are upright and decent, as is mentioned in *Chullin* 133a, "Whoever teaches a student who is not proper, is considered as having thrown a stone to the idol *Markolis*." Therefore, when Avraham Avinu wanted to separate people from their idolatry and convert them to recognize the One G-d, he was required to ascertain that they were fit. He verified their fitness to be his students by seeing how they treat each other.

⊷§ Ridiculing Others Results in Spiritual Decline

People who do not treat others respectfully and act derisively toward others will eventually fall into spiritual decline. We deduce this from the story of Yishmael, who went astray in spite of his upbringing in the home of Avraham, his father. It is hard to understand how such a depraved person can emerge from such a holy home. R' Simcha Zissel Broide suggests that Yishmael's entire spiritual and social decline resulted from his ridicule and mockery of others, for it is written: וַתֵּרֶא שָׂרָה אֶת בֶּן הָגָר הַמִּצְרִית אֲשֶׁר יָלְדָה לְאַבְרָהָם מְצַחֵק, *Sarah saw the son of Hagar, the Egyptian, whom she had born to Abraham, mocking (Bereishis* 21:9).

Ramban explains that the word *metzachek* should be understood in its most literal sense, concluding, "This occurred on the day that Yitzchak was weaned. Sarah saw him mocking Yitzchak, as a slave mocks his master." The mockery and derision of Yitzchak, and — by implication — of Avraham and Sarah, on the day of the feast that they had made for Yitzchak, were the cause of his decline and spiritual degeneration. A person must take to heart just how destructive ridicule and incivility toward others can be!

✑ May I Not Fall into the Hands of Men

It is appropriate to conclude this chapter with the verse (*II Shmuel* 24:14) וַיֹּאמֶר דָּוִד אֶל גָּד צַר לִי מְאֹד נִפְּלָה נָא בְיַד ה' כִּי רַבִּים רַחֲמָיו וּבְיַד אָדָם אַל אֶפֹּלָה, *David said to Gad, "I am exceedingly distressed. Let us fall into Hashem's hands for His mercies are abundant, but let me not fall into human hands,"* as explained by R' Chaim Shmulevitz:

> It is possible that David intended to say that it is better "to fall" from — to violate, Heaven forbid — the word of G-d, meaning a mitzvah between man and G-d, for His mercies are abundant and it is still possible to repent and Yom Kippur can atone. However, David pleads that he not "fall" into "human hands," meaning he should not violate an interpersonal mitzvah, because then there is no mercy; the punishment is harsh and repentance is difficult.

6

Interpersonal Mitzvos as the Basis of True Repentance

Every year, when the month of Elul arrives and the days of judgment draw near, many Jews invest enormous efforts to improve their actions and come closer to G-d. This fits well with the allusion to the verse (*Shir HaShirim* 6:3), אֲנִי לְדוֹדִי וְדוֹדִי לִי, *I am to my Beloved and my Beloved is to me*, which — in the Hebrew — forms the acrostic spelling "Elul." In this chapter we will analyze the interpersonal mitzvos from the perspective of *teshuvah* (repentance and return).

⋖ᶳ Recognizing the Need to Repent

In *Hilchos Teshuvah* (2:2), the *Rambam* writes:

> Repentance means that a sinner abandons his sin ... while making a firm resolution that he will never do it again, regretting his wrongdoing ... such that the Omniscient One could affirm that he will never repeat this sin again. A person also needs to verbally confess and declare all resolutions to which he committed in his heart.

Having completed all of the steps of *teshuvah*, one may antici-pate and hope that his repentance will be accepted. The onerous steps of repentance described above are for sins between man and G-d as well as interpersonal sins. However, as difficult as the process of repentance is generally, it is even harder for violations of interpersonal mitzvos.

As discussed earlier, it is easier to realize that a sin was committed toward G-d than to admit a wrongdoing to another person, because ego and self-interest put blinders on most people. Consequently, people tend to repeat sinful interpersonal behavior, to the point that it becomes habitual and normal. The *Rambam* (4:5) enumerates five sinful activities — all related to interpersonal conduct — for which repentance is extremely difficult:

> There are five things that, if one does them, he will be drawn after them continuously, and it will be difficult for him to desist from them. Therefore, a person must avoid them, lest he bond with them. They are all extremely bad attributes: slander, gossip-mongering, anger, evil thoughts, and association with a wicked man (because one learns from his deeds) — and they become etched on one's heart.

Genuine repentance for interpersonal sins — particularly those that have become "etched on one's heart" — that results in enduring change may require altering one's personality attributes. Unlike the common belief that repentance is needed only for sinful acts, the *Rambam* (*Hilchos Teshuvah* 7:3) argues that repentance is needed even for negative personality traits, and that it is within our power to transform our characters:

> Do not say that there is only repentance for bad deeds, for example: illicit relations, robbery, and stealing. Rather, just as a person needs to repent for these violations, so too does one need to identify his bad character traits and to repent for anger, hatred, jealousy, derision, the pursuit of money and honor, and gluttony, etc. A person needs to repent for all these things, and they are more challenging than sins

committed through action, for once a person becomes engrossed in them, it is very hard to desist from them ....

Repentance for interpersonal sins is thus harder for two reasons: It is difficult to recognize that a sin was committed and to decide sincerely to stop doing it, and repentance is needed not just for wrongful actions but also for the underlying negative personal traits that may have caused those actions.

There is another hurdle in the process of repentance for interpersonal sins: the requirement to apologize and beg for forgiveness. The *Rambam* writes in *Hilchos Teshuvah* (2:9):

> Repentance and Yom Kippur atone only for sins between man and G-d, for example: someone who ate prohibited food, etc. However, for interpersonal sins, such as: inflicting bodily harm, cursing his friend, or stealing from him, etc., a person will not be forgiven until he gives his friend what he owes him and appeases him. Even though he returned the money that he owed him, the offender needs to apologize and to beg forgiveness. Even if he only teased his friend with words, a person must apologize again and again, until he pardons him.

Acknowledging wrongdoing is hard enough, but doing so to another human being and then begging forgiveness, and doing everything possible to earn a pardon, is doubly hard.

৵৪ Yom Kippur Will Not Atone Until ...

Our Sages say (*Mishnah Yoma* 8:9), "Interpersonal sins: Yom Kippur does not atone until the wrongdoer has appeased his friend." In *Michtav Me'Eliyahu* (Vol. 1, 264), R' Eliyahu Dessler, *zt"l*, writes that the Mishnah should have said, "Yom Kippur will not atone for the interpersonal sins **themselves** until the wrongdoer has appeased his friend." Since the *Tanna* did not write it this way, R' Dessler deduces that if a person committed an interpersonal sin and did not apologize to his friend and receive his forgiveness, Yom Kippur will not atone even for sins between man and G-d!

R' Dessler raises the possibility that a person's entire atonement on Yom Kippur depends upon his interpersonal conduct: If he repented and requested his friend's forgiveness, he will be pardoned for all his sins, including those between man and G-d; if, Heaven forbid, he does not apologize and appease his friend, his entire array of wrongdoings remains intact and indicts him.

ᎈ§ What Is the Extent of Their Impact?

Hitherto, we addressed personality traits and actions that impact relations and conduct in the interpersonal domain. There is an additional — though less salient — factor that is impacted by one's interpersonal behavior. The *Zohar*, on *Parashas Emor*, says that people's actions in the earthly sphere have an impact on the celestial sphere:

> We learned that actions down "below" have an effect on the actions from "above." If a person acts properly down below, then the appropriate power is activated above. If a person does an act of kindness in this world, then kindness is activated above, and it settles upon that day and it is crowned with kindness for him. If a person acts with compassion below, then he activates compassion upon that day and it is crowned with compassion for him. That day then becomes a shield for him, whenever he needs it. Fortunate is the person who displays a proper act below, for everything depends upon an action that will activate its corresponding higher power.

In *Parashas Pekudei*, the *Zohar* writes a similar idea in regard to gossip:

> There is one spirit that stands upon all those people who gossip, and when people arouse the power of gossip ...

then this evil spirit is awakened above … and with this activation of gossip it unleashes … the sword and killing in the world. Woe unto those people who awaken this power of evil and do not guard their mouths and tongues, who show disregard for this danger, and who do not understand that the reaction above depends upon the activation below, whether for bad or good.

Accordingly, when a punishment upon a person is decreed in the Heavenly Court, it is not executed immediately, but is postponed until someone in this world maligns the accused. Such gossip reinforces the judgment, and indicates that in this world there is affirmation of the verdict from above, and then it will be carried out. Likewise, the opposite is true: When goodness is decreed upon a person, the Heavenly Court will not actualize this good until someone in this world speaks the praises of this person, for by doing so he demonstrates that the "lower" court affirms the decision that was decreed above.

The impact of human speech and interpersonal action is immeasurable. One has the ability to bestow good, or — Heaven forbid — evil upon other people, even unconsciously and unintentionally, simply through the force of speech. It is thus clear that a person must be doubly careful in all matters related to his relationship with all others. The punishment for harming another person is immense, the recognition of the sin is difficult, the repentance that is required is challenging, and it requires a long process contingent upon other people's cooperation for its completion.

⧽ The Difference Between the Heavenly and Earthly Courts

The interpersonal mitzvos can bolster a person as he stands in judgment during the Ten Days of Repentance. Prior to detailing actions that can improve one's standing on the Day of Judgment it is important to understand the essential difference between the principles of adjudication and decision-making in an earthly court, as compared to the Heavenly Court. There are four essential differences:

1) In an earthly court, the adjudication process focuses on two issues: was a crime committed; and if it was, what is the appropriate punishment. In the omniscient Heavenly Court there is no need to deliberate if a sin was committed, for the Divine Judge knows both the act and the intention behind it. Furthermore, we recognize that all fallible humans err, as expressed in *Koheles* (7:20), כִּי אָדָם אֵין צַדִּיק בָּאָרֶץ אֲשֶׁר יַעֲשֶׂה טּוֹב וְלֹא יֶחֱטָא, *There is no man who is righteous on the earth, who does [only] good and will not sin.* As we stand in judgment before the Heavenly Court, all we can ask for is that the compassionate Creator will not exact the letter of the law.

2) In the Heavenly Court, we ask G-d to adjudicate us favorably as His children. This is expressed in the *Mussaf* prayer of Rosh Hashanah: "Today is the conception of the world. Today G-d places in judgment all of the creatures of the worlds — either as sons or as servants. If as sons, have compassion upon us as a father has compassion upon his sons." Presenting ourselves as children of G-d, we beg that our Father love us unconditionally. Obviously, there is no room for such requests in an earthly court.

3) On the Day of Judgment, we ask for compassion in the merit of our forefathers, we coronate G-d, and we blow the shofar. We show unconditional love and faith in G-d, and we hope that these will lead to a lesser punishment and perhaps a total pardon. Praising a judge in an earthly court would be viewed as inappropriate flattery and as a blatant attempt to sway the judge's objectivity.

4) A great gift was given to us: the gift of repentance. Repentance has the ability not only to lighten our judgment, but it has the power to transform sins into merits and to facilitate our acquittal and transformation. The cleansing power of *teshuvah* was granted in G-d's great mercy, and does not figure in any other judicial system.

Aside from these differences between the heavenly and earthly court in the process of adjudicating the case, there is also a huge difference in the criteria for determining guilt vs. innocence, as well as the type and severity of punishment.

❧ Measure for Measure

The Talmud delineates three areas in which one can improve his conduct and, as a consequence, his standing in the Heavenly Court:

1) "A person who does not stand on principle will be forgiven all of his wrongdoings … for whom does G-d forgive iniquity? To one who overlooks the willful sin [of others]" (*Rosh Hashanah* 17a). *Rashi* explains that a person who "does not stand on principle" is someone "who is not exacting with people who cause him grief, overcomes his impulses [for vengeance], and just continues on his way."

   Thus, to someone who does not respond when taunted by others and even forgives them, G-d responds measure for measure, and forgives his sins.

2) The Gemara in *Shabbos* (151b) says, "Rabban Gamliel b'Rebbi [explained]: וְנָתַן לְךָ רַחֲמִים וְרִחַמְךָ וְהִרְבֶּךָ, *He will give you mercy and be merciful to you and multiply you* (*Devarim* 13:18): whoever is compassionate to people, Heaven will be compassionate to him, and whoever is not compassionate to people, Heaven will have no compassion for him."

This implies that a person who empathizes with others, assists them, and thinks of ways to provide help to others will merit G-d's mercy and will be judged with abundant compassion.

3) Our Sages taught: "A person who gives his friend the benefit of the doubt will be given the benefit of the doubt [by Heaven]" (*Shabbos* 127b).

If a person gives his friends the benefit of the doubt (see chapter on this topic), and endeavors to see the positive attributes of others, G-d — in turn — judges all of his actions in a positive light.

Improvement in the three areas delineated above sways Divine judgment and empowers one to plead not only for himself but also for others. The Gemara (*Taanis* 25b) recounts that R' Eliezer, the leader and outstanding sage of his generation, offered twenty-four prayers that rain would fall, but the drought continued unabated. In contrast, when R' Akiva offered a short prayer, the rain fell immediately. The Gemara relates that a Heavenly voice announced, "Not because one is greater than the other, but because this one [R' Akiva] is willing to 'look the other way' and not stand on principle, while the former does not." This vignette demonstrates that when people require Heavenly mercy, the prayers of one who is willing to forgive and forget are more readily received than the prayer of one who stands on principle.

Public prayers, on behalf of sick individuals or in response to tragedies, are common in most communities. It seems that the person selected to lead the prayers should be one of sterling repute in the realm of interpersonal mitzvos. Most importantly, our prayers would awaken the attribute of compassion if we would commit to treat others with more sensitivity.

✑ Resolutions

The *Chasam Sofer* asks a question on the verse, תָּמִיד עֵינֵי ה' אֱלֹקֶיךָ

בָּהּ מֵרֵשִׁית הַשָּׁנָה וְעַד אַחֲרִית שָׁנָה, *The eyes of Hashem, your G-d, are always upon it [the Land of Israel], from the beginning of the year to year's end* (*Devarim* 11:12). Why does the verse use the definite article (the) in referring to the beginning of the year, whereas in referring to year's end the definite article is omitted? He answers that at the beginning of the year, as the Days of Judgment approach, people are accustomed to make resolutions for improvement so that the coming year will be better — it will be *the* year. However, as the days and months go by, the commitment to improve fades, and thus the year ends just like all the other years, as indistinct as any other year — it is no longer *the* year hoped for in the beginning.

We need to understand why resolutions that were so sincere dissipate with the passing of time. Most people genuinely regret their misdeeds of the past, and their resolution for improvement is sincere. If so, why is there no staying power for the initial resolve to improve?

New resolutions for improving one's behavior often require a dramatic change in one's habitual conduct. This entails strenuous effort and significant personal sacrifice. This is not unlike many diets, which begin with great enthusiasm and fizzle before too long, because they demand tremendous discipline and self-control. The only guarantor of sustained success is the recognition of one's deep-seated faults, and the realization that there is no other way to overcome them, except going through this hard process.

The following story can serve as an example to how one can make a decision to change, yet is not willing to depart from "bad" habits.

Fifty years ago, when a hat was stained, it was unthinkable to simply purchase a new one; one went to the haberdasher, who would clean and refresh the hat. At times, he would even turn the felt inside out, "remaking" the hat! Sadly, after three or four months the stains would reappear. People complained to the "hat man" and accused him of cheating by just temporarily covering the stains with some cream. Responding to the customers' complaints, the "hat man" retorted:

I clean the hat well. However, the person who wears the cleaned hat is the same person who wore the hat before, and he still has the same old habits. On Friday night, as he eats his fish with condiments, he absentmindedly adjusts the position of the hat on his head, leaving a greasy imprint on the brim. Then he touches the horseradish on his plate, and once again adjusts his hat, leaving another stain … These are really new stains, just in the same location as the old stains.

Jews purify themselves on Rosh Hashanah and Yom Kippur. How does it happen that shortly thereafter they look and act just the same as before? If a person does not change his habits — the stains are likely to return! As such, only if a person makes a fundamental change in the causes and patterns of behavior can he expect an enduring transformation in the future.

◆§ The Test of Repentance

Another test to verify if repentance is genuine and sustainable can be found in a person's attitude and actions in the realm of interpersonal mitzvos. So asserts R' Tzvi Elimelech Shapira (*Bnei Yisaschar*) in *Agra D'Kallah*, as he explains the verses (*Devarim* 20:10-12):

כִּי תִקְרַב אֶל עִיר לְהִלָּחֵם עָלֶיהָ וְקָרָאתָ אֵלֶיהָ לְשָׁלוֹם. וְהָיָה אִם שָׁלוֹם תַּעַנְךָ וּפָתְחָה לָךְ וְהָיָה כָּל הָעָם הַנִּמְצָא בָהּ יִהְיוּ לְךָ לָמַס וַעֲבָדוּךָ. וְאִם לֹא תַשְׁלִים עִמָּךְ וְעָשְׂתָה עִמְּךָ מִלְחָמָה וְצַרְתָּ עָלֶיהָ.

When you draw near to a city to wage war against it, you shall call out to it for peace. It shall be that if it responds to you in peace and opens for you, then the entire people found within it shall be a tribute for you, and they shall serve you. But if it does not make peace with you, but makes war with you, you shall besiege it.

Explaining this selection metaphorically, the *Bnei Yisaschar* indicates that the human body is considered a small city (*Nedarim* 32b). Accordingly, when a person examines himself and his evil inclinations, and he wants to repent, he should first קָרָאתָ אֵלֶיהָ לְשָׁלוֹם, *call out to it for peace* — he should first introspect and examine his genuine desire for peace with others. וְהָיָה אִם שָׁלוֹם תַּעַנְךָ, *It shall be that if it responds to you in peace* — if you introspect and find that [your] attribute of peace responds by genuinely loving others, always giving them the benefit of the doubt, and always looking for their positive traits; then, וּפָתְחָה לָךְ, *and opens for you* — this will be an opening and an opportunity for [your own] genuine repentance and transformation. וְאִם לֹא תַשְׁלִים עִמָּךְ וְעָשְׂתָה עִמְּךָ מִלְחָמָה, *But if it does not make peace with you, but makes war with you* — referring to the evil inclination, which harasses you with bad character traits, and does not let you love others and see their positive traits; וְצַרְתָּ עָלֶיהָ, *you shall besiege it* — you shall be deeply troubled by it; וּבָנִיתָ מָצוֹר, *and you will build a bulwark* (v. 20) — to wage war [against your evil inclination] with strength … until you win this "war."

According to the *Agra D'Kallah*, one can fake behaviors, but one cannot fake feelings. The yardstick to a genuine and long-lasting repentance is the way someone feels toward others. As long as there are misgivings and hatred, genuine repentance cannot be achieved.

If a person discerns a genuine change in his feelings and attitudes toward other people, such that he truly desires their well-being, looking for the positive in each person and overlooking the negative, and giving them the benefit of the doubt, then there is a better chance that his resolutions even in regard to mitzvos between man and G-d will endure. Feelings toward others are a true barometer for genuine change and true transformation, since one cannot fake genuine emotion.

7

The Importance
of the Little Things

R'Yosef Zeinvirt *zt"l*, among the most brilliant and distinguished scholars of Jerusalem, once gave a lecture deeply etched in my memory. He opened with an incisive question: "Our generation is blessed with many people dedicating their lives to Torah study. If so, why have we not merited producing a concomitant quantity and quality of great Torah sages and leaders as in previous generations?" His answer was based on the wisdom of the *Chofetz Chaim*:

> The evil inclination is very clever, and always challenges a person in his "weak" spots. Some people tend to concentrate on grand achievements and overarching issues. They may be very generous and be involved in big philanthropic projects. The evil inclination knows their strengths and, therefore, he tempts and provokes them with small and "trivial" matters. Thus, one can find a magnanimous donor who ignores the pleas of one knocking at his door, or coarsely responds when a neighbor asks for a favor.
>
> In contrast, many people are very good at responding to small requests made of them on a daily basis. They have no problem giving a destitute man a few dollars or loaning

a wrench to a neighbor. However, when a larger community effort and undertaking is required, the evil inclination "advises" them to refrain from getting involved, as this just "too much" for them.

The great sages and Torah leaders of each generation are those individuals who deny the evil inclination entry in any space, and stand before him like a fortress wall, whether in the "small" or the "great" things.

This chapter will focus on the great importance of the "little" things.

◄§ A Small Extra Effort: "The Finishing Touch"

A Talmudic adage (*Chagigah* 9b) captures the value of investing the extra effort: "There is no comparison between one who reviews his learning one hundred times to one who reviews one hundred and one times." This statement affirms the value of the extra effort, as insignificant as it may seem, since such an additional effort of even one percent can, at times, dramatically impact the outcome relative to the total prior effort. This truism is more profound than it seems at first glance.

Without analyzing why the Gemara specifically chose the numbers one hundred and one hundred and one, it is clear that the Gemara wants to define certain stages in which the next smallest step can elevate a person to totally new heights and achievements. An individual who attempts to climb the peak of Mount Everest will find that the one step that brings him to the very top will dramatically change the nature of his accomplishment. If he would stop one step before reaching the peak, then he will not be counted among those who "conquered" the tallest mountain in the world!

Similarly, in all our mundane endeavors, as in the study of the holy Torah, there are times when the "small" extra effort, which sometimes requires tremendous emotional or physical energy, differentiates between success and failure.

⇜§ First Steps

Anyone who has experienced physical therapy knows that rehabilitation is an extended process of small steps that ultimately yields the desired recovery. Comparably, psychologists recognize that it is impossible to penetrate into the inner world of the patient all at once. Only a step-by-step therapeutic process yields a sustainable outcome.

Learning anything new is done in stages. In spite of each step being small, requiring multiple repetitions, there are no short cuts. A child will not learn to walk and run before he crawls and then toddles; a student will not master a subject in one fell swoop. In spiritual challenges, just as in physical challenges, a steady and continuous ascent is better than quick giant leaps. This is because big jumps can lead to big falls. To illustrate, I want to relate a story of an illustrious Rosh Yeshivah and Rabbinic leader of the previous generation, who served as a pulpit rabbi before he opened his yeshivah.

The members of his congregation were generally unlearned, respectful of tradition even though some desecrated the Sabbath publicly. As a young rabbi who had just come from the great yeshivos in Europe, this was a new and shocking phenomenon. However, not one to surrender in the face of a difficult situation, he set out with determination to educate and guide his congregants on the path to proper Torah observance.

Before *Ne'ilah* on Yom Kippur, he delivered a powerful sermon to the entire congregation, in hopes that it would catalyze them to change their ways for the better. Standing at the podium, he opened with the following declaration: "If you repent and become a *tzaddik* this year — I guarantee that you will die in the course of the coming year!" The stunned congregation sat riveted as he continued, "However, if you commit to change yourselves in one area and you uphold it, and then assume one more mitzvah and then another — I promise you a good year!"

Having captured their attention, the Rabbi elaborated with an analogy from the stock market. If one held onto a stock whose value had been very low for an extended time, and wakes one morning to discover that its value has inexplicably doubled, an astute broker would advise him to run and sell the stock immediately. A sudden and dramatic jump in price can just as easily have a rapid decline. However, a stock whose value increased steadily over time will be retained by an intelligent investor, because each day that passes translates into additional value. The rabbi concluded:

> If in one day you are transformed into totally righteous people, G-d will take you immediately, lest you descend as quickly as you ascended. However, if your improvement will be gradual, yet continuous, and each day you will add another step to your growth, G-d will protect and save you from all evil and bestow upon you abundant resources of strength, health, and financial success so that you will be able to continue and grow.

⪧ A Mistaken Exchange of Purim Monies

The preciousness of the small acts in daily life, whether in the context of family, friendship, neighborhood, or community, cannot be overstated. The Gemara (*Avodah Zarah* 18a) quotes an edifying dialogue between two *Tannaim*:

> When R' Yose ben Kisma became sick, R' Chanina ben Teradyon went to visit him. R' Yose said to him, "Chanina, my brother, do you not realize that Heaven has granted hegemony to this nation [Rome]? Behold, she has destroyed His home, burned His Sanctuary, killed His pious ones, destroyed His best sons, and it still exists! How can it be that I have heard that you are sitting and learning Torah, and making public assemblies of Jews, while holding a Torah scroll in your lap [defying Roman decrees]?"

R' Chanina responded, "Heaven will have pity upon us." R' Yose said to him, "I say to you reasonable things and you respond, 'May Heaven have pity upon us?!' I will not be amazed if they burn you and your Torah scroll by fire!'

R' Chanina responded, "Rabbi, what will be my share in the World to Come?" R' Yose responded and asked him: "[Aside from learning and teaching Torah] have you had any opportunity to take action?" R' Chanina answered, "Monies of Purim got mixed up with other charity funds and I gave them all to the poor." R' Yose declared, "If so, may my portion [in the World to Come] be the same as your portion, and may my lot be the same as yours."

Rashi explains:

Monies of Purim: that I collected from the inhabitants of the city to disburse to poor people for the Purim feast, and it is taught (*Bava Metzia* 78b), "A poor person is not allowed to use these monies [for anything but the Purim feast], even to buy a strap for his sandal."

Were mixed up with other charity funds: I thought they were all regular charity funds, so I distributed them to poor people — not for the feast; and the expenses of the Purim feast, I covered with my own money.

This dialogue raises astonishing questions. Why does R' Yose ask R' Chanina whether he has done any good deeds? Isn't the fact that he risks his life to teach Torah to the Jewish people sufficient to ensure his portion in the World to Come?

The response of R' Yose is even more baffling: What prompted him to declare that he wants his Divine reward to be the same as R' Chanina's upon hearing of a small act of charity? Acts of charity such as these happen every day! How could it eclipse his willingness to risk his life to learn and teach Torah? This is particularly puzzling as R' Yose ben Kisma was renowned for the value he put on Torah learning (*Avos* 6:9):

R' Yose ben Kisma said, "One time I was walking on the road, when a certain man met me. He greeted me and I returned his greeting. He said to me, 'Rabbi, from what place are you?' I said to him, 'I am from a great city of scholars and sages.' He said to me, 'Rabbi, would you be willing to live with us in our place? I would give you thousands upon thousands of golden dinars, precious stones, and pearls.' I replied, 'Even if you were to give me all the silver and gold, precious stones, and pearls in the world, I would dwell nowhere but in a place of Torah .... Furthermore, when a man departs from this world, neither silver nor gold nor precious stones nor pearls escort him, but only Torah study and good deeds.'"

Given that R' Yose had such great appreciation for Torah, why didn't he consider R' Chanina's willingness to sacrifice his life for the study of Torah sufficient to earn a share in the World to Come? The *Mishneh Halachos* (*Chelek* 13, *Siman* 149) offers the following answer:

Certainly the study of Torah is preeminent. But, greater yet is learning that brings one to action, and if a person studies, but does not act, even Torah he does not have .... Therefore, R' Yose asked him, "Have you had any opportunity to take action?"

R' Yose wanted to know if R' Chanina's learning translated into action or if it remained an academic exercise, without any impact on his daily life. Study of Torah that does not impel one to action does not have value, and one receives no reward for such learning. When he answered in the affirmative, his reward was not only for the action, but also for all the learning as well as his willingness to risk his life. As such, his reward was very great, and R' Yose yearned to be with him in the World to Come.

However, what still needs to be clarified is: Was this the only meritorious action that R' Chanina ben Teradyon did during the many years of his life? Certainly all the days of his life were woven into one continuous tapestry of good deeds and mitzvos, large and small. If so, why did R' Chanina choose to highlight this simple act of charity from all of his manifold deeds? R' Dessler (*Michtav Me'Eliyahu, Chelek* 3) explains that specifically this act demonstrates R' Chanina's attention to "small" things — matters that so many disregard.

◆§ Small Things Reveal a Man's Essence

R' Yose had no doubt about R' Chanina's greatness as a Torah scholar, and in his fitness to transmit Torah to the next generation, ensuring that Torah should not — Heaven forbid — be forgotten under the oppressive rule of the Romans. For this alone, R' Chanina merited the World to Come; but, in order to know how great was this portion, R' Yose wanted to evaluate R' Chanina's role in the mundane acts of charity and kindness.

Thus, R' Dessler also explains the intent of the Gemara in *Bava Basra* (16b):

R' Yochanan said: What was said about Iyov is greater than what was said about Avraham! About Avraham it is written (*Bereishis* 22:12), כִּי עַתָּה יָדַעְתִּי כִּי יְרֵא אֱלֹקִים אַתָּה ... *for now I know that you are a G-d-fearing man*, whereas regarding Iyov it is written (*Iyov* 1:8), אִישׁ תָּם וְיָשָׁר יְרֵא אֱלֹקִים וְסָר מֵרָע ... *a wholesome and upright man, G-d-fearing, and avoiding evil.* What is the meaning of *avoiding evil*? R' Abba bar Shmuel said: Iyov was forgiving with his money. It is customary that when someone hires a worker for a very small job at a pay of half a *prutah* [the smallest denomination], he will go to the store, buy merchandise for a *prutah*, and split it with the worker as payment for his work. Iyov, however, would just forgo the small change and give him the entire *prutah*.

R' Dessler elaborates on the virtue of "small change":

One cannot recognize the true level of the inner dimension of a person in great acts, for superficial enthusiasm may be the motivator. It is in small things, that seemingly have little value or significance, that the inner dimension of a person is revealed …. The greatness of Iyov was his willingness to forgive half a *prutah*. Character traits express themselves even in the littlest acts, and thus, it is in these acts that the fundamental nature of a man can be discerned. We see that people in general do not care about less than a *prutah* and it is not recorded in transactions, unless it can be combined with another half a *prutah*. Nonetheless, it is the way of merchants to round up less than a *prutah* to a whole *prutah*, and not to deduct it from the account. From here we see that the desire for wealth rules over even the smallest amount of money, and when it comes to actual transactions — whether to add the half *prutah* to his or his friend's account — he will add it to his own! This is the explanation of our Sages' words that the greatness of *Iyov* was his willingness to forgive half a *prutah*. This is the way of all character traits — to control even the littlest things, and this is where the fundamental nature of a man can be discerned.

◆§ Without Masks

The fundamental nature of man is revealed specifically in small details because people usually pay little attention to them; consequently one's conduct in these matters is spontaneous and not an expression of forethought. This idea, in its most basic form, is expressed in the Gemara (*Eruvin* 65b), "In three things the essence of a person is perceptible: in his pocketbook, his cup, and his anger." A person who is intoxicated or angry loses his inhibitions. Uninhibited, one's "hidden" thoughts and feelings are revealed. Similarly, one's attitude toward trivial matters reveals his inner dimensions.

This concept is articulated in the opening word of *Parashas Eikev* (*Devarim* 7:12): *eikev*, as it is used in this context, connotes "as a consequence":

וְהָיָה עֵקֶב תִּשְׁמְעוּן אֵת הַמִּשְׁפָּטִים הָאֵלֶּה וּשְׁמַרְתֶּם וַעֲשִׂיתֶם אֹתָם
וְשָׁמַר ה' אֱלֹקֶיךָ לְךָ אֶת הַבְּרִית וְאֶת הַחֶסֶד אֲשֶׁר נִשְׁבַּע לַאֲבֹתֶיךָ.
As a consequence of hearkening to these ordinances — if you observe and perform them — Hashem, your G-d, will safeguard for you the covenant and the kindness that He swore to your forefathers.

The ensuing verses promise multiple blessings to a person who keeps G-d's commandments. *Rashi* notes the double entendre of the word *eikev,* which literally means *heel.* He explains that the verse refers to "the easy mitzvos that a person tramples with his heels." Accordingly, the blessings promised will come for observing and performing the mitzvos that people readily "trample with their heels."

The *Sfas Emes* (*Devarim* 5634) elucidates this verse and explains the idiomatic use of the word *eikev,* which indicates the lowest part of the body:

> There are mitzvos that depend on one's head, heart, and other limbs. There are also mitzvos related to his heel — they are the easy mitzvos. The head is more important than the heel; nonetheless the heels provide the foundation upon which a person stands. Likewise, the "easy" mitzvos have precedence, since the whole foundation [of Judaism] rests upon them.

The *Sfas Emes* suggests that the "easy" mitzvos are the underpinning upon which the entire edifice of our humanity rises. *Issurei Torah* cites an exposition of the *Sfas Emes's* words, in the name of R' Itzele Blazar *zt"l:*

> A person needs to know that sometimes even a small action can determine his lot in this world and the next. This can be analogized to a man trying to reach a city, but he only has enough money to buy a ticket to the last station before his destination. Because he is lacking this small amount of

money, he will need to get off the train … and he will not reach his destination. Similarly in heavenly matters: there can be a small deed that a person neglects and consequently all of his other good deeds may prove insufficient to tilt the Heavenly scale in his favor.

Given that the small things reveal the authentic nature of a person, one needs to take note of them in business matters and, most certainly, in *shidduchim*. The true test of an individual is his unprepared response to trivial matters that arise quite unpredictably.

A distinguished businessman was offered a promising partnership opportunity. To evaluate the offer, he flew to the prospective partner's town. To best utilize their limited time together, they decided to meet several times over the weekend in the lobby of a hotel and in long walks. During these meetings the businessman was very impressed by his host — both for his conversational skills and his business acumen. However, there were several minor issues that needled at him. His host never asked, as they returned from a walk, if perhaps he was tired or thirsty. Moreover, his host was habitually late to their appointed meetings and offered faint excuses.

After much reflection, the businessman decided that the prospective partner lacked interpersonal skills crucial for business networking. Fearful that this could be a liability at any crossroads of disagreement in the future, he rejected the offer. As he discussed his decision with his wife, he pointed out:

> From our bitter experience we know that we could have spared our daughter much grief if we had only paid attention to the seemingly little things that we heard about our son-in-law. We ignored them and focused on his virtues. Since this business partnership will require frequent and almost daily contact, I decided that I do not want to repeat that mistake.

The small things reveal otherwise hidden character traits, and they should figure in choosing candidates for leadership.

❧ Choosing Leaders

Our Sages in *Midrash Rabbah* (*Shemos, Parashah 2, Siman 3*) discuss criteria for choosing a leader:

> G-d does not give greatness to a person until He tests him in a "small" thing. Only afterwards does He elevate him to prominence. There were two outstanding men who were tested by G-d in "small" things. They were found faithful and were raised to distinction.

G-d selected Moshe and David for their respective positions of leadership based on their behavior as shepherds:

> He tested David with a flock and found him to be a fine shepherd, as it is written (*Tehillim* 78:70), וַיִּקָּחֵהוּ מִמִּכְלְאֹת צֹאן, [*He*] *took him from the sheep corrals*. David held back the older sheep so the lambs could graze first from the soft grass, afterwards he let the oldest sheep graze from the mid-grade grass, and then the strongest sheep were sent to graze from the coarsest grass. G-d said, "One who knows how to properly graze the sheep, each according to its strength, will come and shepherd My nation!"

The *Midrash* relates that G-d also tested Moshe's worthiness for leadership. As Moshe Rabbeinu tended Yisro's sheep in the wilderness, one kid-goat fled the fold. Moshe ran after it and found it at a pool of water. Understanding that the kid-goat fled because he was thirsty, Moshe lifted him and carried him back to the flock. Observing this tenderness, G-d said, "Given your compassion in tending sheep … you will tend My sheep, Israel!"

It is very interesting to note that in many biographies of great Torah sages there are multiple anecdotes attesting to their attention to details, reflecting genuine concern about each and every person they encountered.

❧ How Are You?

When I first settled in America, a member of the shul I began to frequent welcomed me warmly with an outstretched hand, and then asked about my well-being. As I began to answer him, he had already turned away, and it occurred to me that his question was just a hollow social courtesy. He really didn't care.

At the same time, I met people who were truly concerned, and made it clear they wanted to reach out and help me get acclimated. These were the few who always said something pleasant at the right time and place, and they immediately sensed when I was having a rough time. All this was done without condescension, and reflected a genuine desire to assist. My experience as a newcomer made me particularly sensitive to the plight of visitors and immigrants who feel estranged.

I recall an anecdote told by a friend, a renowned paradigm of kindness, who traveled from Bnei Brak to Switzerland — as he was accustomed to do — to aid a needy Israeli family that had traveled there for their child's medical treatment. As he checked in at the hotel in Zurich, he met another couple sitting glumly with their daughter in the lobby. He greeted them, introduced himself, and asked how they were doing and if they needed help of any kind. When they reassured them that everything was fine, he went about his business.

In the evening, he returned to the hotel, eager to get a good night's rest, and was surprised to find the same family sitting in the same spot in the lobby, with their luggage, ready to depart, yet lingering silently. He approached them and asked why they were still sitting in the lobby, and had not left for their destination. The father responded that their flight was delayed well past midnight, and it would be a waste to pay for another night in the hotel, so they chose to bide their time in the lobby.

My friend responded, "I cannot accept that you will sit here in the lobby and that I will sleep comfortably in my hotel room! You must be hungry and need something to eat before the return flight to Israel." He hurriedly ran to his room and brought down some cake and chocolate to share with them. He sat with them in the lobby making small talk for hours until they departed, though he had never met these people before, and had no idea what brought them to Switzerland.

A while later my friend received a wedding invitation. On the top of the invitation was a hand-written request that he participate in the celebration, as he would be their "most important guest." My friend could not recollect the names on the invitation; the bride and groom were unknown to him. He figured that there must have been a mistake and he was not the intended recipient.

To his amazement, on the following day, his home phone rang and on the line he heard the voice of the father of the bride, who reminded him of their nocturnal meeting in the hotel lobby in Switzerland. The father said to him, "My wife and I came to Switzerland in search of our daughter — she's the one who was with us that night. She had abandoned Jewish tradition during her studies in Europe, and was going to marry a non-Jew in Switzerland. We had spent two weeks attempting to convince her to change her mind. We were going to depart Zurich that night, despondent as our daughter remained steadfast in her decision to marry the non-Jew, though she had finally agreed to come home.

"On that night, when you sat with us in the lobby, reached out to us and shared whatever food and sweets you had, you made an indelible impression on us — and more importantly, on our daughter. On the way to the airport, our daughter could not stop talking about the warmth of your heart and your genuine goodwill to help a stranger. You launched a transformation in her heart, and during the whole flight she could not stop talking about you. When we landed in Israel, our daughter said — to our amazement — that if this is the way a religious Jew lives, and this is the joy of his life, she wants to be like him!

"That began her return to tradition. Later, she promised that she would marry only a Jew — a G-d fearing and good man like you!" The father concluded, "Do you understand why you are the most precious guest at the wedding of our daughter?"

Indeed, the extra effort and special attentiveness to meet the needs of another can change the trajectory of someone's entire life.

8

Sanctifying G-d's Name One Moment at a Time

A few years ago, at the conclusion of a periodic meeting with an important client, he asked me to stay for a private discussion. This client is renowned for honesty and trustworthiness, living up to all his commitments and promises. He opened our private session by thanking me for the superb and reliable service we provide his company, and then added a startling statement, "You shattered one of my preconceived notions about observant Jewish businessmen." He continued to explain:

> See, I am not familiar with many Orthodox Jews since I grew up in a home that was alienated from Judaism. There was one observant Jew with whom I partnered on a deal, believing that because of his strict adherence to faith he would be very trustworthy. I was very surprised and disappointed to find that very often he did not stand by his words. I mistakenly concluded that my own personal ethics were not congruent with religious ethics, and decided to stop doing business with observant Jews. I was, therefore, very hesitant to meet with you initially, and finally acquiesced because of my respect for our mutual friend who so vehemently vouched for you.

I am happy we met and I gave your company a shot, not just because of your great service and the outstanding results, but because it is now clear to me that my own ethical standards are in complete harmony with the Jewish view. I asked for this private meeting so you could explain to me how seemingly observant and G-d-fearing people can engage in unethical and sometimes outright deceitful behavior.

I could not sense one iota of enmity or cynicism in his question. Initially, I avoided responding, and explained that I cannot comment without knowing the specific circumstances. He brushed aside my reticence, and I proceeded to explain that dressing like an Orthodox Jew does not mean that one is truly G-d-fearing; I declared that the majority of Orthodox Jews are ethical individuals, who are upright and trustworthy, and that it is very unfortunate that his initial encounter was with a person whose conduct was inappropriate.

Though I was gratified that my response was accepted, I felt ashamed to be associated with one who caused such a terrible desecration of G-d's Name.

◆§ The Torah View of the Desecration of G-d's Name

The phrase "desecration of G-d's Name" is mentioned several times in the Torah. In *Vayikra* (19:12) the Torah admonishes: וְלֹא תִשָּׁבְעוּ בִשְׁמִי לַשָּׁקֶר וְחִלַּלְתָּ אֶת שֵׁם אֱלֹקֶיךָ אֲנִי ה', *You shall not swear falsely by My Name, thereby desecrating the Name of your G-d — I am Hashem.* Later, it is written (22:32), וְלֹא תְחַלְּלוּ אֶת שֵׁם קָדְשִׁי וְנִקְדַּשְׁתִּי בְּתוֹךְ בְּנֵי יִשְׂרָאֵל, *You shall not desecrate my Holy Name, rather I should be sanctified among the Children of Israel.* While both verses mention "desecration of G-d's Name," the practical meaning of this phrase is different in each context. Regarding the latter verse, *Rashi* comments that the phrase *I should be sanctified* teaches "that one should sacrifice one's life" and thereby "sanctify My Name."

Sefer HaChinuch writes (*Mitzvah* 296):

> We are commanded to sanctify G-d's Name, as it is written
> (*Vayikra* 22:32), וְנִקְדַּשְׁתִּי בְּתוֹךְ בְּנֵי יִשְׂרָאֵל, *I should be sanctified*
> *among the Children of Israel.* This means that we must risk
> our lives for the fulfillment of the mitzvos of our religion.

Sefer HaChinuch enumerates the three mitzvos for which one
must die rather than violate: idolatry, adultery, and murder.

The former verse (*Vayikra* 19:12) speaks about the desecration of
G-d's Name in connection with swearing falsely for illicit monetary
gain. The *Rashbatz* (*Magen Avos* 4:4) explains why swearing falsely
is deemed a desecration of His Name:

> There is no greater desecration of G-d's Name than this
> — he steals his friend's money by using G-d's honored
> and awesome Name! So our Sages said that if a person,
> who is great in the wisdom of Torah, does things that are
> inappropriate and causes everyone to be appalled, he
> desecrates G-d's Name.

The essence of swearing is an attempt by an individual to
authenticate his claim by saying that just as the existence of G-d is
true, so too are his words. If, Heaven forbid, it becomes clear that
his oath was taken falsely, he has gone far beyond a lie, and has
exploited G-d's Name to execute a despicable plot. Furthermore, by
virtue of his false oath, a person casts aspersion upon the existence
and eternity of G-d, and there is no more profound desecration of
G-d's Name than this!

The Gemara in *Yoma* (86a) brings examples of the desecration of
G-d's Name:

> What qualifies as the desecration of G-d's Name? Rav said,
> "For someone like me, if I buy meat from a butcher and I
> do not pay him right away." When Abaye would buy meat
> from two partners … he would pay each one and afterwards
> he would bring them together, and settle the account.

Rashi explains that Rav felt that when he postpones payment the butcher may suspect that he plans to steal from him, and will learn to disregard thievery. Abaye was afraid that one partner may not know that Abaye already paid the other one, suspecting that Abaye is not planning on paying at all.

Rav and Abaye assumed extremely high standards of ethical conduct, knowing that, as leaders of their generation, all of their actions were highly scrutinized. They wanted to avoid at all costs any possibility — remote and mistaken as it may be — that their actions may result in the desecration of G-d's Name. The Gemara's discussion continues by explaining the verse in *Devarim* (6:5) — וְאָהַבְתָּ אֵת ה' אֱלֹקֶיךָ, *You shall love Hashem, your G-d* — "which teaches us that the Name of Heaven should be beloved through you."

> A person should study Torah and Mishnah, serve Torah sages, and conduct his business congenially. What do people say about him? "Fortunate is his father who taught him Torah; fortunate is his rebbi who taught him Torah. Woe unto people who do not study Torah. This person who studied Torah — look how pleasant are his ways, and how appropriate his actions!" About him the verse (*Yeshayahu* 49:3) says, עַבְדִּי אָתָּה יִשְׂרָאֵל אֲשֶׁר בְּךָ אֶתְפָּאָר, *You are My servant, Israel! Through you I will be glorified.*
>
> However, someone who studies Torah and serves Torah sages, but does not conduct his business with integrity, and his speech with others is not pleasant — What do people say about him? "Woe unto a person who studied Torah, woe unto his father who taught him Torah, and woe unto his rebbi who taught him Torah! This person who studied Torah — look how corrupt are his actions and how disgraceful his ways!"

Abaye teaches that sanctifying or desecrating His Name is determined by how others judge our actions, and that yardstick applies to all people — not just to the highly visible sages.

The *Rambam* in *Hilchos Yesodei HaTorah* (*Perek* 5, *Halachah* 11) rules that one does not have to actually commit a sin in order to desecrate G-d's Name. The greater and more famous a person is, the greater is his responsibility to be careful in all aspects of his behavior:

> There are other things that are also considered a desecration of G-d's Name — presuming they are done by a man who is great in Torah and famous for piety. [If he does] things that people gossip about, even though they are not sins, he has desecrated G-d's Name .... if his speech with others is not congenial and he does not greet them nicely, he is quarrelsome and prone to anger, etc. All this depends upon the greatness of the sage, he must be meticulous and go beyond the letter of the law.
>
> Similarly, if he is meticulous in his behavior, speaks congenially and gets along with others, maintains a refined demeanor, greeting them with a pleasant countenance, and does not respond in kind when insulted — even to those who ridicule him — and conducts business with integrity ... to the point where everyone praises and loves him, and values his actions, behold this individual sanctified the Name of G-d. About him, the verse (*Yeshayahu* 49:3) says, *You are My servant, Israel! Through you I will be glorified.*

Indeed, our Sages' expectations from those who are being scrutinized are so high that even a visible garment stain is deemed a desecration of G-d's Name (*Shabbos* 114a).

A Torah scholar is viewed as a representative of G-d. If he is not dressed appropriately, people may disrespect him, and by association the Torah and the values he represents. A particular behavior of a Torah scholar could be considered a desecration of G-d's Name, whereas the same behavior by a layman will not be considered a desecration of G-d's Name. Furthermore, there is no middle ground in a situation that requires sanctifying His Name. If a person does not fulfill his expected obligation to sanctify G-d's

Name, then by default he is desecrating G-d's Name.

Consequently, one may reconcile an apparent difficulty in the verse (*Vayikra* 19:12), וְלֹא תִשָּׁבְעוּ בִשְׁמִי לַשָּׁקֶר וְחִלַּלְתָּ אֶת שֵׁם אֱלֹקֶיךָ אֲנִי ה', *You [in plural] shall not swear falsely by My Name, thereby you [in singular] shall not desecrate the Name of your G-d.* The *Meshech Chochmah* asks, "Why does the verse open in the plural form, yet conclude in the singular form?" Based on the sources quoted above, one can deduce that the prohibition of swearing falsely applies to all people equally, and therefore the Torah wrote it in the plural form. In contrast, the criteria for what is considered desecration of G-d's Name changes from person to person. A stain on a sage's clothing, or an unfulfilled promise by a prominent Torah scholar, can be classified as a desecration of G-d's Name, though comparable behavior from an anonymous common person may not be classified as such. Since the magnitude of the desecration of G-d's Name changes from one person to the next, the Torah wrote the prohibition to desecrate G-d's name in singular form.

৵৽ The Desecration of G-d's Name in Private

According to Rabbeinu Yonah, desecrating G-d's Name is possible not just in public, but also in front of an individual. Rabbeinu Yonah, in *Sefer HaYirah*, writes:

> Do not do anything unbecoming in front of your friend. If others did something in front of you and you were disgusted, forgive them .... If you found spit lying around, remove it or cover it and forgive the person who made it, lest someone else come and see it and not be forgiving. Be careful that no dirt, oil, or anything disgusting be found on your clothes, because someone who gets soiled and is not careful about his cleanliness, makes G-d's beloved ones hated.

The *Rambam* goes even further, asserting that it is possible to desecrate G-d's Name even in total privacy. Every action that demonstrates a person's disdain or disregard for G-d is considered desecration of His Name. Conversely, a person who refrains from committing a wrongdoing because of his love for G-d — and not because of his concern about what people will say — sanctifies G-d's Name. In *Hilchos Yesodei HaTorah* (5:10) he writes:

> Whoever intentionally violates any of the mitzvos written in the Torah, with disdain and spitefully, desecrates G-d's Name .... If he committed this sin in the presence of ten Jews, he has desecrated G-d's Name in public. Likewise, anyone who refrains from doing a sin or does a mitzvah, not for any worldly reason: not out of fear, trepidation, or loss of honor, but solely for the sake of the Creator — like Yosef's withstanding the temptations of his master's wife — such a person has sanctified G-d's Name.

The source for the ruling of the *Rambam* is a Mishnah in *Avos* (4:5):

> רַבִּי יוֹחָנָן בֶּן בְּרוֹקָא אוֹמֵר: כָּל הַמְחַלֵּל שֵׁם שָׁמַיִם בְּסֵתֶר, נִפְרָעִין מִמֶּנּוּ בְּגָלוּי. אֶחָד שׁוֹגֵג וְאֶחָד מֵזִיד בְּחִלּוּל הַשֵּׁם, R' Yochanan ben Beroka says, "Whoever desecrates G-d's Name in secret, punishment will be exacted from him in public; unintentional or intentional, both are alike regarding the desecration of G-d's Name."

Clearly this Mishnah implies that it is possible to desecrate His Name in private. The *Tiferes Yisrael* writes on this Mishnah:

> There are two kinds of desecrators of G-d's Name: A person who commits a sin in public, even to satisfy his sensual desire, nonetheless desecrates and dishonors G-d's Name, because he is telling everyone that he is not concerned about G-d's commands. Even a person who was overwhelmed by his evil inclination or committed a sin to satisfy his sensual desire, at least should have done the act in private with concern for the honor of his Maker, and not desecrated G-d's Name in public ....

But, there is another form of the desecration of G-d's Name which our Mishnah is referring to, and that is [people] who sin brazenly in hiding, even when they derive no benefit ... to deny the existence of G-d, or that Torah is from Heaven, or that there is Divine Providence, or that there is reward and punishment. Nonetheless, he does not sin in public out of concern for his own honor, because he wants to pretend that he is a righteous man.

The punishment for someone who desecrates G-d's Name in secret is greater, for he has no fear of G-d and sins only to demonstrate his total disdain for the Creator of the universe. This person commits his iniquities in private to protect his reputation and appear to others as a Heaven-fearing individual. The retribution for such a person will be in public, in order to remove the pious mask from his face.

✌§ The Reward for Sanctifying G-d's Name

The Gemara (*Sotah* 10b) details the reward that is given for sanctifying G-d's Name in private and in public:

> Yosef, who sanctified G-d's Name in private, merited that one letter from G-d's Name was added to his name, as it is written (*Tehillim* 81:6), עֵדוּת בִּיהוֹסֵף שָׂמוֹ, *He appointed it as a testimony for* **Yehosef** ... Yehudah, who sanctified the Name of Heaven in public, merited that his name is composed of the four letters of G-d's Name.

Though Yosef's refusal to sin was private, his resistance of temptation was deemed a sanctification of G-d's Name. Any person who stands strong and does not capitulate to his evil inclination, due purely to his fear of Heaven, is considered to have sanctified the Name of G-d. On the other hand, Yehudah's public admission of guilt was considered a public sanctification of G-d's Name. He not only admitted wrongdoing, but went a step further and vindicated Tamar, disregarding his honor or reputation. Concerned only with uncompromising truth, Yehudah's public act exemplifies sanctification of G-d's Name.

⋘ Emulating G-d

Ramban presents a novel definition of the concepts of the sanctification and desecration of G-d's Name, by quoting *Devarim* 28:9, וְהָלַכְתָּ בִּדְרָכָיו, *go in His ways*:

> Since all of our actions [are meant to] emulate the acts of G-d, so long as we are doing that which is good and upright, we are sanctifying His great Name .... Whenever we do not behave appropriately and commit transgressions, we desecrate the Name of Heaven (*Iggeres HaKodesh*).

An upright person, who conducts himself appropriately, is deemed to be emulating G-d and thus faithfully fulfills his purpose for being — having been created in G-d's image. However, if, Heaven forbid, a person does not conduct himself suitably, and, as such, is not going in the ways of G-d, he has failed in his principal role.

We need to realize that as Jews, and especially as observant Jews, we have a significant responsibility. Many have great expectations of us, particularly in the way we treat others. Expectations and perceptions are critical in determining the magnitude of sanctification or desecration of the Name of G-d. Each individual has ample opportunity to sanctify G-d's Name each day, by demonstrating integrity, respect and decency in interactions with others. If, Heaven forbid, we do not do so, it is quite likely that we cause the desecration of G-d's Name, a sin that eludes atonement.

9

A Person as Judge

The Torah is very explicit and specific in its demands of a court of law. Judges are obligated to carry out a thorough and fair investigation in their efforts to get all the pertinent facts: וְדָרַשְׁתָ וְחָקַרְתָ וְשָׁאַלְתָ הֵיטֵב, *You shall seek out and investigate, and inquire well* (*Devarim* 13:15). *Midrash Tannaim* elucidates that in obtaining testimony the judges need to engage in multiple inquiries to substantiate the credibility and accuracy of the witnesses:

> Seven inquiries: In which cycle of the sabbatical year? In which year? In which month? On which day of the month? On which day of the week? At what hour? In which place? … — to the exclusion of any doubt … — the testimony of the two witnesses must be compatible, for if either the inquiries or the cross-examinations are contradictory, their testimony is invalid.

The court has the responsibility to question and cross-examine the witnesses on all of the pertinent details of the incident. If there is any contradiction in their testimony, even in one small detail — their entire testimony is dismissed!

⊷§ Transparency in Judicial Procedure

In addition, the court must ensure that judicial procedures are transparent, such that there are no questions about their fairness. In explaining the verse in *Parashas Kedoshim*, לֹא תַעֲשׂוּ עָוֶל בַּמִּשְׁפָּט לֹא תִשָּׂא פְנֵי דָל וְלֹא תֶהְדַּר פְּנֵי גָדוֹל בְּצֶדֶק תִּשְׁפֹּט עֲמִיתֶךָ, *You shall not commit a perversion of justice; you shall not favor the poor and you shall not honor the great; with righteousness shall you judge your fellow* (*Vayikra* 19:15), the *Mechilta* comments:

> Do not say, "Since the litigant is a poor man ... I will decide in his favor and this way he will be supported without shame." Therefore, it is written, לֹא תִשָּׂא פְנֵי דָל, *you shall not favor the poor* .... Do not say, "He is a *nazir*, he descends from a great family, how could I embarrass him?" Therefore, it is written, וְלֹא תֶהְדַּר פְּנֵי גָדוֹל, *you shall not honor the great.*

The Gemara in *Shevuos* (30a) adds:

> R' Yehudah said, "I heard that if they want to seat both of the litigants, they may do so. What is prohibited? For one to sit and for the other to stand; for one to speak his full, yet to say to the other litigant, 'Make your words brief!'"

Accordingly, judges have a duty to treat the litigants equally. Judges must ensure that no litigant feels disadvantaged or discouraged in his standing in the court. Furthermore, it is the judges' responsibility to make sure that justice is transparent, avoiding any suspicion that any litigant is treated unfairly.

In addition to these understandable requirements, the Torah demands that a religious and faith-based perspective is manifest in every court session. The Gemara in *Sanhedrin* (6b) says:

> The witnesses must know ... before Whom they are testifying, and Who will exact retribution from them in the future, as it is written (*Devarim* 19:17), וְעָמְדוּ שְׁנֵי הָאֲנָשִׁים אֲשֶׁר לָהֶם הָרִיב לִפְנֵי ה׳, *The two men who have the grievance shall stand before Hashem.* The judges must know who they are judging, before Whom they are judging, and Who will exact retribution from them in the future, as it is written

(Tehillim 82:1), אֱלֹקִים נִצָּב בַּעֲדַת קֵל, *G-d stands in the Divine assembly.* Perhaps a judge will say, "Why do I need this grief?" The Torah answers, וְעִמָּכֶם בִּדְבַר מִשְׁפָּט, *He is with you in the matter of judgment* (II Divrei HaYamim 19:6). A judge is held accountable only for what his eyes can see.

Every judge must realize that he is not the only judge in the courtroom, and that the ultimate Judge, the Almighty, is also present in the court, carefully inspecting every step of the proceedings. The Almighty expects the judges to do whatever is humanly possible to discover all the facts, and reach an appropriate decision. Any slack in the efforts to discover the facts, in deliberating and reaching a verdict, or in guaranteeing equal treatment to both sides, will not be tolerated by G-d, and is deemed a direct affront to the honor of the Creator, Whose essence is Truth.

⋇§ The Heavenly Court

The judicial process in the Heavenly Court is completely different than the one described above. The Mishnah in *Avos* (2:1) says, דַּע מַה לְמַעְלָה מִמְּךָ, עַיִן רוֹאָה, וְאֹזֶן שׁוֹמַעַת, וְכָל מַעֲשֶׂיךָ בְּסֵפֶר נִכְתָּבִים, *Know what is above you — a watchful Eye, an attentive Ear, and all your deeds are recorded in a Book.* In the Heavenly Court the facts are clearly known, and there are no doubts about the accused's intentions or motivations, as everything is revealed before the Heavenly Throne. In Heaven there is no need for witnesses or warnings, for G-d know whether an appropriate warning would have made a difference. As the Yom Kippur prayers clarify:

> You know the mysteries of the world, and the hidden secrets of every living thing. You reveal all the inner chambers of the belly and You examine the kidneys and the heart. Nothing is hidden from You and nothing is concealed from Your eyes.

It is clear that in the Heavenly Court a person is judged not only for his actions, but also for his intentions and hidden emotions. All of these are taken into consideration when a person is judged by G-d, and they determine his reward or punishment.

✍§ A Person as Judge

Besides the "official" courts of law — the Heavenly and the earthly — there is another large group of judges and magistrates. These judges do not require authorization, and they do not function in an official judicial system, yet their power and influence are huge. This group includes all men and women who continuously engage in making judgments about the people and events they encounter daily.

As we observe people around us, we gauge their deeds and behaviors and determine whether they are right or wrong, appropriate or not. Based on our evaluations — often made subconsciously — we draw conclusions about how righteous or wicked they are. We make decisions about every person we come in contact with — neighbors, friends, spouse, children, business associates, religious leaders, etc. The conclusions we reach about people and events have a considerable impact on our daily lives, and in many cases on the lives of those we judge. Therefore it behooves us to ascertain that we have the appropriate attitude and tools to properly judge others, since the ramifications of a faulty and misguided judgment can be enormous.

In our roles as everyday "judges," we are not obligated to use the elaborate tools and procedures required in a courtroom, and obviously we do not have access to the tools of the Heavenly Court, for כִּי הָאָדָם יִרְאֶה לַעֵינַיִם וַה׳ יִרְאֶה לַלֵּבָב, *man sees what his eyes behold, but Hashem sees into the heart* (I Shmuel 16:7). The question is, what approach can we use? What can we do to arrive at a proper and accurate judgment? What are the guidelines provided to us by the Torah and Sages when judging another human being?

✄ Giving Someone the Benefit of the Doubt

The Torah's command, בְּצֶדֶק תִּשְׁפֹּט עֲמִיתֶךְ, *with righteousness shall you judge your fellow* (*Vayikra* 19:15), is not intended only for professional judges in an official court of law, as *Rashi* explains (based on the Gemara in *Shevuos* 30b):

> The verse does not refer to litigants in court; rather it refers to a person who sees his friend doing something that could be interpreted either in a negative or positive way — you must give him the benefit of the doubt and judge him favorably, and not suspect him of committing a misdeed.

Giving a person the benefit of the doubt is not just a recommendation, but rather an obligation that is counted as one of the *Taryag* [613] mitzvos.

The *Sefer HaChinuch* (*Mitzvah* 235) explains that though they are not permitted to serve as professional judges in a halachic court of law, women are nonetheless also obliged in this mitzvah. The *Korban Aharon*, on *Toras Kohanim* (*Parashas Kedoshim, Perek* 4), explains why the Sages saw fit to interpret this verse as a commandment directed to all people, and not just to professional judges:

> … the verse should have said, *"your fellows"* in the plural and not just *"your fellow"* in the singular! For this reason the Sages interpreted this verse as not referring to litigants, but to the application of logical reasoning in judgment …. if a person sees his friend doing something that could be interpreted in a positive or negative manner — he must judge him favorably … the verse says, *"your fellow,"* because this obligation applies only to someone who is like you — if he is known to be an evil person, then there is a mitzvah to judge him unfavorably ….

Laymen — much like professional judges — must seriously deliberate the manner in which they gauge the conduct of another person, and be extremely cautious in drawing conclusions: is this a good or a bad person, righteous or wicked? In this sense each individual is comparable to the judge in a courtroom, as rash judgment in either arena can lead to wrong conclusions and to a betrayal of our task as "justices of the peace."

⋖§ Do Not Judge Your Peer Until You Have Reached His Place

Aside from giving our peers the benefit of the doubt, there is an additional responsibility when we judge the behavior of others. *Avos* (2:5) warns, וְאַל תָּדִין אֶת חֲבֵרְךָ עַד שֶׁתַּגִּיעַ לִמְקוֹמוֹ, *Do not judge your fellow until you have reached his place*. Even when the facts are clear, and point incontrovertibly to a negative conclusion, we are prohibited from drawing conclusions about the person before we have "reached his place." The phrase "reached his place" connotes understanding the state of mind, the social and emotional circumstances, and the background surrounding the person and the event witnessed. Indeed, the *Sfas Emes* goes so far as to posit that the intent of the Mishnah is to prohibit all negative judgment of another person, since it is impossible to fully comprehend and empathize with the wide gamut of variables affecting behavior.

Clearly, refraining from drawing conclusions based on the evidentiary facts would be a miscarriage of the duties of a professional judge. However, for laymen, the Sages place stringent restrictions on their propensity to judge their peers.

⋖§ Three Levels in Judging Righteously

Based on the above, it appears that there are three distinct categories of circumstances in which we are enjoined to judge others with great caution:

1) It is forbidden to suspect honorable people by attributing negative intentions or meaning to their action, as Reish Lakish warned, "One who suspects honorable people

will suffer bodily harm" (*Shabbos* 97a). This refers to an honorable person whose actions are usually acceptable, but in this case there is a possibility of interpreting the behavior in a negative way. This directive prohibits us from any tenuous suspicion.

2) We are enjoined to judge someone favorably — even when it appears on the surface that the act is wrong and inappropriate. If there is a possibility, even a remote one, to interpret the behavior positively, then it is our obligation to give a peer the benefit of the doubt.

3) Do not judge your fellow until you have reached his place — there is a prohibition to draw negative conclusions about the person, even when his actions are clearly inappropriate and there is no reasonable way to explain his actions positively. The restriction in judgment is not related to the behavior, but about the person, without knowing the background and circumstances of his action, and without ever having experienced similar conditions.

As stringent and burdensome as the requirements of a judge in a courtroom seem, they pale in comparison to the responsibilities incumbent upon every person as a judge. We judge people and their actions all day long, and not just during limited court hours; yet the Torah puts ironclad limits on our freedom to draw negative conclusions about others.

Understandably, these restrictions are very challenging! However, we also need to remember, that every judge — whether he be an official or informal one — has a Judge Who accompanies him: the Almighty G-d, in all His glory. Therefore, it is incumbent upon us to be extremely careful before drawing any conclusions about another person. Exercising extreme caution in judging others will also protect us, as we are judged with the same yardsticks that we judge others. Our Sages (*Sanhedrin* 90a) taught us, "All the attributes of G-d are manifest as measure for measure." If we want G-d to judge us favorably, our only hope is to judge our peers favorably.

In the coming chapters we will broaden the discussion of the obligations of a person as he judges and evaluates all that surrounds him.

10

One Who Suspects Virtuous People

When G-d appoints Moshe Rabbeinu as the leader charged with taking *Bnei Yisrael* out of Egyptian bondage and bringing them to the Promised Land, Moshe demurs (*Shemos* 4:1):

וְהֵן לֹא יַאֲמִינוּ לִי וְלֹא יִשְׁמְעוּ בְּקֹלִי כִּי יֹאמְרוּ לֹא נִרְאָה אֵלֶיךָ ה׳.

But they will not believe me and they will not heed my voice, for they will say, "Hashem did not appear to you."

G-d showed him the miracle of turning his staff into a snake, and then turning it back into a staff, to prove that Moshe was sent by G-d. Then G-d showed him another miraculous event:

וַיֹּאמֶר ה׳ לוֹ עוֹד הָבֵא נָא יָדְךָ בְּחֵיקֶךָ וַיָּבֵא יָדוֹ בְּחֵיקוֹ וַיּוֹצִאָהּ וְהִנֵּה יָדוֹ מְצֹרַעַת כַּשָּׁלֶג. וַיֹּאמֶר הָשֵׁב יָדְךָ אֶל חֵיקֶךָ וַיָּשֶׁב יָדוֹ אֶל חֵיקוֹ וַיּוֹצִאָהּ מֵחֵיקוֹ וְהִנֵּה שָׁבָה כִּבְשָׂרוֹ.

Hashem said further to him, "Bring your hand to your bosom," and he brought his hand to his bosom; then he withdrew it and behold, his hand was leprous like snow. He said, "Return your hand to your bosom," and he returned his hand to his bosom; then he removed it from his bosom and behold, it reverted to be like his flesh (ibid. vs. 6-7).

Our Sages (*Shabbos* 97a) explained why G-d chose to show Moshe Rabbeinu a miracle associated with leprosy.

> Reish Lakish said, "One who suspects virtuous people will suffer bodily harm." For it is written, וְהֵן לֹא יַאֲמִינוּ לִי, *But they will not believe me* .... G-d said to Moshe, "They are believers, the sons of believers, but you, in the end, will not believe" .... as it is written, לֹא הֶאֱמַנְתֶּם בִּי, *Because you did not believe in Me* (*Bamidbar* 20:12).

Based on the above Gemara, one who suspects innocent people is punished twofold: First, his body becomes weak and sickly, as happened to Moshe Rabbeinu when his hand became leprous. Besides the chastisement of the physical malady, there awaits him an additional retribution — he will ultimately commit the very wrongdoing of which he accused the other, who was truly blameless. This is actually what happened to Moshe, who was punished for lack of faith when he hit the rock instead of speaking to it, as it is written, לֹא הֶאֱמַנְתֶּם בִּי, *Because you did not believe in Me.*

⊷§ Why Was Moshe Punished?

The *Maharsha* (*Shabbos* 97a) questions the Gemara's assertion cited above, given that Moshe had substantive reasons to assume that the Israelites in Egypt will not believe him. After all, why should a reasonable person believe someone who claims to be a prophet, without corroboration? Furthermore, the fact that the Torah affirms that they believed in Moshe *after* he performed the wondrous acts is not a contradiction to the concern he expressed, as he was the one who asked G-d to give him a sign to prove his authenticity. Clearly these wondrous acts worked to earn the Israelites' belief. So what exactly was Moshe's mistake?

The *Maharsha* answers that the Israelites held fast to a Divine message passed from father to son among the Elders, that the appointed messenger will announce the code words: פָּקֹד פָּקַדְתִּי,

pakod pakadti (*Shemos* 3:16), proving that G-d had sent him and that their redemption was imminent. Apparently, Moshe was not aware of the significance of these words, and therefore he asked for a sign or wonder to guarantee that the Israelites would believe in him. We need to understand: How could Moshe be punished for something he did not know, and for making a very reasonable and logical assumption?

The *Maharsha* answers that Moshe was punished since G-d hinted to him, וְשָׁמְעוּ לְקֹלֶךְ, *they will listen to your voice* (ibid. v.18), connoting that the people will believe him. Given Moshe's spiritual level, it was expected that he would decipher that very discreet hint, and comprehend that there is a secret code that would be understood by the leaders of *Bnei Yisrael*.

An alternative explanation suggests that Moshe was punished because he suspected a collective entity, lumping together the virtuous with the morally weak. Our Sages admonished, "One who suspects virtuous people" — while the subject and verb are singular, the object of the verb is in plural form: "virtuous people." It seems, then, that being suspicious of a group of people, stereotyping them in a negative way, is deemed an abrogation of the power of discernment. Perhaps this is the reason Moshe was punished: He faulted an entire people, rather than just those specific individuals whom he justly surmised would not listen to him.

Nonetheless, the prohibition of suspecting virtuous people is not limited to a suspicion of an entire group, and also applies to false suspicion of individuals. The Gemara (*Yoma* 18b) relates that as the Temple service on Yom Kippur commenced, the elders of the priesthood made the high priest swear that he would not deviate from their instructions regarding the Yom Kippur service. The concern was that perhaps he was a clandestine Sadducee, and he might do the service of Yom Kippur according to their practices, and not according to the guidelines of the Sages. The Gemara continues:

> He goes to the side and cries because they suspected him
> of being a Sadducee, and they go to the side and cry, for

R' Yehoshua ben Levi said, "One who suspects virtuous people will suffer bodily harm."

We see clearly that suspicion of a virtuous individual leads to the severe punishment of bodily harm. There are several explanations for the twofold punishment for those who suspect innocent people of evil intentions.

❧ The Punishment of One Who Suspects Virtuous People

The *Chasam Sofer* on *Maseches Shabbos* (97a) explains why G-d punishes with physical illness those who suspect innocent people of wrongdoing. He explains that as a rule, G-d, as Master of Compassion, gives wrongdoers the benefit of the doubt, and therefore He usually forgoes punishing the body of a sinner and exacts initial retribution on his property. However, G-d also judges people "measure for measure" — and where someone does not give others the benefit of the doubt, and rashly suspects the worst of others, G-d also withholds the benefit of the doubt. Therefore, He punishes and inflicts bodily harm right away, as retribution for baseless suspicion of others.

In *Parashas Korach*, the *Kli Yakar* suggests that the reason one who suspects others will be found guilty of the selfsame offense of which he accused others is a function of the dictum, וַעֲשִׂיתֶם לוֹ כַּאֲשֶׁר זָמַם לַעֲשׂוֹת לְאָחִיו, *And you will do to him as he conspired to do to his fellow* (*Devarim* 19:19):

> According to the letter of the law, it is proper to do to the one who suspected his friend as he "conspired" to do to the accused. If so, he suffers the same punishment that would have been given to the accused, if his suspicion had been proven true.

The *Kli Yakar* applies the law that witnesses who conspire against another person and provide false testimony are actually punished exactly as they had conspired to do to the defendant. So too here, the punishment of the one who baselessly suspects others of wrongdoing is that he will actually commit the self-same sin.

The *Kli Yakar* (*Vayikra* 14:4) provides an additional explanation as to why one who baselessly accuses others of misconduct will ultimately commit the exact same wrongdoing:

> Shlomo (*Koheles* 10:1) said, זְבוּבֵי מָוֶת יַבְאִישׁ יַבִּיעַ שֶׁמֶן רוֹקֵחַ, *Dead flies putrefy the perfumer's oil* — referring to those who gossip and slander, who are compared to flies ... because their whole intent is to discredit righteous people; יַבִּיעַ שֶׁמֶן רוֹקֵחַ, *putrefy the perfumer's oil* .... This individual speaks even against a person of integrity, whose pleasantness wafts like the perfumer's oil .... In the gossip's eyes, יָקָר מֵחָכְמָה מִכָּבוֹד סִכְלוּת מְעָט, ... *a little folly outweighs wisdom and honor* — the little bit of "folly" that he discerns in the other person outweighs all of the wisdom and honor that the other possesses.

The *Kli Yakar* contends that gossips take pleasure in finding fault in others, and when they can perceive some "folly," they allow that to outweigh all of an individual's virtues. His position is supported by the Talmudic adage, "Whoever finds fault in others possesses the same fault" (*Kiddushin* 70b). The Talmud suggests that we are most likely to notice faults that are projections of our own. Accordingly, the *Kli Yakar* explains, one who is suspicious of innocent others will find that he ultimately commits the same offense of which he accused others.

> This fool, who suspects others of misconduct, knows inside himself that the same fault and vice which he "casts" upon his friend, he has too .... By blemishing others, he *proclaims to all that he is a fool*, and he projects the same imperfection — which he knows is really in him — upon others. The fool reasons, since he does foolish things, that everyone else probably does these kinds of folly as well.

This is not a function of the punitive principle of "measure for measure," but rather a natural consequence. Since people project their imperfections on others, it is probable that they will eventually commit the wrongdoings they perceive in others.

✎§ Repentance for Suspecting the Virtuous

The *Rosh* in *Orchos Tzaddikim* rules that when a person is aware that people suspect him of inappropriate behavior, he needs to make every effort to clear his name; on the other hand, if someone suspected a virtuous person and it became clear that his suspicion was unjustified, he is obligated to apologize to his fellow, even if the latter is totally unaware that he was the subject of suspicion. Additionally, he is required to bless him, as Eli HaKohen did to Chana, whom he had suspected of being drunk. After she clarified to him that she was not intoxicated, but rather childless and was passionately praying for a child, he sent her off and blessed her that her plea for children would be answered (*I Shmuel* Ch. 1).

Perhaps suspicion of others originates from an innate disdain — howsoever unconscious — toward them, and therefore, the usual regret and the asking of forgiveness are insufficient for repentance. Restoration of spiritual equilibrium requires more: a genuine blessing from the depths of the heart for the suspected victim, as a means of expressing that he truly values and recognizes his virtues.

Someone who has developed a jaundiced eye and cynical approach to people naturally tends to suspect others of wrongdoings; he tends to concentrate on their imperfections, and to associate them with undesirable acts and intentions. Therefore, he does not realize that he is doing anything wrong. Furthermore, he convinces himself that since he has not acted, just "suspected," no wrong was committed, and there is no need to repent. Finally, attributing evil intent may become second nature to a person who tends to denigrate or disregard others, even righteous people.

Cynics rarely heed the admonitions of the Torah and its scholars. The *Rif* (*Yoma* 6a) writes:

There are twenty-four things that impede repentance ....
One who argues with the words of the Sages, one who is
suspect of virtuous people, one who despises admonition,
and one who mocks the mitzvos.

Whereas the *Rif* uses the language of "impedes," the *Rambam*
uses much sharper language and writes that one who suspects
virtuous people "is most likely not to repent." The *Rambam* explains
his position (*Hilchos Teshuvah, Perek* 4, *Halachah* 4):

One who is suspicious of a virtuous person says in his
heart that he is not sinning, because he thinks: "What have
I done to him? Is there anything here more than suspicion?
Maybe he did it or maybe not." He does not recognize that
it is a transgression — though he turns a righteous man
into an evildoer in his mind.

The *Meiri* in *Chibur HaTeshuvah* wrote another reason why
repentance and atonement will be difficult for those who tend to
suspect others.

Even though there is not a physical action in being suspicious
of an innocent, for he did not rob him or embarrass him,
behold this wrongdoing will bring about an attitude that
the righteous are no different than the wicked; and he will
not listen to the rebuke of the Sages, because he suspects
that they are guilty of the self-same offense for which
they admonish others. Therefore, our Sages warned us to
always judge people favorably (page 87).

According to the *Meiri*, suspicion of virtuous people stems from
disdain of others and the feeling that there really are very few, if any,
genuinely righteous people; and virtually all of them are guilty of
the very things they preach about to other people. Accordingly, it is
understandable why the suspecting person will not think he needs
repentance and will not listen to others and their call to repent.

❧ Virtues and Not Faults

In our days, maligning people and suspecting the worst of others has become very commonplace. Presuming malevolent intentions for even benign actions is normative in the popular media, and in our private and public lives. We are quick to categorize people and to disqualify them based on their dress or on an isolated incident.

To summarize, suspecting others is a very serious wrongdoing for which a person may suffer bodily harm, as well as spiritual downfall, as he will eventually commit the selfsame offense he alleged others had done. Besides the punishments that befall one who suspects virtuous people, a person like this develops bad character traits and accustoms himself to seeing only the faults of others, condemning and distrusting others in his heart. These are habits that generate severe consequences, for this person will refrain from repenting — whether because he does not understand the evil in his conduct, or because he will not listen to the sages of the generation and their advice.

It is possible that due to the severity of the matter and because a negative outlook on others manifests itself in our relationship to everything around us, the Rebbe R' Elimelech of Lizhensk composed the liturgical masterpiece preceding Shacharis that includes the prayer, "that we should see the virtue of our friend and not his faults." A positive outlook on other people has far-reaching effects on our entire day and on our behavior toward those we encounter.

11

The Obligation to Judge Everyone Favorably

The obligation to judge someone favorably is sourced in the verse (*Vayikra* 19:15), בְּצֶדֶק תִּשְׁפֹּט עֲמִיתֶךָ, *with righteousness shall you judge your fellow,* as it is interpreted in the Gemara (*Shevuos* 30a). The *Rambam* in *Sefer HaMitzvos* counts this as one of the 613 mitzvos for which every Jew is obligated:

> In this mitzvah the judges were commanded to treat the litigants equally …. Another element of this mitzvah is to judge one's friend favorably, and not to interpret his actions and deeds other than as an expression of goodness and kindness.

Rabbeinu Yonah, in *Sha'arei Teshuvah* (*Sha'ar* 3), rules the same way:

> As our Sages (*Shabbos* 127b) said, "One who judges his friend favorably will be judged favorably by the Omnipresent." **This is a Torah obligation**, as it is written (*Vayikra* 19:15), בְּצֶדֶק תִּשְׁפֹּט עֲמִיתֶךָ, *with righteousness shall you judge your fellow.* If the matter is inclined to a negative interpretation, let it be a doubt for you, and do not judge him unfavorably.

While both the *Rambam* and Rabbeinu Yonah concur that there is a Torah obligation to judge others favorably, the *Rambam* goes a step further, and writes (based on *Avos* 6:6) that judging someone favorably is a necessary condition in acquiring the Torah. The *Rambam* writes in *Hilchos Dei'os* (5:7):

> A Torah scholar should not shout and scream … [nor] raise his voice too loud, but his speech should be pleasant with all people. When he speaks softly, he should be careful that it should not be too soft, lest he appear haughty. He should greet every person so that they should be pleased with him. **He must judge every person favorably.** He should speak about the praises of his fellow, and not [mention] his shame at all. He should love peace and pursue peace.

◄§ Pursuit of Righteousness vs. Judging Favorably

The obligation to judge another person favorably — even when the facts point to a likely misdeed — seems to contradict the Torah's command to always search for and speak the truth, and to distance oneself from any falsehood, or even something that has the appearance of non-truth, as it is written (*Shemos* 23:7), מִדְּבַר שֶׁקֶר תִּרְחָק, *Distance yourself from a false word.* Furthermore, the word בְּצֶדֶק, b'tzedek (translated as "with righteousness") in the commandment to judge favorably, implies the search for that which is just, true, and honest. If so, how did our Sages derive from this same word the obligation to bend the facts and search for a favorable decision? R' Samson Raphael Hirsch *zt"l* addresses this question:

> The verse, בְּצֶדֶק תִּשְׁפֹּט עֲמִיתֶךָ, *with righteousness shall you judge your fellow* (*Vayikra* 19:15), is the source for two seemingly contradictory laws. A judge is obligated to operate in a system of absolute justice; whereas outside of the courtroom — in regard to the personal evaluation

of another person — our Sages derived from these words to "judge your friend favorably" (*Shevuos* 30a). However, this is not a real contradiction. Judicial law and social evaluation are different .... A judge needs to examine only the facts of the case ... he must ignore all of the personal and private circumstances, and all of the motives behind the incident.

On the other hand, society is primarily interested in character and personality. The same attribute of righteousness which dictates that a judge should ignore personalities and only judge the facts of the case, also dictates that society should weigh all of the possible circumstances which advocate in favor of the personalities and their character. It declares: "Do not be quick to pass judgment on your friend! Judge your friend favorably!" This is the same attribute of righteousness which when applied to the social construct says, וְאַל תָּדִין אֶת חֲבֵרְךָ עַד שֶׁתַּגִּיעַ לִמְקוֹמוֹ, *Do not judge your fellow until you reach his place* (*Avos* 2:5).

According to R' Hirsch, the standards used by the judges in court are totally different from those that are used by a person when he "judges" his fellows on a daily basis.

The judges in court are obliged to use the "judicial" criteria, by examining the facts and ignoring all the hidden circumstances and intentions surrounding the case. On the other hand, a private individual who is judging the actions of his friend is obligated to judge him based on the "social justice" criterion. According to this criterion, there is an obligation to consider all the possible circumstances and motives, the social and psychological state of the person, etc., and then give the person the benefit of the doubt. These two standards, the judicial and the social, strive together to achieve "righteousness."

To What Extent Must We Judge Others Favorably?

The obligation to judge a person favorably is not without its limits. It does not apply to a criminal, whose actions are detestable. For example, a convicted serial killer is not deserving of favorable judgment. The *Rambam*, in his commentary to the Mishnah quoted above, offers us sound guidance in this matter:

> If the subject is a person unknown to you — you do not know if he is righteous or wicked .... In this case interpret his action in the way that reflects well on him, and do not consider him an evil person .... If he is a wicked man and his misconduct is well-known, and we saw him do an action which all signs indicate was good, but there is a remote possibility that it was a misdeed — one needs to be wary of him and not to assign good motives ... as it is written (*Mishlei* 26:25), כִּי יְחַנֵּן קוֹלוֹ אַל תַּאֲמֶן בּוֹ כִּי שֶׁבַע תּוֹעֵבוֹת בְּלִבּוֹ, *Though his voice is ingratiating, do not trust him, for there are seven abominations in his heart.*

While we do not have to give a proven wicked person the benefit of the doubt and judge him favorably, we need to be very cautious before labeling someone as a "wicked person." If there is the slightest doubt of whether or not someone is wicked, we must also give him the benefit of the doubt. We need to know a person's background, and a great deal of details about his upbringing and about his current circumstances, before labeling him in a negative way, otherwise we may be transgressing a Torah obligation to give people the benefit of the doubt and judge them favorably.

May G-d Judge You Favorably

The reward for one who judges others favorably is tremendous: one who judges others favorably will also be judged by Heaven favorably. This is a manifestation of what our Sages said, "The criteria by which you measure others, is how you will be measured." Consequently, the Gemara in *Shabbos* (127b) relates:

> Whoever judges his friend favorably, is judged favorably by Heaven. There is a story of a man who came down from the upper Galilee and hired himself out to work for three years for a businessman who lived in the South. On the Eve of Yom Kippur he said to him, "Give me my wages, so that I may go and provide for my wife and children." He responded, "I do not have any money." He said to him, "Give me fruit." He responded, "I do not have any." "Give me land." "I do not have any." "Give me animals." "I do not have any." "Then give me pillows and blankets." "I do not have any." He swung his bags over his shoulders, and went home extremely disappointed.
>
> After Succos, the businessman took the overdue wages and three donkeys laden with goods — one of food, one of drink, and one of delicacies — and traveled to the house of his employee. After they ate and drank, he gave him his wages. He said to him, "When you asked me to give you your wages and I said that I did not have any money, what did you suspect?" "I said [to myself], 'Maybe you had a chance to purchase a lot of merchandise cheaply and you used the money for that.'" "When you asked me to give you animals, and I said that I do not have any, what did you suspect?" "I said [to myself], 'Perhaps they are rented out to other people.'" "When you asked me to give you land, and I said that I did not have any land, what did you suspect?" "I said [to myself], 'Perhaps they are leased to others.'" "When I said to you that I did not have any fruit, what did you suspect?" "I said [to myself], 'Perhaps they have not been tithed.'" "When I said to you that I did not have any pillows or blankets, what did you suspect?" "I said [to myself], 'Perhaps he dedicated all of his possessions to Heaven.'"

The businessman said to him, "I swear by Heaven, that is exactly what happened! I had put a ban on all of my possessions with a vow because of Horkonus, my son, who was not studying Torah. When I came to my friends in the South, they released me from my vow. As for you — just as you judged me favorably, may the Omnipresent judge you favorably!"

The *Kedushas Levi* explains, in the name of the *Ba'al Shem Tov,* that the notion that G-d relates to a person as he relates to others is hinted in the verse, ה׳ שֹׁמְרֶךָ ה׳ צִלְּךָ עַל יַד יְמִינֶךָ, *Hashem is your Guardian, Hashem is your protective Shadow at your right hand* (*Tehillim* 121:5), clarifying as follows:

> *G-d is your protective Shadow*: G-d relates to a man like a shadow. Just as everything that a man does, his shadow does as well, so too, G-d conducts Himself with man.

Consequently, when a person judges his friend favorably, not only does he fulfill a mitzvah from the Torah, but he also benefits himself because Heaven will judge him favorably.

This view is supported in the *Midrash* (*Mishlei, Perek* 12) which stresses the virtue of thinking positively about someone else:

> If you see a man who speaks positively about his friend, the ministering angels also speak positively about him. If you see a man who speaks disparagingly about his friend, the ministering angels also speak disparagingly of him.

Chassidic writings further elaborate on the impact that judging others favorably has in this world — such that an awakening from this lower realm arouses Heaven to also judge favorably.

The *Sfas Emes* poses several questions about the Mishnah in *Avos* (1:6), וֶהֱוֵי דָן אֶת כָּל הָאָדָם לְכַף זְכוּת, *Judge every man favorably*:

1) The language of "judge" implies that there is an obligation to judge others. Who empowered any person to judge? Isn't it better not to judge at all?

2) What difference does it make how a person judges his friend? Is not judgment passed by G-d? Whatever is decided in Heaven will determine one's fate. If so, why is it so important how a person judges his friend?

The *Sfas Emes*, citing his grandfather, the *Chidushei HaRim*, explains that the Torah commands us to judge, and endows great power to human speech. When an individual judges his peer favorably, Heaven affirms his words and judges the peer favorably. Thus, one is obligated to judge his friend favorably in order to help exonerate him in the Heavenly judgment.

ᓫᏜ Inspiration from Below

R' Levi Yitzchak of Berditchev, in *Kedushas Levi*, elaborates on this obligation to judge others favorably:

> G-d judges the Jewish people upon the Day of Judgment with abundant compassion and kindness. However, inspiration from below is necessary to awaken the Sublime Attribute of Compassion; and by virtue of our acts of kindness and judging others favorably, the Sublime Attribute of Kindness is awakened, as well. Consequently, [in Heaven] they apply kindness to him and all the Jewish people. If so, a person's actions awaken the "upper gate," to open the gates of kindness, and to bestow blessing upon the Jewish people.
>
> This is the meaning of the verse, (*Devarim* 16:18), שֹׁפְטִים וְשֹׁטְרִים תִּתֶּן לְךָ בְּכָל שְׁעָרֶיךָ, *Judges and officers shall you appoint in all of your gates,* which implies that you yourself will prepare and affix the Heavenly judgment by your "gates," referring to the things that you do, and awaken by your actions. Consequently, the verse concludes, וְשָׁפְטוּ אֶת הָעָם מִשְׁפַּט צֶדֶק, *and they shall judge the people with righteous judgment,* meaning that every person will teach himself to judge others with righteous judgment, to apply charity and

merit to all the Jewish people. In so doing, a person awakens the Sublime Gate, and through this he emerges exonerated in the Heavenly judgment, for by the "measure" which one judges others, he is "measured" by Heaven (*Sotah* 8b).

These words teach us that a person may seal his judgment by the very breath of his mouth, and to have an impact on the judgment of the entire Jewish nation. For there may come a time when a person may plead in the Heavenly Court, "Why was I found guilty for a certain action, and I was not judged favorably?" The response will be, "You judged your friend by the same 'measure' to be guilty, and you are being judged by the same criteria you applied to others!"

When the holy Rebbe of Berditchev was on his way to the synagogue to say *Selichos* on the eve of Rosh Hashanah, he passed a coffee house from which emanated loud voices in Yiddish. The Rebbe remarked to his attendant, "How beautiful are the Jewish people! As they rise so early to say *Selichos*, they drink coffee before they come to pray so that they will be wide awake!" The attendant clarified, "The Rebbe must be in the company of sublime angels, for I overhear them conversing about their acts of thievery ...." The Rebbe exclaimed excitedly, "How amazing these Jews are! They gather together before *Selichos* to publicly confess their misdeeds!" (R' Aharon Perlow, *Otzroseihem shel Tzaddikim*).

⋖§ Bringing Peace

There is another beneficial aspect to the performance of this mitzvah of judging others favorably; namely, it generates peace between a man and his fellow. Our Sages (*Sotah* 27a) teach that when a Jew judges his fellow favorably, he removes the seeds of hatred:

> There are six acts whose benefits a person consumes in this world and the principle remains for the World to Come: hospitality, visiting the sick, concentration in prayer, rising early to the synagogue, raising one's sons to study Torah, and judging one's friend favorably.

Rashi explains that judging one's friend favorably brings about peace in human society: "Since he judges him favorably and says 'He did not sin against me'; 'it was beyond his control'; or 'he intended for the good,' there will be peace between them."

The *Orchos Chaim* writes that R' Chaim of Volozhin introduced a novel idea about the power of the mitzvah to judge others favorably:

> If a person, Heaven forbid, has enemies, he should convince himself, and accept in his heart, that these people are righteous and judge them favorably. Then their hearts will immediately be transformed and they will become his friends.

By judging others favorably, one not only fulfills the mitzvah of *with righteousness shall you judge your fellow,* but can also transform an enemy into a friend, thereby increasing peace in the world. Such transformation is a function of the wisdom of *Mishlei* (27:19), כַּמַּיִם הַפָּנִים לַפָּנִים כֵּן לֵב הָאָדָם לָאָדָם, *As water reflects a face back to a face, so one's heart is reflected back to him by another's.*

◄§ Do Not Judge Your Friend — He May Be Your Brother

The following true story illustrates the great need to judge others favorably even in difficult circumstances. It teaches us how a person needs to think twice before he judges another, because sometimes, that "other" is not really an "other"....

In one of the local schools, the staff met to discuss various educational issues, among them the disruptive behaviors of a few students. The principal, who was careful not to defame any student, described in great detail some disruptive behaviors, without mentioning the names of any of the students. Discussion centered on the behavior of one particular child and its impact on the entire classroom, such that the classroom teacher lost control of his students. Asking for suggestions to restore order in the class, the principal invited discussion among the teachers.

Among the teachers advocating a "tough" approach to this student was one of the most experienced and revered teachers in the school. He demanded that the school deal with that child in the most stringent manner, punishing him for his mischief and threatening him with expulsion, suggesting that any leniency will yield chaos in the school. The meeting ended with a decision to reconvene in two days, giving the faculty time to reflect and consider the issue.

The teacher heading the group demanding the tough measures was summoned to the principal's office, who discreetly informed him that the student in question is none other than his nephew. The teacher's tone, demeanor, and his suggestion of how to respond all changed drastically and instantly. He started to describe his nephew's troubled home and the abuse he suffers from his siblings, claiming, "We need to treat this child differently. The child is not at fault — there are contextual conditions that require a more sensitive approach."

12

Do Not Judge Another Until You Have Reached His Place

Beyond the prohibition of baseless suspicion of virtuous people, and the obligation to judge others favorably, Hillel warned: וְאַל תָּדִין אֶת חֲבֵרְךָ עַד שֶׁתַּגִּיעַ לִמְקוֹמוֹ, *Do not judge your fellow until you have reached his place* (*Avos* 2:5). Various interpretations have been suggested for the phrase "until you have reached his place." Chief among them is that of the *Bartenura*, "If you witnessed your friend encounter a trial and fail, do not judge him unfavorably until you encounter such a trial and succeed." As long as a person has not been in a similar situation and successfully withstood a comparable challenge, he cannot know how he would have responded in such conditions. Hence, he should not judge his friend's actions.

The *Meiri*, in addressing the rationale behind this prohibition of judging the misbehavior of others, explains that unless one understands the motivations and context, it is impossible to condemn observable actions. He explains that "There is no guarantor against sinning, and perhaps even you, if the same [temptation] would occur, would not control yourself, for not every person is able to withstand a test" (*Beis HaBechirah*). Just as our Sages (*Kesubos* 13b) said, "There is no guarantor against illicit relations," to indicate that everyone is prone to fail in this transgression, so too, "there is no guarantor against sinning [in general]." When one judges another's actions as improper, there is an underlying assumption that he would have behaved differently in a similar situation. That assumption is invalid as long as he did not confront a similar situation with all the surrounding circumstances.

Rabbeinu Yonah explains why the Mishnah links the following two prohibitions: וְאַל תַּאֲמִין בְּעַצְמְךָ עַד יוֹם מוֹתְךָ, *Do not believe in yourself until the day you die,* and וְאַל תָּדִין אֶת חֲבֵרְךָ עַד שֶׁתַּגִּיעַ לִמְקוֹמוֹ, *Do not judge your fellow until you have reached his place*:

> Even though you have been faithful and of proper spirit, do not consider yourself righteous. Do not say, "I have not done anything wrong for several days. I have coerced my evil inclination, and I have overcome and conquered temptation …." Therefore, the Mishnah says, "Do not believe in yourself until the day you die," presuming you can withstand the arguments of heretics and the temptation of sin …. [Furthermore] "Do not judge your fellow until you have reached his place" — this too derives from the same issue; as [judging others self-righteously] comes from relying too much on his intellect.

According to Rabbeinu Yonah, the tendency to judge others negatively is rooted in exaggerated self-confidence and in the secure belief that any decent person would have acted differently. A person should be humble and doubt his ability to overcome trials and tribulations. Only then can he understand that he must not judge the actions of his friend unless he has successfully overcome a comparable challenge.

The *Mirkeves HaMishneh* on *Maseches Avos* adds an interesting twist to Rabbeinu Yonah's explanation:

> The concept of this admonition is that a person should not think that everyone in the world is a fool and only he is intelligent. Moreover, this attitude will cause him to despise other people, and others will despise him. Thus,

Hillel, consistent in his philosophy, advises, הֱוֵי מִתַּלְמִידָיו
שֶׁל אַהֲרֹן, אוֹהֵב שָׁלוֹם וְרוֹדֵף שָׁלוֹם, *Be among the disciples of
Aharon — loving peace and pursuing peace* (*Avos* 1:12).

The *Mirkeves HaMishneh* adds two points: First, a person judges
another's behavior negatively because of his disdain for others and
because of his attitude that others are inferior to him. Moreover,
one who judges his friend unfavorably before trying to "stand in
his shoes" increases hatred and quarrels in the community.

⇜§ The Obligation of Mutual Responsibility

R' Mattatia HaYitzhari on *Avos* (6:38) provides another
explanation for not judging someone without having "reached his
place":

> … a person should not say, "Why should I make an effort
> and empathize with his pain? He brought this [suffering]
> upon himself … as his intentions [and actions] were
> malevolent." Do not say this! Judge him favorably. Perhaps,
> if you had been in the same situation, your response would
> have been even more foolish.

Underlying this explanation is the belief in the mutual
responsibility that exists between all members of the Jewish
people. Collective responsibility demands that each one attempt to
advocate for another, putting the other's deeds and motives in a
positive light, and to judge him favorably.

Pirkei Moshe on *Avos* suggests that the obligation of reaching his
friend's place is based on the Torah's mitzvah (*Vayikra* 19:18), וְאָהַבְתָּ
לְרֵעֲךָ כָּמוֹךְ, *You shall love your fellow as yourself.*

> When someone quarrels with another because he shamed
> him, or caused him monetary loss, or did some other
> bad thing to him, it is not right to condemn him, until he
> strives to imagine that he was in the place of this person
> … in the spirit of *you shall love your fellow as yourself.* This

is the meaning of "until you reach his place": Do not pass judgment against him until you imagine that you reached his place, as if you were actually in his place.

Accordingly, the obligation to postpone judgment until one can empathize with the other and actually "reach his place" is inherent in the mitzvah to love your fellow "as yourself." A person must imagine himself in the same situation of his friend, and try to understand his feelings and actions.

R' Moshe b'R' Yehudah Even Machir adds yet another dimension to "reaching his place":

A person should not promote hatred in his heart, and he should consider things from the perspective of his friend, not according to his own viewpoint, for not all minds think alike. Even when there seems to be no room for giving the other party the benefit of the doubt, he should perceive the matter from the viewpoint of the mind and sensitivity of his friend. Perhaps he will find that he bears no guilt or blame, for he acted through innocent intent and not with malevolence or spite. This is a profound matter — for a person will not come to argue with his friend or spouse when he contemplates things from their vantage point. This is the meaning of "Do not judge your fellow until you have reached his place" — "place" refers to his mindset and way of thinking …. It will be considered an act of righteousness, and by the measure he judges others, so will he be judged by Heaven (*Seder HaYom*).

According to this view, "until you have reached his place" includes the emotional state and intellectual capabilities of the other person at the time he committed the act.

·§ "His Place" — Where He Resides

Many commentators explain that the intent of the words, "until you have reached his place," refers to his place of residence.

Thus, the fundamental assumption of this mitzvah is that the true character of a person is most discernible in his own community and home. When someone is outside of his regular surroundings, his behaviors may not reflect his true essence. There is a double warning here: On the one hand, if we see a person outside of his natural surroundings acting improperly, we should postpone judgment of him until we observe his behavior in comparable situations in his usual domicile. Conversely, if we observe a guest or stranger acting like a righteous individual, elevated above the common folk, we should credit him with great virtue only after we've observed him at his regular dwelling, where we can see his "natural" behavior. These are the words of the *Meiri*:

> Some of my rabbis explained this to me as follows: "Do not judge your fellow until …": If you see a stranger in your city, and you see him display splendor and outstanding, sterling character, nonetheless, do not judge him to truly possess these virtues until you "reach his place" in which he lives and you see his conduct "at home," if it confirms them ….

The notion that a person is best recognized in his own community is also written regarding the mitzvah of appointing judges: הָבוּ לָכֶם אֲנָשִׁים חֲכָמִים וּנְבֹנִים וִידֻעִים לְשִׁבְטֵיכֶם וַאֲשִׂימֵם בְּרָאשֵׁיכֶם, *Provide for yourselves distinguished men, who are wise, understanding, and well-known to your tribes, and I shall appoint them as your heads* (*Devarim* 1:13). *Rashi* explains the phrase *well-known to your tribes*:

> … to exclude [the one who] would come before me wrapped in his *tallis*, and I would not know who he is, from what tribe he comes, or if he is proper. But you are well-acquainted with him and you raised him, therefore it says, *and well-known to your tribes*.

⋽ The Place He Frequents Most

The *Ba'al HaTanya* (*Likutei Amarim, Perek* 30) presents a fascinating interpretation of the words "his place":

One must also take to heart the obligation to fulfill the words of our Sages (*Avos* 4:12), וֶהֱוֵי שְׁפַל רוּחַ בִּפְנֵי כָל אָדָם, *Be of humble spirit before every person.* This should be taken literally — "before every person" — even the lowliest of the low. This is based on the words of our Sages, "Do not judge your fellow until you have reached his place." Because his place causes him to sin, since his livelihood requires him to walk in the marketplace all day among commoners, where his eyes see all the temptations — the eye sees, the heart desires, and his evil inclination burns like a fiery oven, as it is written in *Hoshea* (7:6), הוּא בֹעֵר כְּאֵשׁ לֶהָבָה, ... *it burns like a blazing flame.* This is not so when a person rarely goes into the market and spends most of his time at home.

Furthermore, the *Ba'al HaTanya* notes, even among those who spend most of their day in the marketplace there is great variance in their ability to respond to temptation.

Clearly, the expectations from a person who spends most of his day in the *beis medrash* are very different. A person who frequents the marketplace and is subjected constantly to its temptations is more likely to behave improperly, given his exposure to the vices of "the street." Therefore, we should not judge this person by the same criteria that we judge a person who sits at home or in the *beis medrash*. The *Ba'al HaTanya* continues and says that we must know that "the place" also includes the personality of the individual and his way of thinking. People respond differently to identical situations; therefore, it is very difficult to judge another person without "entering his world."

The *Sfas Emes*, in explaining the Mishnah, writes succinctly that since "it is impossible to ever reach the place of your friend given that not all people are of one mind, do not judge your friend at all!" Similarly, R' Nachman of Breslov in *Likutei Moharan* (*Tinyana Torah* 1) writes that the right to judge people belongs exclusively to G-d.

When a person sits to speak to his friend, this is like a mini-

Rosh Hashanah, which is the Day of Judgment, for he sits and judges his friend. A person needs to be very careful ... in this situation, to look at himself well, if he is worthy of judging his friend. Judgment belongs to G-d, for only He is truly worthy of judging a human being. As our Sages (*Avos* 2:5) said, "Do not judge your fellow until you have reached his place." Who is capable of knowing and reaching the place of his friend, but G-d?!

Based on the above, it is quite clear that it is forbidden for a person to judge another even when it is most difficult to give his actions any positive spin. Even if the person judging had been in a similar situation yet acted differently, he still is not allowed to judge his friend, since every person comes from a different background and has a unique personality, and there are many things that influence his motivations and behavior: the style and setting of his upbringing, his relationship with parents and teachers, his daily pressures.

◆§ Judging Others Is Really Judging Oneself

The *Ba'al Shem Tov (Parashas Kedoshim, Os* 5) takes the concept of "not judging your fellow until you have reached his place" to higher domains. Commenting on the case of Nosson the Prophet, who admonished David for his behavior with Batsheva by relating the parable of the poor man's lamb, the *Ba'al Shem Tov* taught:

> ... *the poor man had nothing except one small lamb that he had acquired* [and the rich man *took the poor man's lamb*]. David responded, "*He deserves to die ...*" (*II Shmuel* 12:3). Afterward the prophet said to him, "*You are that man.*" Likewise, when Heaven wants to judge a person for some wrongdoing, they show him the self-same misdeed performed by another person. He gets angry at this person and condemns him to some punishment. The way he judged his friend is the way that he will be judged by Heaven. Unconsciously he was judging himself!

Thus our Sages said, "Do not judge your fellow until you have reached his place." ... you should know that ... you are shown your friend's actions so that you should judge him, and as you render judgment, such will be done to you. According to this principle, ensure that you always judge the other person favorably, and by doing so, you will judge yourself favorably.

A person must realize that whenever he judges others, he actually renders his own verdict.

The *Ba'al Shem Tov* uses the notion that judging others is in fact judging oneself to explain the order of the words in the Mishnah (*Avos* 3:1), וְלִפְנֵי מִי אַתָּה עָתִיד לִתֵּן דִּין וְחֶשְׁבּוֹן, *and before Whom you will give judgment and reckoning*. He notes that the logical order should be "reckoning" and afterward "judgment" since deliberation always precedes the verdict. Answers the *Ba'al Shem Tov*, the word "judgment" refers to the case when a person first sees his friend's misdeeds and then renders a judgment about his friend and his behavior. After he rendered a "judgment" on his friend, the Heavenly Court uses that judgment in "reckoning" his own case.

The conclusion is that we cannot judge another person, as we never could emulate the exact circumstantial, social, and emotional variables that determined a person's behavior, and hence we can never know how we would have reacted under similar circumstances. Passing judgment on others is not only prohibited, but can be really dangerous to ourselves, as we provide the Heavenly Court a guideline of how to judge our own actions.

⇜§ A Tishah B'Av Conversation of Holocaust Survivors

One Tishah B'Av morning two young yeshivah students, who did not *daven* regularly at our *shtiebel*, came to recite *Kinnos* with us. They were reciting *Kinnos* with great devotion, enunciating each word. During the recitation, two elderly men stood outside talking quietly. Their voices could not be heard, as the glass doors were closed. Suddenly, the students stepped out, admonished them for not reciting *Kinnos*, and asked them if they do not feel the pain of the destruction of the *Beis HaMikdash*.

The eldest of the two gentlemen turned to the students and asked, "Who is your Rosh Yeshivah?" One of the young men told him the name of the Rosh Yeshivah. The elderly man continued:

> See, my "rosh yeshivah" was Hitler, may his name be obliterated. Afterward, I studied with the cursed Mengele. My friend's "rosh yeshivah" was Himmler, may the name of the wicked rot. Yes, these were our "roshei yeshivah." You fellows read the *kinnos* about the destruction that our forefathers experienced, and it is doubtful if you truly empathize with their pain, and if you are even capable of understanding what they went through. But, we are talking about our "*kinnos*" — about the tragedies, the destruction, and the devastation that we actually experienced.
>
> Our destruction and pain are so great that even the most moving of the *kinnos* cannot express what we went through, and the immense sorrow that we feel for our parents, our wives, and our children whom we lost. Therefore, instead of reciting the printed *kinnos*, we stand and bespeak our personal lamentations, as we feel the pain of the destruction more vividly than you are able to feel, even if you recite the *kinnos* with concentration and at length …. Can you understand, young men, how great is our sorrow? With G-d's help, never!

Deeply embarrassed, the boys returned to their places. Several years ago, I met one of those "young men," and he is still ashamed of his behavior on that Tishah B'Av more than four decades ago. He confessed to me that ever since that incident, he is doubly careful to avoid judging others.

13

The Person of Integrity

The word *"yashar"* — mentioned frequently in the *Tanach* — literally means *straight*, but its connotations change in various contexts. The most common meanings of the word are: forthright, honest, just, decent, and upright. In this chapter we will address the following:

1) The requirement that people be "straight" and behave with integrity.

2) The meaning of the attribute of "straight" as it relates to G-d: צַדִּיק וְיָשָׁר הוּא, *Righteous and upright is He* (*Devarim* 32:4).

3) The definition of the attribute of "straight" as it relates to moral decisions.

The Torah uses the word *yashar* as related to human behavior in three places:

In *Shemos* (15:26) it is written: אִם שָׁמוֹעַ תִּשְׁמַע לְקוֹל ה' אֱלֹקֶיךָ וְהַיָּשָׁר בְּעֵינָיו תַּעֲשֶׂה . . . כָּל הַמַּחֲלָה אֲשֶׁר שַׂמְתִּי בְמִצְרַיִם לֹא אָשִׂים עָלֶיךָ כִּי אֲנִי ה' רֹפְאֶךָ, *If you hearken diligently to the voice of Hashem, your G-d, and do what is just (yashar) in His eyes ... then any of the diseases that I brought upon Egypt, I will not bring upon you, for I am Hashem, your Healer.*

In *Devarim* (6:18) it is written: עָשִׂיתָ הַיָּשָׁר וְהַטּוֹב בְּעֵינֵי ה׳ לְמַעַן יִיטַב לָךְ, *You shall do what is fair (yashar) and good in the eyes of Hashem, so that it will be good for you …*

In *Devarim* (12:28) it is written: שְׁמֹר וְשָׁמַעְתָּ אֵת כָּל הַדְּבָרִים הָאֵלֶּה אֲשֶׁר אָנֹכִי מְצַוֶּךָ לְמַעַן יִיטַב לְךָ וּלְבָנֶיךָ אַחֲרֶיךָ עַד עוֹלָם כִּי תַעֲשֶׂה הַטּוֹב וְהַיָּשָׁר בְּעֵינֵי ה׳ אֱלֹקֶיךָ, *Safeguard and hearken to all these words that I command you, in order that it be well with you and your children after you forever, when you do what is good and right (yashar) in the eyes of Hashem, your G-d.*

In all of the aforementioned citations, a reward is promised for being *yashar* — a term that remains nebulous. In explaining the verse (*Devarim* 12:28), *what is good and right in the eyes of … your G-d*, *Rashi* writes: "**good** — in the eyes of Heaven; **right** (*yashar*) — in the eyes of men." According to *Rashi*, the word "good" refers to fulfillment of religious mitzvos, whereas "*yashar*" refers to interpersonal mitzvos — to act properly toward another person. Comparably, in *Shemos* (15:26) *Rashi* writes:

וְהַיָּשָׁר בְּעֵינָיו תַּעֲשֶׂה, *and do what is just (yashar) in His eyes:* This refers to business matters, and teaches us that whoever conducts his business with integrity and people find him pleasant and amenable, is considered as if he fulfilled the entire Torah.

Clearly, integrity and proper interpersonal behavior are essential components in the fabric of the mitzvos, and they are a necessary condition for Divine reward.

⇜§ Comprehensive Integrity

According to the *Ramban*, the command to be *yashar*, upright, is an all-encompassing ethical principle, which requires one to go beyond the letter of the law. He explains this principle in his comment to *Devarim* (6:18): *You shall do what is fair and good:*

Our Sages have a beautiful interpretation for this: it refers

to compromise and going beyond the letter of the law …
since it is impossible to specify in the Torah all the possible
scenarios of a person's interactions with his neighbors and
friends … so, after the Torah mentioned many of them,
for example: לֹא תֵלֵךְ רָכִיל, *You shall not be a gossipmonger*
(*Vayikra* 19:16); לֹא תִקֹּם וְלֹא תִטֹּר, *You shall not take revenge
and you shall not bear a grudge* (ibid., v. 18); לֹא תַעֲמֹד עַל דַּם
רֵעֶךָ, *You shall not stand aside while your fellow's blood is shed*
(ibid., v. 16) …. and similar ordinances, this verse reiterates
a general principle that a person should do what is good
and right in all matters, including compromise and going
beyond the letter of the law; and … one's speech should be
pleasant with people, until he will be esteemed by all as a
wholesome and upright person in all matters (*Yoma* 86a).

As customs and social norms vary from one place to another,
and as each situation is unique and not specified by Torah law, one
must adjust and modulate his behavior such that people will deem
him a person of integrity and upright in all matters.

ও§ Righteousness and Integrity

Tehillim 33:1 opens with: רַנְּנוּ צַדִּיקִים בַּה׳ לַיְשָׁרִים נָאוָה תְהִלָּה, *Sing
joyfully to Hashem, O righteous (tzaddikim); for the upright (yesharim),
praise is fitting*. The *Alshich HaKadosh* asks why the verse opens with
a call to the *righteous*, yet concludes with a call to the *upright*, and
what the difference is between them. He answers:

> … the righteous are those who practice justice by the letter
> of the law, and the upright are those who go beyond the
> letter of the law, conducting themselves with integrity
> …. This is the ultimate perfection, as our Sages (*Yalkut
> Shimoni, Tehillim* 656) have said, "They are the greatest
> of the seven groups in *Gan Eden*, and they will see the
> innermost sanctum … (*Tehillim* 140:14), יֵשְׁבוּ יְשָׁרִים אֶת פָּנֶיךָ,
> … *the upright will dwell in Your Presence*."

The *Alshich* continues:

> … the upright ones are greater than them [the righteous], since unto them praise is due — both for their piety and their upright hearts, for they do not question [the ways of G-d] even in the absence of good in Israel.

According to the *Alshich*, the attribute of *yashar* is immeasurably greater than the attribute of righteousness, for the upright person is filled with faith and accepts both good and bad with equanimity, as gifts from the Creator of the universe. These are the people for whom "praise is fitting," and who know how to praise G-d, and therefore they are rewarded with the revelation of the Divine Presence.

✏️ "Fair and Good": Halachic Implications

The principle inherent in the mitzvah to do *"what is fair and good"* has many halachic implications. Following are a few of them:

1) *Bar Meitzra*

The law of *bar meitzra* dictates that when a man wants to sell land, the holder of an adjacent field has the right of first refusal for purchasing the field. He can force the owner to sell him the land under the same conditions open to any other buyer (*Shulchan Aruch, Choshen Mishpat, Siman* 175).

The *Maggid Mishneh* (*Hilchos Shecheinim* 14:5) explains that this halachah, among others, derives from two guiding principles specified in the Torah:

> Our perfect Torah gave general principles for the rectification of character and man's conduct in the world in the statement, קְדשִׁים תִּהְיוּ, *You shall be holy* (*Vayikra* 19:2), the intent of which is "sanctify yourself even in those things that are permissible to you" (*Yevamos* 20a) …. Likewise, the Torah said, וְעָשִׂיתָ הַיָּשָׁר וְהַטּוֹב, *You shall do what is fair and good* (*Devarim*

6:18), meaning that a person should conduct himself in a fair and good way with other people. It was not appropriate to legislate details, because the mitzvos of the Torah apply at all times, in all places, and in all situations; and every person must fulfill them, despite the fact that the personality traits and conduct of men change according to time and person. Our Sages wrote several beneficial details, which fall under these two general categories: some of them were established as fixed laws and some as preferences and acts of piety.

The above is an elaboration of the *Ramban's* position cited earlier, that the Eternal Torah provides direction that applies to varying times and places. The right of first refusal granted to a neighbor is a derivative of the command *to do what is fair and good.*

2) *Shuma Hadar*

Another halachic manifestation of the requirement to do *what is fair and good* is *shuma hadar.* This ruling deals with the case of a person who borrowed money and could not repay his loan, in which case the court appropriates some of his assets, valued at the full amount of the loan, and transfers them to the lender. If the transferred assets were real estate (land or buildings), the borrower can later reclaim his property in exchange for repaying the loan. The Sages took into consideration the financial and emotional distress of a borrower who has had his land and home foreclosed, and ruled that the mitzvah to do *what is fair and good* dictates that the borrower can at any time retrieve his property if he repays the loan in cash (*Bava Metzia* 35a). This option can be exercised only if the lender had not sold the real estate and/or the value or condition of the transferred assets have not changed.

3) Beyond the Letter of the Law

Another ruling derived from the principle of *what is fair and good* is *lifnim mishuras hadin* — beyond the letter of the law. Among the numerous examples cited in the Talmud for this is the case related in *Bava Metzia* 83a: Rabbah bar Bar-Chanan's workers, who were very poor, unintentionally broke some of his wine barrels. According to the letter of the law, the workers must pay him for the damage. Rav exempted them from payment of the damage, and furthermore, he required Rabbah bar Bar-Chanan to pay them their withheld wages, based on the verse in *Mishlei* (2:20): לְמַעַן תֵּלֵךְ בְּדֶרֶךְ טוֹבִים וְאָרְחוֹת צַדִּיקִים תִּשְׁמֹר, *in order that you may walk in the way of the good and keep the paths of the righteous.* According to Rav, this verse, along with the Torah's directive to *do what is fair and good*, compel one to abide by a different set of norms. Even if a person has legal rights to demand payment from another, in certain circumstances this is improper and even prohibited. In some situations, ethical sensitivity demands that one relate to needy people with fairness and goodness, above and beyond cold logic.

It is interesting to note that Rav obligated Rabbah bar Bar-Chanan to pay his workers, as if nothing wrong had happened. If Rav had only been concerned with the welfare of the workers, he could have commanded Rabbah bar Bar-Chanan to give them the money as charity since his workers did not earn their wages, given the damage they caused. However, Rav apparently understood that the responsibility to *walk in the way of the good and keep the paths of the righteous* encompasses not only the duty to care for his poor employees, but also to do it in a way that protects their dignity.

◆§ Righteous and Upright Is He

The *Song of Ha'azinu (Devarim* 32:4) describes G-d as, הַצּוּר תָּמִים פָּעֳלוֹ כִּי כָל דְּרָכָיו מִשְׁפָּט ... צַדִּיק וְיָשָׁר הוּא, *The Rock! — perfect is His work, for all His paths are justice ... righteous and fair (yashar) is He*. In his introduction to *Ha'amek Davar*, the *Netziv* of Volozhin writes:

> ... *Sefer Bereishis* is called by the prophets, *Sefer HaYashar* (the Book of the Upright) .... R' Yochanan explains (*Avodah Zarah* 25a): This is the book of Avraham, Yitzchak, and Yaakov, who were called "the upright ones," as it is written (*Bamidbar* 23:10), תָּמֹת נַפְשִׁי מוֹת יְשָׁרִים, *May my soul die the death of the upright.*
>
> ... why did Bilaam call our forefathers by the name "the upright ones" and not the righteous or pious ones? ... The answer is found in our Sages' explanation of the verse (*Devarim* 32:4), *The Rock! — perfect is His work ... righteous and fair is He.* The accolade, *fair is He*, was said as a validation of G-d's judgment during the era of the Second Holy Temple's destruction, which was deemed a "perverse and twisted" generation.

The *Netziv's* evaluation of the Jews in that era and how they brought about the destruction of the *Beis HaMikdash* is based on the Gemara (*Yoma* 9b):

> They were engaged in Torah study, mitzvos, and acts of lovingkindness, so why was it destroyed? It was destroyed because of baseless hatred. This teaches you that baseless hatred is equivalent to the three cardinal sins: idolatry, adultery, and murder.

The *Netziv* elaborates on the words of the Gemara:

> ... they were righteous and pious people, who toiled in Torah learning; however, they were not upright in worldly matters. Therefore, because of the baseless hatred that was in their hearts toward each other, they suspected someone

who they saw acting not in accordance with their concept of worshiping G-d, of being a Sadducee or a heretic. Through this they came to virtually committing murder and all of the evils of the world, leading to the destruction of the Temple. For this tragedy [our Sages] validated the Divine judgment: G-d is upright and fair (*yashar*) and does not tolerate such "righteous" people, unless they also follow the path of fairness in worldly matters, and not with crookedness — even if it be for the "sake of Heaven" — for this causes the devastation of Creation and the ruin of civilization.

This was the praise of the forefathers: In addition to being exceptional righteous and pious men and lovers of G-d, they were also upright — meaning they dealt with the nations of the world, even unworthy idolaters, with love and concern for their well-being — as this is the perpetuation of Creation. As we see how fervently Avraham Avinu pleaded on behalf of Sodom, though he consummately hated them and their king for their wickedness ... nonetheless he desired their survival.

Sadly, the *Netziv's* words ring so true in our times too. People are very quick to label others as "inferior in worshiping G-d" and not as "worthy," even when they follow the guidance of *Shulchan Aruch* and the age-old customs of their forefathers. Such people delude themselves that their denigration of others pleases the Creator, when in reality, G-d cannot tolerate this type of "righteousness," which brings destruction upon the world. The words of the *Netziv* also clarify a verse in *Mishlei* (14:12), יֵשׁ דֶּרֶךְ יָשָׁר לִפְנֵי אִישׁ וְאַחֲרִיתָהּ דַּרְכֵי מָוֶת, *There is a way that seems right to man, but at its end are the pathways to death. Rashi* explains that the verse refers to a reprobate sinner who refuses to acknowledge that he has done something wrong.

❧ A Sinner Who Says He Has Done No Wrong

The *Alshich HaKadosh* also harshly condemns those who are sincerely desirous of pleasing G-d and following His ways, yet remain blind to the sinfulness of their denigrating attitude toward other people, particularly to those who may be different than them in dress or custom. He is particularly critical of those who harden their hearts to the needy, justifying their indifference to suffering by presuming that poverty or disease are afflictions from G-d, and that it would be an act of rebellion against G-d to help those whom He condemned.

He refers to the story of Tornus Rufus (a Roman governor credited with wreaking the final devastation on Jerusalem), who challenged R' Akiva (*Bava Basra* 10a), "If G-d loves poor people, why does He not provide for them?" According to this Roman tyrant's view, by addressing the ills of society, men such as R' Akiva are perverting Divine will:

> There is an "upright" path before a man to prohibit himself from giving his bread to the poor, by saying that since G-d is angry at him and has withheld bread from him, would it not be considered a violation of the will of the King were he to give him bread to eat!?

They justify not providing for the needy as an act of submission to G-d's wishes to have these people stay poor and hungry. It is about this corrupt attitude that Shlomo HaMelech says (*Mishlei* 14:12), וְאַחֲרִיתָהּ דַּרְכֵי מָוֶת, *at its end are the pathways to death.*

Perhaps that is the intention of the verse, כִּי יְשָׁרִים דַּרְכֵי ה' וְצַדִּקִים יֵלְכוּ בָם וּפֹשְׁעִים יִכָּשְׁלוּ בָם, *For the ways of Hashem are straight; the righteous will walk in them and sinners will stumble in them* (Hoshea 14:10). One may ask why the verse says that the sinners *will stumble "in them"* — it should have said, "they will stumble by not following the ways of G-d." Such is *Rashi's* interpretation; however, based on the *Alshich*, one can interpret the verse to mean that sinners stumble by deluding themselves that their corrupt actions are the "ways of G-d." Such individuals always find a good reason to despise and bicker with other people, and in their brazenness claim that this is the will of G-d.

14

Man of Law, Man of Justice, and Man of Faith

There is a common belief that decisions rendered by courts reflect reality, at least inasmuch as the judges see it. Court decisions in favor of a plaintiff are viewed in much broader terms than mere determinations of who is guilty and who is innocent, or who owes money to whom. Oftentimes, people interpret a verdict in a dispute between two litigants as vindication of one party, and to a large degree as an incrimination of the other party. As this chapter will clarify, such impressions are far from the truth.

In most legal systems, and particularly in a Jewish court of law, the power of rendering and enforcing decisions by the judges is severely restricted. It is quite possible that judges will acquit someone due to lack of credible or legally admissible evidence, despite their conviction that he is guilty. Often, even when the facts are clear to the court, due to technical reasons the judges lack the authority to adjudicate and impose a ruling.

For example, according to Jewish law, the testimony of only one witness — regardless of his virtue or credibility — is insufficient to convict a person of a crime punishable by the court. Similarly, if Moshe and Aharon should both witness a crime, the court cannot rule based on their testimony, because the Torah does not accept the testimony of two brothers in the same case. As these two examples demonstrate, the Torah limits the decision-making power of the court. The fact that the court is not able to convict the defendant based on faulty testimonies does not imply that the defendant is without any moral guilt that requires repentance and restitution. Oftentimes, a court may not have the authority to convict a man, though by any measure of truth and justice he is indeed guilty.

The Talmud (*Bava Kamma* 55b-56a), recognizing the limitations of human judicial courts, applies the term "exempt according to the judgments of man, but liable according to the judgments of Heaven" to a variety of cases in which a verdict in court is not congruent with the high moral codes of behavior required of a person.

> R' Yehoshua said, "There are four acts for which the offender is exempt from the judgments of man, but liable in the judgment of Heaven. They are: breaking the fence in front of his neighbor's animal, bowing his neighbor's grain toward a fire, hiring false witnesses, and having evidence to exonerate another but refusing to testify on his behalf."

The Gemara continues with other examples of culpability that cannot be adjudicated in a human court, such as: placing lethal poison in front of his friend's animal, and startling his friend and inadvertently causing injury or property damage as a result of shock. The common denominator in all of these cases is that damage was caused only indirectly by the offender, rendering him exempt according to the human courts, but liable according to the judgment of Heaven.

R' Samson Raphael Hirsch succinctly explains this rule in his commentary (*Vayikra* 25:14):

> The laws of Israel often differentiate between the legal and moral domains. In those cases in which the court's ruling will exempt an offense based on objective justice, but deem it morally liable, the Sages express displeasure with this offender.

Accordingly, if the court will rule that Reuven is exempt from paying Shimon, he may still need to pay Shimon's claim if he wishes to appease G-d and the Heavenly Court. *Rashi*, among others, contends that exemption in a human court does not absolve one from Divine punishment.

The Gemara in *Bava Kamma* (103b-104a) describes a scenario in which an individual admits to two people, "I stole [a *maneh*] from one of you, but I do not know which one." The Gemara's ruling is that this individual must pay both claimants the full amount, since he already admitted he stole. *Rashi* comments:

> [He must pay both] … if he wants to satisfy the Heavenly Court, even though a [human] court cannot force him to pay both, but could instead tell him to place the amount stolen before them. Nonetheless, he is not exempt from [Divine] punishment until he pays both of them, since otherwise, he would not necessarily have returned the stolen item to its rightful owner.

According to *Rashi*, the admitted thief cannot attain atonement in the Divine court, and remains liable for stealing until he pays each one the full amount that he stole, since according to the law of the Torah, he has a responsibility to return the stolen item to its proper owner, as it is written (*Vayikra* 5:23), וְהֵשִׁיב אֶת הַגְּזֵלָה אֲשֶׁר גָּזָל, *he shall return the robbed item that he robbed.*

◆§ Meiri: A Heavenly Monetary Obligation

The *Meiri* presents a more stringent view, arguing that the ruling, "exempt according to the laws of men" is comparable to the ruling of "exempt" regarding restrictions on Shabbos. In the laws of Shabbos, exemption does not mean the act is permitted — on the contrary, the general law is: "exempt, but prohibited." The *Meiri* applies the same principle in monetary cases, claiming that wherever the ruling is "exempt according to the judgment of man, but liable according to the judgment of Heaven," the offender remains morally culpable. Moreover, the *Meiri* claims that so long as the offender has not satisfied the judgment of Heaven and made full restitution, he retains the status of criminal even in the human court, and he is disqualified as a witness under Jewish law (*Beis HaBechirah, Bava Kamma* 56a).

Consequently, it is possible that a law-abiding citizen, whom the court exempted from any monetary claim, will still be considered a wicked person and a robber and is therefore disqualified to serve as a witness in the same court. According to the *Meiri*, the ruling "exempt according to the judgment of man, but liable according to the judgment of Heaven," is nothing more than an admission of the court's inability to coerce restitution.

⟩ Exempt in a Human Court and Brings Destruction to the World

Many generations and civilizations were eradicated though they conducted themselves according to the letter of the law, for they failed to internalize both the difference between "exempt" and "morally right" and the fact that one can be found not guilty in court and still be wrong. When equating legal and ethical standards becomes the prevailing norm, it facilitates the disintegration of the society's moral fabric and arouses the wrath of G-d.

The Generation of the Flood exemplified this attitude, and therefore G-d decreed utter devastation to the world. Our Sages (*Sanhedrin* 108a) explained that though the Torah relates (*Bereishis* 6:12), וַיַּרְא אֱלֹקִים אֶת הָאָרֶץ וְהִנֵּה נִשְׁחָתָה כִּי הִשְׁחִית כָּל בָּשָׂר אֶת דַּרְכּוֹ עַל הָאָרֶץ, *G-d saw the earth, and behold it was corrupted, for all flesh had corrupted its way upon the earth,* the Flood was decreed only for robbery: וַיֹּאמֶר אֱלֹקִים לְנֹחַ קֵץ כָּל בָּשָׂר בָּא לְפָנַי כִּי מָלְאָה הָאָרֶץ חָמָס מִפְּנֵיהֶם, *G-d said to Noach, "The end of all flesh has come before me for the earth is filled with robbery* (ibid., v. 13). Though the Generation of the Flood violated every moral prohibition, it was the small acts of robbery that sealed their fate (*Talmud Yerushalmi, Bava Metzia* 4:2).

Bereishis Rabbah (31:5) presents an illustration of such petty crimes that cannot be adjudicated in courts:

> This is what the people of the Generation of the Flood would do: A peddler would bring his cart of legumes into the marketplace. One person would come and steal legumes valued at less than a *prutah* [an amount that could not be claimed in court], and then another person would come and steal legumes valued at less than a *prutah* [until there were no legumes left].

The people that were wiped out by the Flood were law-abiding citizens who knew how to evade legal action. Therefore, they were careful to steal only the meager amount worth less than a *prutah* so as to avoid prosecution in court. According to their mindset, if an act is not prosecutable, it is permissible; and exemption from restitution means that the act is legal and just.

A society based on dispassionate and dry application of the law — without the illumination of moral justice — will ultimately self-destruct and disappear from the world. In a society in which the code of justice can be turned on its head, criminals can view themselves as ethical paragons who conduct their affairs according to the law. Such a society is beyond repair, and is doomed to annihilation.

◆§ Mi Shepara

There are instances in which the court does not have the authority to enforce compensation, but is able to threaten a litigant with the curse of *Mi Shepara*. In Jewish law, there are instances in which a transaction is not finalized even after the buyer paid the full purchase price. In such cases, the buyer or seller can revoke the transaction, even if this causes a significant loss to either party.

While the court does not have the authority to enforce the original transaction, it can express its disapproval by issuing the following admonition (*Mi Shepara*): "The One Who exacted retribution from the Generation of the Flood and the Generation of the Dispersal will exact retribution from anyone who does not stand by his word" (*Mishnah Bava Metzia* 4:1). There is a dispute between Abaye and Rava in *Bava Metzia* (48b) if this is just a judicial admonition or is an actual curse and evocation of Divine punishment for the one who does not stand by his word.

It is noteworthy that the curse of *Mi Shepara* makes specific mention of both the Generation of the Flood and the Generation of the Dispersal, though people in both eras committed sins much graver than reneging on their transactional commitments. The *Torah Temimah* (*Bereishis* 6:13) explains that the parallel between these two generations and someone who does not keep his promise is that all of them committed wrongful acts that could not be adjudicated or punished by a court of law:

> ... the law demands that a person stand by his word .... However, since this is merely a verbal guarantee, the claim cannot be enforced by the court. As has been explained, the Generation of the Flood committed minor theft that could not be redressed in court, and G-d exacted retribution from them. Therefore, they [the judges] say to one who goes back on his word: "The One Who exacted retribution from the Generation of the Flood and the Generation of the Dispersal"... since he too violated something that cannot be adjudicated in court.

R' Yechezkel Panet (*Mar'eh Yechezkel*) condemns people who have the "exultation of G-d in their mouths and the sword of deceit in their hands":

> ... I see in our times: people slaughter newborn calves and are not careful to wait eight days after their birth, as required by the Torah, and consequently feed non-kosher meat to Jews .... the root of this misconduct is because people do not conduct their business with integrity; therefore the [butcher] is reluctant to buy a newborn calf and leave it with the owner to nurse for a few days lest

his competitor might offer more money, and buy it .... I daily confront such cases of deceitful behavior; e.g., a person gives money to his friend to buy him an ox or a horse, and he goes and buys it for himself; or two partners acquired a business and afterward one of them forces the other out of joint ownership ... and many others like these, that according to Torah law one cannot recover the loss ... this common practice of deceit ... is worse than stealing, because one can be wary of a thief, but it is impossible to be wary of a cheater.

... this is what our Sages intended when they cursed the deceiver, "The One Who exacted retribution from the Generation of the Flood and the Generation of the Dispersal will exact retribution from anyone who does not stand by his word." [This] wickedness is very great, for it destroys the world ... a person cannot provide for himself without engaging in business relationships with others, and when people deceive one another, it is impossible to conduct any manner of business.

As such, the *Mar'eh Yechezkel* stresses, a society that is not established on the foundations of justice and morals, and in which people cannot trust one another, does not have the ability or merit to sustain itself. Consequently, our Sages attribute destruction of the Second Commonwealth to the deterioration of social trust.

❧ The Destruction of the Temple

The Gemara in *Bava Metzia* (30b) provides an intriguing explanation for the destruction of the Second Temple:

R' Yochanan said, "Yerushalayim was destroyed only because they rendered decisions based on the letter of the law." [The Gemara counters:] "What should they have done, rendered decisions based on rules of superior strength?" Rather ... they abided by the letter of the law and did not conduct themselves by going beyond the letter of the law.

This Gemara should give any reader pause. It is almost incomprehensible that an entire generation was destroyed, and the city of Yerushalayim and its glorious Temple were laid to ruin, because law-abiding people refused to go beyond the letter of the law. Yet, there is another explanation in *Maseches Chagigah* (14a):

Yerushalayim was not destroyed until men of integrity were not to be found within it, as it is written (*Yirmiyahu* 5:1), שׁוֹטְטוּ בְּחוּצוֹת יְרוּשָׁלַם וּרְאוּ נָא וּדְעוּ וּבַקְּשׁוּ בִרְחוֹבוֹתֶיהָ אִם תִּמְצְאוּ אִישׁ אִם יֵשׁ עֹשֶׂה מִשְׁפָּט מְבַקֵּשׁ אֱמוּנָה וְאֶסְלַח לָהּ, *Walk about in the streets of Yerushalayim, see now and know, and seek in its plazas; if you will find a man [of authority], if there is one who dispenses justice and seeks truth, then I will forgive her.*

In the continuation of the discussion, the Gemara points that even though they were learned Torah scholars, they lacked integrity in their business dealings.

As these passages in the Gemara point out, mere obedience to the letter of the law cannot save a society from ruin and destruction. A society cannot be sustained unless there is trust and faithfulness in interpersonal interactions, and that those interactions be among people who are willing to make concessions and do what is "right" above and beyond the basic expectations of the law.

◆§ The Man of Law, the Man of Justice, and the Man of Faith

In summation, people can be categorized as follows:

The Man of Law: A person who knows and adheres to the particulars of the law according to the *Shulchan Aruch*. He also knows the ways to circumvent the law without actually violating the law. He may steal less than a *prutah* value, or cause indirect damage to his friend, and by so doing evade legal action and compensation. The Man of Law rationalizes that whatever a court cannot enforce is an act that is permitted and proper.

The Man of Justice: This person is prepared to assume patterns of behavior above the minimum requirements of the law. Having a well-developed sense of social justice and a strong sense of moral responsibility, he understands that to steal less than a *prutah* value or to deceive and fail to live up to his word are despicable acts. His behavior is dictated by the law and modulated by his personal ethics, though faith in G-d may not necessarily enter his moral deliberations. However, he will not necessarily engage in demanding behaviors that arise from a deep-seated faith that everything comes from the hands of the Almighty.

The Man of Faith: This person believes profoundly that everything that he has is from the hand of G-d. In his view, human endeavor is nothing more than "an attempt" whose outcome is determined in Heaven. Believing that his purpose in life is to *walk in the ways of G-d,* he tries to adhere to the commandment to *do what is fair and good,* and to ensure that all of his actions are consistent with the will of G-d. For such a person, failing to keep his word or causing even unintentional damage to another are not merely ethical transgressions, but expressions of a lack of faith in G-d. Trying to please his Creator in everything he does, he holds himself up to even higher standards of behavior.

It is incumbent upon every believing Jew to aspire to conduct himself like the man of faith — behavior that is driven by higher standards than the requirements of the law or justice. In the coming chapters, we will explicate those things that are expected from the man of faith.

15

Business with Integrity

The importance of conducting business with integrity and good faith cannot be overstated, as this is among the first questions that are asked when a person comes before the Heavenly Court after leaving this earth. The Gemara in *Shabbos* (31a) says:

> When a person is brought for judgment [before the Heavenly Court] they ask him, "Did you conduct your business in good faith? Did you set aside fixed times for the study of Torah? Did you engage in procreation? Did you anticipate redemption? Did you discourse in wisdom? Did you deduce one thing from another?"

The importance of conducting one's business with integrity is further emphasized in the words of the *Mechilta*:

> ... whoever conducts his business with integrity and people find him pleasant and amenable, is considered as if he has fulfilled the entire Torah.

Apparently, conducting business in good faith and with integrity is a prerequisite for fulfilling the fundamental precepts of Torah, such that such a person is considered as if he has fulfilled the entire Torah. One can deduce, therefore, that the opposite also is true: A person who disregards this matter is considered as if he disregarded the entire Torah.

৵§ What Constitutes Conducting Business with Integrity?

The author of *Aruch HaShulchan* defines the meaning of conducting business in good faith and with integrity, and he outlines the halachic parameters in *Orach Chaim (Hilchos Masa U'Matan, Siman* 156:3):

> The intent is not just that a person should not steal, rob, or falsify his weights and measures. These things are not included in this precept, for one who does any of these things is actually an evil person. It is forbidden to steal, rob, or commit fraud, whether to a Jew or non-Jew … as the *Rambam* wrote in the first chapter of *Hilchos Geneivah* and the *Tur/Shulchan Aruch in Choshen Mishpat, Siman* 348.
>
> Rather, the intention is that an individual's "yes" and "no" should be absolute. When he says that this merchandise costs him a certain amount, or that it is good quality material, he should not lie by an iota. He should negotiate congenially, speaking pleasantly — he should not shout, curse, or get angry. The result will be that his business will acquire a good reputation, his financial success will be sustainable, and everyone will trust him, for וְהַבּוֹטֵחַ בַּה' חֶסֶד יְסוֹבְבֶנּוּ, *one who trusts in G-d, kindness surrounds him (Tehillim* 32:10).

According to *Aruch HaShulchan*, the interrogation of a departed soul is not to clarify whether one cheated or stole, for those are criminal acts, and one who refrains from them deserves no prize. Rather, the intent of the Gemara is to emphasize the responsibility of a person to be decent and fair, not just in business matters, but in all of his interactions with others.

Honest business dealings are consistent with the fundamental tenet to be a decent, honest, and truthful person, who means what he says and fulfills his promises and commitments, in the spirit of כְּכָל הַיֹּצֵא מִפִּיו יַעֲשֶׂה, *according to whatever comes from his mouth shall he do* (*Bamidbar* 30:3). *Eliyahu Rabbah* (*Siman* 156:2) elaborates on this obligation:

> A person who promises his friend, even casually, to do a favor, or service, or to give him a gift, is obligated to stand by his word. If he incurs a debt, he must repay at the set date, and if he is concerned that he may not be able to repay, he should extend the time *a priori* in order to avoid being a liar. A salesman should not overpraise his merchandise, and when buying one should not disparage the goods exceedingly. Whoever speaks truth in his heart, and does not lie, his words will be realized even if he did not intend them, as it is written (*Iyov* 22:28), וְתִגְזַר אֹמֶר וְיָקָם לָךְ, *You would utter a decree and it would be done*. A person should initially say his intentions, be it in trade, loans, or monetary transactions.

Accordingly, a person must be totally honest and forthright, fulfilling promises without compromise. Instead of making promises on the hope that all will go smoothly, a person must take into account the mishaps and difficulties that may occur, articulating his promise in a fashion that will prevent excuses as to why the promise was not fulfilled. Ultimately, it is better not to make promises, and when unavoidable to promise less.

Eliyahu Rabbah stresses that there is special Heavenly support for a person who stands by his word and keeps his promises. Even when a commitment was misunderstood to mean something unintended, G-d helps one who fulfills his commitments to live up to his words as others understood it, so that his reputation remains intact, for רַגְלֵי חֲסִידָיו יִשְׁמֹר, *He guards the steps of his devout ones* (*I Shmuel* 2:9).

The *Radak* and the *She'iltos of Rav Achai* add another important level to the expectation of integrity in the conduct of business. They rule that even if one did not verbally promise, but only thought to do an action, commitment to integrity requires the person to fulfill even those unspoken intentions. In his comment to the phrase, וְדֹבֵר אֱמֶת בִּלְבָבוֹ, *speaks the truth from his heart* (*Tehillim* 15:2), the *Radak* writes:

> This means that he speaks the truth and will never lie, and that the truth that he speaks with his mouth will be in his heart, because he is never hypocritical …. Included … is that he will fulfill even the mere thought in his heart to do a favor for someone in business …. Needless to say, this applies when he tells someone that he will sell him something; but even if he only thought to sell him some item, yet did not verbally articulate his intent, he will not renege, but rather will fulfill his thought.

If one must fulfill unexpressed intentions or implied promises, all the more so, someone who uttered a promise or commitment must not profane his words, and should fulfill it completely.

⊷§ Reishis Chochmah: Seven General Principles

The *Reishis Chochmah* (*Perek Masa U'Matan Be'Emunah*) expounds on matters that are included in this important and sensitive topic, identifying seven general principles that ensure that business is conducted with complete integrity:

1) One should be happy with his portion and not pursue wealth, in contrast to those who think that the goal of amassing wealth justifies any means.

2) A person should avoid deceit; for example, inviting his friend, though in his heart he does not really want him in his home and the invitation is mere lip service. Deceiving people is tantamount to deception of the Almighty.

3) A person should give a little bit more to his customers than they actually purchased. Since the sin of theft brings drought, one should not be punctilious and give a little bit more.

4) A person should refrain from verbal oppression, such as reminding someone of his past to gain some psychological advantage in business dealings.

5) A person should go beyond the letter of the law, making concessions and compromises that benefit the other.

6) A person should work for his employer faithfully. "Just as it is a mitzvah to give a worker his wages at the proper time, so too, is it a mitzvah for the employee to do his assigned work without deceit."

7) A person should not trespass upon the livelihood of his friend.

✑ The Importance of Trustworthiness and Incorruptibility

The tremendous importance attributed to honest and impeccable business dealings finds expression throughout *Tanach*. In *Tehillim*, David identifies the virtues that ensure eternal life:

מִי יַעֲלֶה בְהַר ה' וּמִי יָקוּם בִּמְקוֹם קָדְשׁוֹ? נְקִי כַפַּיִם וּבַר לֵבָב אֲשֶׁר לֹא נָשָׂא לַשָּׁוְא נַפְשִׁי וְלֹא נִשְׁבַּע לְמִרְמָה, *Who may ascend the mountain of Hashem, and who may stand in the place of His sanctity? One with clean hands and pure heart; who has not sworn in vain by My soul, and has not sworn deceitfully* (24:3-4).

Metzudas David explains that the expression "clean hands" refers to one "whose hands are pure from money that was not earned honestly, and his heart is pure with the fear of G-d and not the fear of man." Similarly Rav Achai notes that only such people of integrity are called נֶאֶמְנֵי אֶרֶץ לָשֶׁבֶת עִמָּדִי, *faithful of the land, that they may dwell with me* (*Tehillim* 101:6), and they "will merit and dwell in the inner sanctum with G-d" (*She'iltos, Parashas Vayechi, She'ilta* 36).

Midrash Rabbah (*Shemos* 4:1) attributes the phrase, נְקִי כַפַּיִם וּבַר לֵבָב, *clean hands and a pure heart*, to Moshe Rabbeinu, who did not exploit his powerful position for even the smallest favor. Apparently, Moshe was concerned that a sense of obligation for any favors received might compromise his objectivity as leader of the nation.

Rabbeinu Bachya, in his book *Kad HaKemach*, explains that dealing with integrity and good faith were among the commandments given to Adam HaRishon; and while it is expected of all human beings, it is a precondition for acceptance of sacrificial offerings at the Temple:

> … someone who has stolen goods in his possession is distanced from the mountain of G-d and His holy place …. There is tremendous inspiration for this from the concept of sacrifices, where the Torah rejected the innards of birds from being brought on the altar, but accepted those of an animal …. This is because an animal is fed from the feedbag of its owner, but a bird is nourished by stealing … a person who has stolen goods in his possession will not approach the altar of G-d, will not ascend, and will not appear before Him, but he will be abhorred and detested by G-d.

Eliyahu Rabbah (*Choshen Mishpat, Siman* 156:3) explains the reason for placing the obligation to conduct business as the first question in the Heavenly Court:

> Why is this question [Did you conduct your business with integrity?] asked prior to the question about the study of Torah? I heard in the name of my grandfather, the *Gaon Maharash*, that if one's business is not conducted with integrity, then his study of Torah is a desecration of G-d's Name, as is stated in the Gemara (*Yoma* 86a): "What do people say about him? Woe unto his father who taught him Torah!"

When a person's appearance and garb give the impression of

someone who observes Torah and mitzvos, yet his business dealings are not meticulously honest, he besmirches the Torah way of life. There is no greater public desecration of G-d's Name than this!

It is interesting to note that the obligation to conduct business with integrity is not enumerated among the *Taryag* (613) mitzvos. Rabbeinu Bachya (*Kad HaKemach, Erech Gezel*) clarifies the awesome significance of trustworthiness, as it is rooted in the fundamental duty of every Jew to live with total faith in the Creator of the world:

> It is known that all of the mitzvos depend upon faith, for if a person does not treat his friends with faith in all matters, whether in his business dealings with him or a partnership, behold he is lacking in His faith in G-d. Regarding this David HaMelech said that the person who merits to live in the "tent of G-d" — to be in His domain, and to dwell on His holy mountain — is the individual who fulfills these mitzvos.

A person who firmly believes in G-d knows that whatever he has is from G-d; thus, he has no temptation to cheat or deceive, knowing such acts will not be effective and will yield nothing.

Further on, Rabbeinu Bachya explains that the Creator is One, and His essence is truth, and every person is obligated to emulate his Creator and to channel all of his actions to the truth. If he does not emulate his Creator, he distances himself from and severs his relationship with G-d:

> Included in faith is that a person should love the truth and choose to speak it …. This verse admonishes people to be pure in their speech and to speak only the truth — even when telling a commonplace story, even when the account is not critical and does not make a real difference. Needless to say, one's business dealings should be conducted with faith, to stand by one's word, such that his yes and no are true ….
>
> There is in this matter a way of life to all those who listen

and contemplate it — they should be careful in their speech, for great is the power of truth, and whoever embraces the attribute of truth his prayers are heard. So too did David HaMelech write (*Tehillim* 145:18), קָרוֹב ה' לְכָל קֹרְאָיו לְכֹל אֲשֶׁר יִקְרָאֻהוּ בֶאֱמֶת, *Hashem is close to all who call upon Him, to all who call upon Him with truth.* Whoever directs their actions to the truth becomes closer to their Creator, Who is the One Truth.

R' Bakshi Doron clarifies this thesis. He says that the essential question posed in a soul's final judgment is not merely: Did a person conduct himself faithfully when relating to another Jew? Rather, the intent is much deeper and it is to ask: When you conducted business with another individual, was it done with faith in G-d? If, indeed, your faith in G-d is all-embracing, then also your business dealings will be done with trustworthiness, because only G-d determines the extent of your success.

> The demand that is impressed upon a believing Jew is: Did you conduct your business with integrity? Not only did you conduct your business with integrity, but that your business should be guided by a belief in Divine Providence, and not just the ethical norm of fairness and truth which society requires. The belief in Divine Providence, that everything comes from His hand, totally changes the nature of business and the relational construct between people. In business done with integrity there is not just the buyer and the seller. The main component is the belief in G-d — that only His Will shall decide the success and potential of the venture (*Binyan Av, Siman* 76).

ⰷ The Reward of One Who Conducts Business with Integrity

As great and comprehensive as the demands of dealing with

integrity are, so too are the rewards for the person who fulfills them. First, the spiritual rewards are immense, since only a person who conducts his business with integrity merits to ascend the mountain of G-d and to stand in His holy place and sit in the inner sanctum with G-d, as was discussed earlier in this chapter. Aside from the spiritual reward, his benefit in this world is immense. In *Mishlei* (28:20) it is written, אִישׁ אֱמוּנוֹת רַב בְּרָכוֹת וְאָץ לְהַעֲשִׁיר לֹא יִנָּקֶה, *A man of integrity will increase blessings, but one impatient to be rich will not be exonerated. Metzudas David* explains:

> **A man of integrity:** A person who does business with integrity and does not deceive other people is destined to an abundance of blessings, but one who hurries to enrich himself will not stop cheating, and he will not be exonerated from his just retribution.

Rabbeinu Bachya in *Kad HaKemach* adds:

> A person who has "lips of truth" and is mindful that his speech should only be aligned with truth will always attain success with such speech, and it will last forever. People will always trust his words because people will perceive him as a man of truth, since he has been accustomed all his days to speak the truth.

The Gemara in *Maseches Niddah* (69b) asks, "What should a person do that he may be rich?" He [R' Yehoshua ben Chananya] responded, "He should increase his business dealings and conduct his business with integrity."

The *Shelah HaKadosh* praises those who conduct business with integrity and points out that:

> A person should not think that by conducting his business with integrity he will be losing. On the contrary, G-d blesses the work of his hands ... It is written (*Devarim* 25:15), אֶבֶן שְׁלֵמָה וָצֶדֶק יִהְיֶה לָּךְ, *A perfect and honest weight you shall have* — if you do so, then you will have what to negotiate,

what to buy and sell, as it says, יִהְיֶה לָךְ, *you shall have* (*Shnei Luchos HaBris, Chullin*).

Hence, there is a promise of special Divine support for the person who conducts his business with integrity. *Menoras HaMaor* (Chapter 12) elaborates on this thesis:

> It is stated in *Midrash Mishlei*: "A man of integrity will increase blessings, but one impatient to be rich will not be exonerated." One who conducts his business with integrity will find blessing in his possessions, and G-d prepares his livelihood because other people trust him and his faith, and their money will always be available to him. Not only will he be provided for by virtue of his faith, but he will be called a righteous man, as it says (*Chavakuk* 2:4), וְצַדִּיק בֶּאֱמוּנָתוֹ יִחְיֶה, *the righteous man shall live through his faith*.

Accordingly, one who conducts his business with integrity is promised that his possessions will be blessed. The *Menoras HaMaor* explains that the blessing will derive from the trust that people place in him and their willingness to invest money in his enterprises. Apparently, this is the intent of the verse in *Koheles* (7:1), טוֹב שֵׁם מִשֶּׁמֶן טוֹב, *A good name is better than good oil*. A person's good reputation will stand him in good stead, yielding even more than just good oil (material things).

The words of the *Chofetz Chaim* highlight the seriousness of violating trust in business dealings. He was asked once by his students: "Why was a law that deals with the prohibition of idolatry affixed in the reading of *Shema* [*Devarim* 11:16: וְסַרְתֶּם וַעֲבַדְתֶּם אֱלֹהִים אֲחֵרִים, *lest you turn astray and worship other gods*]? Given that the drive for idolatry hardly exists anymore, why do we need to mention this prohibition twice every day, morning and evening?" He answered:

> To my chagrin, almost every Jew is liable to stumble at any moment upon the severe prohibition of idolatry. If you will ask me, "How could that be?" I will explain it to you. A person owns a supermarket and every day he receives a

shipment of fresh fish. Sometimes, he has a fish left from the previous day. What does the average storeowner do? He places yesterday's fish on top of the pile so that it will be sold first.

The fish that he has from yesterday is no longer fresh, and he really should sell it at a lower price. However, the storekeeper sells it as if it is fresh, at the full price. This happens because the storekeeper thinks that if he will sell the fish for less, his livelihood will not be forthcoming.

At this point the *Chofetz Chaim* raised his voice to a thunderous pitch. "What does this shopkeeper think?!" He continued:

Was it not G-d Who left him this fish from yesterday? Did not G-d establish exactly what would be his income on that day? Behold, everything is from His hand and is decided from Rosh Hashanah to Rosh Hashanah .... Apparently, the storekeeper does not think so, and hopes that G-d will not know his doings. This is a heretical thought! This is a thought of absolute idolatry! On the other hand, if the storekeeper believes in G-d and knows that it is prohibited to go astray after other gods, and on the contrary, places his entire belief in G-d, then he will maintain the integrity of his merchandise and will sell yesterday's fish at its real price, and by doing so, his livelihood will be completely from the hand of G-d in abundance.

✺ Business with Integrity and Setting Aside Fixed Times for Torah Study

Based on the above, it is possible to explain the juxtaposition of the question regarding conducting business with integrity with the question about setting aside fixed times for Torah study — the first two questions asked of a person after his death. As will be elaborated in a later chapter, the question implies an expectation that one makes Torah study a permanent fixture — at an appointed time each day — such that it will become the central pillar of his day. Prioritization of Torah study — if only for an hour or two — is the most salient manifestation of a person's belief that his entire livelihood comes from the Creator of the world, and his responsibility is only to make a meaningful effort, and not more. Should a business opportunity arise, demanding the cancellation of his fixed time for learning, one should maintain his regular learning schedule in firm faith that he will suffer no loss, and that the Creator will provide him with what he deserves.

If so, the two questions: Did you conduct your business with integrity, and did you set aside fixed times for Torah study, are inexorably bound by the faith that the ultimate power is in G-d's hand. With genuine belief that this is reality, every person can set aside times for Torah study, making them the most important part of his day.

16

Great Is the Person Who Lives from His Own Labor

Commonplace chatter among friends and acquaintances often includes the topic of one's job or workplace. Very often such idle conversation focuses on complaints about the boss and his mistreatment of employees. Rarely do people talk about the mistreatment of employers by their employees. Conventional thought presumes that the employer has greater means and power relative to his subordinates, and therefore his legal and ethical obligations are much greater than those of the employees. Indeed, the case in *Bava Metzia* (83a) seems to substantiate this view:

> Rabbah bar Bar-Chanan's hired porters broke a barrel of wine. He took their coats in lieu of payment for the damage that they caused through their negligence. The porters complained to Rav. Rav said to Rabbah bar Bar-Chanan, "Return their coats to them." He retorted, "Is that the law?" He [Rav] responded, "Yes, as it is written (*Mishlei* 2:20), לְמַעַן תֵּלֵךְ בְּדֶרֶךְ טוֹבִים, *in order that you may walk in the way of the good.*" He returned their coats. The porters complained to Rav, "We are poor and we worked the entire day. We are hungry and have no money for food." Rav said to Rabbah bar Bar-Chanan, "Go and pay them their

wages." He reacted, "Is that the law?" Rav answered, "Yes, as it is written (ibid.), וְאָרְחוֹת צַדִּיקִים תִּשְׁמֹר, *keep the paths of the righteous.*"

This case demonstrates the tremendous responsibility of an employer, not just to follow the letter of the law, but to go beyond the letter of the law when dealing with employees and their basic needs. However, as delineated in this chapter, the employee bears considerable responsibility toward his employer.

✍ Workers' Conduct

I have occasionally conversed with other employers about their workers' conduct. Aside from the usual complaints about their employees' lack of effort and inability to meet agreed-upon deadlines, many of my peers complain about common inappropriate behaviors. Here are some examples:

1) **Tardiness:** Workers excuse themselves for coming late, but are punctilious in leaving the workplace precisely at the official time.

2) **Private telephone conversations during work hours:** Employees spend significant time on private telephone conversations during work hours. The following is an amusing, yet true, anecdote to illustrate how pervasive this practice has become.

   Coming home after a hard day's work, a man found an envelope with his monthly phone bill. He opened the envelope and shouted, "Why is our phone bill so high?! Who talks so much? I," he said to his wife and children, "make all of my private calls at work, such that I have no portion whatsoever in this inflated bill." His wife countered, "I also make all of my personal calls at work and not from home. This bill is not because of me!" The housekeeper also chimed in, in her naiveté, "I also make all of my phone calls from my place of employment ...."

3) **Non-Work-Related Conversations:** Employees discuss personal matters, completely unrelated to the job, during work hours.

4) **Absenteeism:** Employees allow themselves a great deal of leeway to be absent from work.

5) **Coffee and Lunch Breaks:** Employees extend these breaks beyond the allotted time.

6) **Usage of company computers and software programs for personal matters at the expense of work.**

7) **Employees come to work tired.**

Of course, workers have a variety of rationalizations for these self-made allowances. These are the most common:

1) Everyone does it.

2) I do not take anything from the employer.

3) The employer does not mind.

Following is a general outline of the ethical obligations of an employee, and how an employee can enhance his service of the Almighty through ethical behavior at the workplace.

᥍ Employees' Responsibilities

Some Jewish laws relating to the obligations of employees in the workplace are derived from Yaakov's harsh rebuke of Lavan, and from his conversation with his two wives, Rachel and Leah. In *Bereishis* (31:6) Yaakov describes his hard labor for his father-in-law Lavan: וְאַתֵּנָה יְדַעְתֶּן כִּי בְּכָל כֹּחִי עָבַדְתִּי אֶת אֲבִיכֶן, *You have known that it was with all my might that I have served your father*; followed by (ibid., v. 40): הָיִיתִי בַיּוֹם אֲכָלַנִי חֹרֶב וְקֶרַח בַּלָּיְלָה וַתִּדַּד שְׁנָתִי מֵעֵינָי, *By day scorching heat consumed me, and frost by night; my sleep drifted from my eyes.*

Yaakov Avinu attests that he worked for Lavan with all of his strength by day, despite the heat and his thirst, and by night, despite the fierce cold. Yaakov fulfilled all of his obligations to his employer, even though Lavan tricked him many times and deceitfully coerced him into working seven additional years. While Yaakov used the idiomatic terminology "with all my might," the *Rambam* translated this into practical halachah. He writes in *Hilchos Sechirus* (*Perek* 13:7):

> Just as the employer is admonished not to withhold the wages of a poor man and not to delay their payment, so too, the poor man is admonished not to steal from his employer — wasting a little bit of time here and wasting a little bit of time there — spending the entire day cheating his employer. Rather, he is obligated to be exacting of himself in regard to time, for behold the Sages prohibited him from reciting the fourth blessing of the *Birkas HaMazon*. Likewise, he is obligated to work with all his strength, for behold the righteous Yaakov said, בְּכָל כֹּחִי עָבַדְתִּי אֶת אֲבִיכֶן, *with all my might I have served your father*. Therefore, he received a reward even in this world, as it is written (*Bereishis* 30:43), וַיִּפְרֹץ הָאִישׁ מְאֹד מְאֹד, *the man* [Yaakov] *became exceedingly prosperous*.

According to the *Rambam*, the words "with all my might" have a double meaning: an obligation to dedicate all of one's time to his work without wasting any time, and likewise an obligation to dedicate all of his physical strength, energy, and talent to perform his duties during working hours.

The Gemara cites many additional laws regarding the responsibilities of an employee during worktime. For example: A worker is permitted to recite *Shema* when he is standing at the top of a tree or on top of a wall [in lieu of coming down], though fear of falling may impair his ability to concentrate properly (*Mishnah Berachos* 2:4). Likewise, it is prohibited for an employee to rise before Torah Sages [who are passing by] to interrupt his work (*Kiddushin* 33a). The common denominator of all these laws is the heavy emphasis that our Sages placed upon the importance of not wasting any time during working hours at the expense of the employer, even for spiritual activities. Obviously, the employer can at his discretion grant permission to conduct such activities during working hours.

Moreover, the *Rambam* rules that an employee's responsibilities vis-à-vis his employer do not cease at the end of the work day (*Hilchos Sechirus* 13:6):

> He is not allowed to starve or deprive himself in order to have food for his family, since this will result in his "stealing work" from his employer, as he and his mind will be weakened and he will not be able to labor with full strength.

Hagahos Maimonios on the *Rambam* (ad loc.), citing the *Talmud Yerushalmi* (*Demai* 26b), relates an incident in which R' Yochanan saw a teacher looking weak and sickly. When asked about his health, the teacher explained that he undertook a pious fast. R' Yochanan told him that it was forbidden for him to do so. He explained that if a regular worker, whose job is for a human employer, is not allowed to do anything that diminishes his ability to do his job, then certainly it is forbidden for a teacher of small children to do so, since his work is in the service of Heaven.

Accordingly, an employee may not go to sleep late; he may not assume an additional job if it will compromise the quality of his work the following day; and he is required to eat and drink properly so that he is in full physical and mental strength when he comes to work the next day. Many in the secular world will think that extending his obligations beyond working hours is an excessive intrusion into the private life of an employee. The halachic view is that while the employee may do whatever he pleases in the hours after work, he is not permitted to do anything that he knows will diminish his ability to do his job properly the following day.

The Gemara in *Taanis* (23a) relates a story about Abba Chilkiya, renowned for his ability to beseech Heavenly compassion so the rain would fall. Once, during a severe drought, the Sages sent two Torah scholars to beg his intercession for rain. They found him working in the field. When they greeted him, he did not respond and continued working. At the end of the day, after he returned from work, they asked him to explain why he refused to respond to their greetings. He explained, "I am a paid day-worker, and I reasoned that it was forbidden for me to pause in my work!"

R' Ben-Tzion Chai Uziel, the first Chief Sephardi Rabbi of Israel, summarized the obligations of an employee to his employer in his work, *Shus Piskei Uziel (Siman* 46):

> A worker must recognize that he is obligated, physically and mentally, to work for his employer .... This is a clearly stated halachah: Craftsmen, who are working for others, are not permitted to stand before the elderly or a Torah sage ... in order that they do not interrupt their work.
>
> Just as a worker must be meticulous to account precisely and faithfully for the time at work, so too, does he need to approach his work with all of his energy. It is self-evident that a worker has an obligation to do his work with love, respect, and friendship toward his employer, and to maintain a relationship of love toward his craft. He should not be like a machine, or even like a person who feels commanded to do the work, or like a hired person, who does it only for the money. Rather, he should be like a partner in this constructive and creative endeavor.

◄§ Work Is Torah

When an employee faithfully fulfills all obligations to his employer, then his work is also deemed a form of service of G-d. Rabbeinu Bachya on the verse (*Shemos* 20:9), שֵׁשֶׁת יָמִים תַּעֲבֹד וְעָשִׂיתָ כָּל מְלַאכְתֶּךְ, *Six days shall you work and accomplish all your work,* writes:

> It is possible throughout six days for you to serve G-d through the accomplishment of your work, like the

Forefathers who served G-d by caring for their flocks and other physical labor. But on the seventh day, which is the Sabbath and dedicated entirely to G-d, you may not do any work at all. I heard this in the name of the *Rambam*.

Rabbeinu Bachya provides a new perspective on being a faithful employee: Not only is it possible to serve G-d through employment, but we are commanded to do so! It appears that this is also the intention of the *Sfas Emes* on the Torah (*Chukas* 5631):

> The Gemara states that the pious ones of earlier generations made their Torah learning permanent [the central and fixed activity of each day] and their work temporary [a necessary act to make a living], and they were successful in both [Torah learning and work]. It appears that the meaning of this is that even in all of the work that they did, the paramount thing was the "learning," for a person can learn the will of G-d from all things. A person who does everything for the sake of Heaven will find the radiance of Torah ... because the toil in a physical act that is done in full accord with the Torah is called the "Torah of man."

According to the *Sfas Emes*, when a person's job is performed with the intent to fulfill G-d's will, his workday is also considered "a part of Torah."

What emerges from all of this is that a Jew who works for his living can transform his mundane work into the "service of G-d." Certainly the aspiration of every Jew should be to study Torah day and night. However, most people do not merit this status and are required to work for a living. Nonetheless, these people should not be discouraged, for they have the potential to transform their material pursuit into an activity that is the fulfillment of the will of G-d.

Such a perspective on employment may illuminate the Mishnah in *Avos DeR' Nosson* (*Nuscha* 1, *Perek* 11):

Shemaya says, "Love work" … This teaches us that a person should love work, and he should not hate work. Just as the Torah was given with a covenant, so too, work was given with a covenant, as it is written (*Shemos* 20:9-10): שֵׁשֶׁת יָמִים תַּעֲבֹד וְעָשִׂיתָ כָּל מְלַאכְתֶּךָ, וְיוֹם הַשְּׁבִיעִי שַׁבָּת לַה׳ אֱלֹקֶיךָ, *Six days you shall labor, and do all your work; but the seventh day is Sabbath to Hashem, your G-d.*

The words "Just as the Torah was given with a covenant, so too, work was given with a covenant" begs explanation, for it seems to imply an equivalence between Torah and work. Torah study is the primary goal and objective of our lives. How can there be any kind of equivalence between our life ambition and mundane labor?

It seems that the Mishnah provides a novel insight: The Torah is the elixir of our lives, and we have a covenant to learn and toil in it. But we also have a covenant to perform our work properly when we are at the workplace. If properly performed, work activities can become a spiritual endeavor by performing the will of G-d. Servitude of G-d is expressed not just through learning Torah, but is intertwined in the time well spent at the workplace.

◆§ And Its Top Reached Heavenward

Understandably, there are varying levels of work. People whose "ladder is standing on the ground" though "its top is reaching heavenward" are men of distinction, who choose not to derive benefits from gifts and donations, and therefore engage in some work for their livelihood. However, while they are occupied with work, their minds roam in the upper spheres, as they apply holy names and Kabbalistic meaning to every physical act.

Many mystical works cite the Midrash about Chanoch, whom the Torah describes by saying, וַיִּתְהַלֵּךְ חֲנוֹךְ אֶת הָאֱלֹקִים, *Chanoch walked with G-d* (*Bereishis* 5:22):

Chanoch sewed shoes, and with every stitch he would have intent and say, "Blessed is the Name of His glorious kingdom for all eternity" (*Asarah Ma'amaros*, 28, *Chelek* 3, *Siman* 22).

Only a few can reach such a high level of spirituality such that they can perform mundane work activities and simultaneously focus on Divine service. Nonetheless, those who perform their work with faith and trustworthiness are also blessed. The *Ba'al Shem Tov* on the Torah (*Parashas Behar*) writes:

> Business is also a form of Divine service and Torah, because there are many laws that relate to it. If someone studies Torah for the sake of the Creator, for example, the Mishnah (*Bava Metzia* 100a), "One who exchanges a cow for a donkey…," he is very precious to his Creator. All the more so, if he actually performs the action of exchanging a cow for a donkey according to the laws of the Torah; it certainly is considered a higher form of service. This is because everything that exists in the world was created for His glory ….

According to the above, one can explain an apparent contradiction in the words of R' Shimon Bar Yochai. In *Maseches Berachos* (35b) he says:

> If a person will plow at the time of plowing, plant at the time of planting, reap at the time of reaping, thresh at the time of threshing, and winnow when the wind blows — what will become of Torah? However, when people do the will of G-d — their work is done by others …. When people do not do the will of G-d — their work is done by themselves … [and in addition they must also do] the work of their enemies. Abaye said, "Many people did like R' Shimon bar Yochai and were not successful.

In contrast, the Gemara *Menachos* (99b) states:

> R' Yochanan said in the name of R' Shimon bar Yochai, "Even if a person only recited *Krias Shema* in the morning and the evening, he has fulfilled the verse (*Yehoshua* 1:8),

לֹא יָמוּשׁ סֵפֶר הַתּוֹרָה הַזֶּה מִפִּיךָ, *This Book of the Torah shall not depart from your mouth."*

R' Shimon bar Yochai's pronouncements seem to contradict one another. In *Maseches Menachos* he is satisfied with the recitation of *Krias Shema* in order to fulfill the verse, לֹא יָמוּשׁ סֵפֶר הַתּוֹרָה הַזֶּה מִפִּיךָ, *This Book of the Torah shall not depart from your mouth;* whereas in *Maseches Berachos* he demands that anyone who is able should exclusively engage in Torah study, presuming that the work will be done by others!

It is possible that R' Shimon bar Yochai is addressing two distinct groups. In *Maseches Berachos* he addresses those who engage in Torah study day and night, such that Torah study consumes their waking day. If indeed a person is worthy and capable of doing so, he merits that his work is done by others. Those individuals who are talented and capable of sustaining this responsibility, yet choose not to do so, will not be successful in their endeavors.

However, the majority of people are not able to spend the entire day learning Torah, as the Gemara states, "Many people did like R' Shimon bar Yochai and were not successful." These individuals, who work for their livelihood, should not consider themselves as second-class Jews. These are the Jews whom R' Shimon bar Yochai addresses in *Maseches Menachos.* In effect, his message to these workers is: The recitation of *Shema* with sincere intention is sufficient to fulfill the commandment, לֹא יָמוּשׁ סֵפֶר הַתּוֹרָה הַזֶּה מִפִּיךָ, *This Book of the Torah shall not depart from your mouth.* By reciting *Krias Shema* properly, understanding its full meaning, one may accept upon himself the yoke of Heaven. Such a person understands that mundane work, which is mentioned in the second paragraph of *Krias Shema*, can be elevated to become the service of G-d.

◈§ Know Him in All of Your Ways

It is possible and obligatory to be a servant of G-d every moment of one's mundane existence — not only during working hours. It is possible to transform every endeavor into a mitzvah and the fulfillment of the will of G-d, even habitual matters like eating, drinking, sleeping, and ordinary conversation. Such is the position of the *Rambam* in *Hilchos Dei'os* (3:3):

> A person who conducts himself in accord with good medical practice, if he focuses on having a healthy body and limbs alone, and that he should have children who will do his work and toil on his behalf, [he has not chosen] a good path. Rather, he should desire that his body will be whole and strong so that his soul may be directed to knowing G-d; for it is impossible that a person should understand and discern wisdom if he is hungry, sick, or one of his limbs is hurting. He should desire a son who may become a sage and great leader of the Jewish people. Consequently, a person who follows this path his whole life, serves G-d continuously, even when he engages in business … because his intent in all of this is that his physical needs should be satisfied so that his body is whole to serve G-d. Even when he is sleeping, if he sleeps so that his mind should rest and his body be refreshed, so that he does not become sick and incapable of serving G-d, then his sleep is also the service of G-d. Thus, the Sages commanded us, "All of your actions should be for the sake of Heaven." This is what Shlomo said in his wisdom (*Mishlei* 3:6), בְּכָל דְּרָכֶיךָ דָעֵהוּ וְהוּא יְיַשֵּׁר אֹרְחֹתֶיךָ, *In all your ways know Him, and He will smooth your paths.*

The service of G-d does not end at the conclusion of a study session or upon leaving the walls of the *beis medrash*. The Torah is a Torah of Life and it encompasses all human activities throughout the day and night, such that לֹא יָמוּשׁ סֵפֶר הַתּוֹרָה הַזֶּה מִפִּיךָ, *This Book of the Torah shall not depart from your mouth* (*Yehoshua* 1:8).

This theme resonates in the words of *Yalkut Shimoni on Tehillim* (116:9), אֶתְהַלֵּךְ לִפְנֵי ה' בְּאַרְצוֹת הַחַיִּים, *I shall walk before Hashem in the lands of the living.* R' Yehudah said, "This refers to the marketplace." King David indicates that even when he walked through the marketplace — a setting filled with distractions and inappropriate behavior — there too, he sustained the status of "walking before G-d."

The *Kedushas Levi's* words, in his commentary to *Maseches Avos*, serve as an apt summation of this chapter:

Rabban Gamliel, the son of R' Yehudah HaNasi, says: יָפֶה תַּלְמוּד תּוֹרָה עִם דֶּרֶךְ אֶרֶץ שֶׁיְגִיעַת שְׁנֵיהֶם מַשְׁכַּחַת עָוֹן, *Torah study is good together with an occupation, for the exertion of them both makes sin forgotten* (*Avos* 2:2). Ostensibly, this statement is very puzzling — why link the study of Torah with an occupation? However, it seems there is an explanation. Let us first clarify the question of *Tosafos* (*Sanhedrin* 7a) regarding the first questions they will ask a man in the Heavenly Court: "Did you conduct your business with integrity? Did you set aside fixed times for the study of Torah?" Elsewhere, our Sages said, "The initial stage of a man's judgment [in the Heavenly Court] is on knowledge of Torah." Perhaps these questions are really one — for one depends on the other: When a person engages in business with integrity, he can properly engage in Torah study.

... for people who scurry around engaged in business ventures ... how can they be engaged in Torah study at the same time? ... [However] Shlomo HaMelech said, בְּכָל דְּרָכֶיךָ דָעֵהוּ, *In all your ways know Him* (*Mishlei* 3:6). When a man walks in the marketplace and encounters a woman or colorful female clothing, and he does not want to look, because of the Sages' admonition (*Avodah Zarah* 20a), "It is prohibited to look at a woman and it is prohibited to look at the colored clothing of a woman," he is [actually] learning the halachah at that time.

In the market, which is a place of wickedness, a person is prone to lie, yet if he does not, remembering the verse

(*Vayikra* 19:11), וְלֹא תְכַחֲשׁוּ, *you shall not deny falsely*, he is learning the verse at that time ....

Likewise, when he comes to his store and a customer comes to buy from him, and he gives him a full measure ... and does not corrupt his weights, then he remembers the verse (*Vayikra* 19:36), מֹאזְנֵי צֶדֶק אַבְנֵי צֶדֶק ... יִהְיֶה לָכֶם, *You shall have correct scales, correct weights ....* As such, if he conducts his business with integrity, he is also learning.

With this understanding, the question of *Tosafos* is answered — the Heavenly Court will ask him: Did you conduct business with integrity, and consequently learn all of the Torah? If so, the first question is also about the study of Torah.

It is quite clear that the obligations of an employee toward his employer are an inseparable part of his service of G-d and constitute a part of "his Torah." A working man has no reason to feel like a second-class citizen; on the contrary, he needs to realize that there are certain aspects of his service of G-d that are more difficult than for a person who toils exclusively in Torah. Whereas the world of the Torah scholar is a spiritual domain, and the study of Torah is the singular important thing in this world, the working world may be estranged from spirituality. The service of G-d in this world and the transformation of the profane into the sacred require tremendous effort and constant vigilance over one's spiritual responsibilities — and thus, earn great reward in this world and the World to Come.

17

Distance Yourself from a False Word

Aside from the Torah's imperative to say the truth and to distance oneself from falsehood, there are a number of fundamental concepts in Judaism that are defined as truth. The Torah is called the "Torah of Truth," the seal of G-d is truth (*Shabbos* 55a), and one of the Names of G-d is Truth, as it is written (*Yirmiyahu* 10:10), ה׳ אֱלֹקִים אֱמֶת, *Hashem, G-d, is truth.*

The obligation to speak the truth and to distance oneself from lying appears twice in the Torah: מִדְּבַר שֶׁקֶר תִּרְחָק, *Distance yourself from a false word* (*Shemos* 23:7), and לֹא תִּגְנֹבוּ וְלֹא תְכַחֲשׁוּ וְלֹא תְשַׁקְּרוּ אִישׁ בַּעֲמִיתוֹ, *You shall not steal, you shall not deny falsely, and you shall not deceive one another* (*Vayikra* 19:11). The *Chofetz Chaim*, in the prologue to his name-sake work, says that if a half-truth was inserted in a small part of a person's speech, he has violated the positive commandment written in the Torah, מִדְּבַר שֶׁקֶר תִּרְחָק, *Distance yourself from a false word.*

Lying is considered a severe transgression, even worse than stealing. Citing *Toras Kohanim* on the verse, לֹא תִּגְנֹבוּ וְלֹא תְכַחֲשׁוּ וְלֹא תְשַׁקְּרוּ אִישׁ בַּעֲמִיתוֹ, *You shall not steal, you shall not deny falsely, and you shall not deceive one another,* Rashi notes that the verse lists the sins in sequential order based on their severity, from lowest to highest.

First a person will steal, then he will continue to deny falsely that he owes money; afterward he will advance to lying, and in the end, he will even swear falsely. It is clear that lying is considered a greater iniquity than stealing.

Furthermore, *Tehillim* (101:7) warns: לֹא יֵשֵׁב בְּקֶרֶב בֵּיתִי עֹשֵׂה רְמִיָּה דֹּבֵר שְׁקָרִים לֹא יִכּוֹן לְנֶגֶד עֵינָי, *In the midst of my house shall not dwell a practitioner of deceit; one who tells lies shall not remain in my presence.* Commenting on this verse, R' Yirmiya bar Abba said (*Sotah* 42a):

> There are four groups that will not greet the Divine Presence: the scoffers, the flatterers, the liars, and the gossips .... The liars — as it is written (*Tehillim* 101:7), דֹּבֵר שְׁקָרִים לֹא יִכּוֹן לְנֶגֶד עֵינָי, *one who tells lies shall not remain in my presence.* And the speakers of gossip — as it is written (ibid. 5:5), כִּי לֹא קֵל חָפֵץ רֶשַׁע אָתָּה לֹא יְגֻרְךָ רָע, *For You are not a G-d Who desires wickedness, no evil dwells with You.*

Deceit cannot remain in the presence of the Almighty, for "His Name is truth and His seal is truth" (*Shabbos* 55a).

R' Zusha of Anapol; commented on the phrase, *Distance yourself from a false word*, that by lying a person distances himself from his Creator. So does *Midrash Lekach Tov* (*Pesikta Zutrasa, Bamidbar, Parashas Nasso, Daf* 86a), adding that a liar not only distances himself from his Creator, but is even considered a denier of his Creator, since the Torah deems deceit as לִמְעֹל מַעַל בַּה', *committing treachery toward Hashem* (*Bamidbar* 5:6). *Menoras HaMaor* (*Perek* 19) writes harshly about liars:

> A deceitful person is despicable and an abomination before G-d, as it is written (*Mishlei* 6:16-19): שֵׁשׁ הֵנָּה שָׂנֵא ה' וְשֶׁבַע תּוֹעֲבַת נַפְשׁוֹ. עֵינַיִם רָמוֹת לְשׁוֹן שָׁקֶר וְיָדַיִם שֹׁפְכוֹת דָּם נָקִי. לֵב חֹרֵשׁ מַחְשְׁבוֹת אָוֶן רַגְלַיִם מְמַהֲרוֹת לָרוּץ לָרָעָה. יָפִיחַ כְּזָבִים עֵד שָׁקֶר וּמְשַׁלֵּחַ מְדָנִים בֵּין אַחִים, *G-d hates these six, but the seventh is the abomination of His soul: haughty eyes, a false tongue, and hands spilling innocent blood, a heart plotting iniquitous thoughts, feet hastening to run to evil, a false witness spouting lies, and one*

who stirs up strife among brothers. Three of the seven things are related to the sin of falsehood: a false tongue, spouting lies, and a false witness.

Thus, one who deceives is considered a traitor to the Creator, for G-d is absolute truth, and through words of falsehood the speaker is transformed into an abomination.

◆§ "Distance Yourself" from a False Word

The Torah's admonition to *distance yourself from a false word* is unique in that in no other area of human behavior is such extra vigilance commanded. Clearly, the tendency to veer, howsoever slightly, from the truth is so prevalent that extra caution is required. The Gemara (*Shevuos* 30b-31a) cites a long list of actions that derive from the obligation to distance oneself from a false word, among which are the following examples:

1. A judge should not vociferously rationalize his decision, when there may be even a small faint reason to doubt it.
2. A judge should not teach unworthy students.
3. A judge should not partner with an unsavory colleague in forming a judicial panel.

Though these examples do not entail any direct falsehood, the Gemara cites them to indicate how stringent is the obligation to avoid any situation or behavior that will prevent the truth from coming to light. Distancing oneself from falsehood requires refraining from any action that is likely to create a mistaken impression, or will result in the corruption of justice, even if the action was technically legal.

Nonetheless, the Talmud cites instances in which it is permissible — and even obligatory — to conceal or "stretch" the truth. The Gemara (*Yevamos* 65b) relates an opinion that justifies Yosef's brothers, when they suggested that their father Yaakov had — on his death-bed — expressed his wish that Yosef refrain from avenging the wrong that had been done to him when his brothers sold him into slavery. Since the Torah makes no mention that Yaakov knew what his other sons had done to Yosef, nor that he ever said such a thing, R' Illa presumes that this was a falsehood — but a justifiable one — since it served to bring peace into familial relations:

> It is permissible for a person to "adjust the truth" for the sake of peace, as it is written (*Bereishis* 50:16), אָבִיךָ צִוָּה ... כֹּה תֹאמְרוּ לְיוֹסֵף אָנָּא שָׂא נָא פֶּשַׁע אַחֶיךָ, *Your father gave orders ... Thus shall you say to Yosef: Kindly forgive the spiteful deed of your brothers ....*

R' Nosson, on the other hand, insists that it is not only permissible, but actually a moral obligation to bend the truth in order to save a life.

> It is a mitzvah, as it is written (*I Shmuel* 16:2-4), וַיֹּאמֶר שְׁמוּאֵל אֵיךְ אֵלֵךְ וְשָׁמַע שָׁאוּל וַהֲרָגָנִי וַיֹּאמֶר ה' עֶגְלַת בָּקָר תִּקַּח בְּיָדֶךָ וְאָמַרְתָּ לִזְבֹּחַ ה' בָּאתִי, *But Shmuel asked, "How can I go? If Shaul finds out he will kill me." So Hashem said, "Take along a heifer and say, 'I have come to bring an offering for Hashem.'"*
>
> *Tanna d'vei Yishmael* taught, "Great is peace! Even G-d made a change: First it is written (*Bereishis* 18:12), וַאדֹנִי זָקֵן, [Sara said] *my husband is old.* But, when relaying Sara's words to Avraham, Hashem quoted her as saying, וַאֲנִי זָקַנְתִּי, *though I have aged* (ibid., v. 13).

Similarly, the Gemara in *Maseches Kesubos* (17a) says that it is permissible and even laudable to praise the bride in front of the groom, even if the words are somewhat exaggerated. The Gemara in *Maseches Bava Metzia* (23b) presents three specific instances in which Torah sages would prefer to hide or adjust the truth: to understate one's knowledge or expertise, to remain silent and discrete on private issues, and in extreme cases, not to praise one's hosts lest they are inundated with hospitality requests which they are incapable of meeting.

Nonetheless, the Torah demands that one "distance" himself

from falsehood, so that even when it is permissible to conceal the truth or stretch it, one needs to do so reluctantly, while "gritting one's teeth." The Gemara in *Maseches Yevamos* (63a) warns against the habit of lying, even for a good reason, relating the following illustrative anecdote:

> Rav's wife was causing him distress. When Rav asked her, "Make me lentils," she prepared him legumes. When he asked for legumes, she prepared lentils. When his son Chiya grew up, he would reverse the instructions: if his father said to him that he wanted lentils, he would tell his mother that his father requested legumes, and if he asked for legumes, he would tell his mother that his father wanted lentils. In this way, Rav's desire was fulfilled.
>
> Rav commented to his son, "Your mother is now good to me and does whatever I ask!" R' Chiya then told his father that he had reversed the instructions to his mother. Rav said to him, "This is an example of the popular idiom: The child that comes from you teaches you wisdom, and does what you were supposed to do." However, my son, do not do this, since it is a lie, as it is written, לָמְדוּ לְשׁוֹנָם דַּבֶּר שֶׁקֶר, *they train their tongue to speak falsehood* (*Yirmiyahu* 9:4).

Explaining why Rav chose to quote from *Yirmiyahu* and not the verse מִדְּבַר שֶׁקֶר תִּרְחָק, *Distance yourself from a false word*, the *Maharsha* writes that Rav wanted to teach his son an important lesson. As much as he enjoyed his son's wisdom, Rav asked his son to stop tricking his mother so that he would not habituate himself to corrupt the truth. If a person becomes accustomed to lie or bend the truth, his moral sensitivity is dulled and his discomfort with falsehood gradually dissipates.

The Aramaic translation of the word "train" in the above verse is "*ilfu*" which connotes a double meaning: to teach and to train or exercise (as in physical therapy). The Torah expects a person to have an innate revulsion to falsehood, presuming that people would find it physically and psychologically difficult, not unlike any physical activity to which they are not accustomed. Such physiological difficulties are discernable by lie detecting machines. However, people who habitually lie minimize their physiological reactions and can thus circumvent the detection of these machines. The *Menoras HaMaor* (*Perek* 19) writes:

> A deceitful person is considered like a dead man, because people do not reckon with his words, since he is accustomed to lying — his life and his death are the same. Our Sages (*Sanhedrin* 89b) said, "This is the punishment of an impostor: even if he says the truth, people do not listen to him. When Yirmiyahu, the prophet, admonished the Jewish people, he only admonished them about deceit, as it is written (*Yirmiyahu* 9:4), לִמְּדוּ לְשׁוֹנָם דַּבֶּר שֶׁקֶר הַעֲוֵה נִלְאוּ, *they train their tongue to speak falsehood, striving to be iniquitous*; after they trained their tongues to speak falsehood, it became like their very nature, and they were unable to depart from it, and they tired from attempting to abandon the way of falsehood for the way of truth.

The prophet Yirmiyahu complained that the people of his generation repeatedly lied, and trained their tongues to lie, until falsehood and deceit became normative.

⌐§ The Boot Factory in Lodz

My upbringing was overseen by my father *z"l*, who modeled integrity and honesty and demanded no less from his family. Indeed, it seemed he was incapable of speaking a false word or insincere compliment, and could not tell a lie even when his very life depended upon it.

My early years were nurtured in the Neve Achiezer neighborhood of Bnei Brak, which was built for survivors of the Holocaust. While many of our neighbors were shattered people haunted by their nightmares, they nonetheless radiated trust in G-d, and faithful hope for a better future in the Land of Israel. Among them was R' Manis Zitnitzky, *zt"l*, whose first wife and six children perished in the Holocaust. When it became clear that he and his second wife would not be blessed with children, they dedicated themselves to building Yeshivas Imrei Emes in Bnei Brak.

I recall that for as long as we lived nearby, I visited Reb Manis' home every Shabbos to eat *kugel* and to be tested on the *parashah*. Even when I objected, preferring to play with friends, my father insisted that I visit Reb Manis to alleviate the sorrow of this childless couple. Not understanding why it was solely my responsibility, I obeyed — sometimes grudgingly. Only after Reb Manis died did my father share the secret of this odd bond between our families.

At the height of World War II, the Germans established a factory in the Lodz Ghetto to manufacture fur-lined boots for their pilots, who often returned from their bombing missions with frostbitten feet. The Germans turned the ghetto into a large forced-labor camp, but in their zeal to secure the safety of their pilots they gave the Jewish shoemakers free rein in choosing their laborers, as well as better conditions and food, because of the urgent need for the fur boots. There was one condition: all of the workers had to be professional shoemakers. Anyone hiring unqualified craftsmen would be killed.

My father risked his life and snuck into the factory trying to join a work team. Production was managed in groups of about ten men, with each group producing a pair of boots from start to finish. My father related:

> I approached the first group and asked if they need another worker. The foreman raised his head and asked me if I am a shoemaker. I shook my head, and he rebuked me and demanded that I immediately go away. This scenario repeated itself several times as I dashed from group to group in the large warehouse. Time was running out, and I feared the Nazi guards who periodically patrolled the factory. Desperately, I decided to approach two more

groups. If the first one rejected me, I would lie to the last group and claim that I was a professional shoemaker.

As I approached the next group, and again asked if they need an additional worker, the foreman lifted his eyes. "Are you a shoemaker?" As I whispered "no" he looked at me again with a penetrating stare and said, "Look, young man, go over to the barrel filled with bootblack, and stir it well to prevent coagulation. Put your hands in and mix the paint well." Relieved yet hesitant, I put my right hand in to mix the paint, and after several minutes of stirring the foreman asked me to show him my hands. When he saw that my left hand was clean, he chastised me and said that this work requires mixing with both hands. After a few more minutes of stirring with both hands, he asked me again to show him my hands, and declared with satisfaction, "Now you are a professional shoemaker and you can join the group."

At that moment a German guard approached our group and asked, "I was told someone entered the factory without permission. Did you see him?" The head of the group responded, "He is right here next to me; he is a professional shoemaker, and I requested his services." The German nodded his head approvingly and let me be. So I stayed in the boot factory and my life was spared.

Then my father fixed his gaze on me and said, "Do you know who was in charge of that group? It was none other than R' Manis Zitnitzky, in whose merit I remained alive."

Shocked, I remained silent for a few minutes, finally comprehending why Reb Manis would occasionally refer to me as "his grandchild." After a few more minutes of reflection, I could not resist and asked my father why did he not lie immediately and say he was a shoemaker since no one would be able to verify his claim? With a puzzled expression, my father exclaimed, "But I was not a shoemaker." I was awestruck by his simple and matter of fact answer. Even when his very life was at risk, he could not bring himself to utter a false word, and decided that only when all alternatives were exhausted, having no other choice, would he lie and say that he was a shoemaker.

⪧ Different Categories of Liars

Menoras HaMaor (*Perek* 19) categorizes liars into seven groups:

1) Deceitful people. Not only do these people lie, they corrupt, abuse and rob those they encounter. Included in this category are those who deny their debts, those who withhold employee wages, and those who swindle their customers and partners.

2) Those who intend to acquire trust and friendship through their lies, so they can cheat and take advantage of people in the future.

3) The smooth talkers and flatterers who use false words to attain a favor or a position originally intended for another. Though they do not directly cheat or steal, they use lies in order to gain some future benefit.

4) People who relate stories that they heard, changing some details or exaggerating, though this behavior yields them no benefit.

5) People who promise to bestow good and gifts on others without any intention to fulfill these promises.

6) People who falsely boast of the favors they did.

7) People who brag of virtues and achievements that they do not possess; for example, one falsely claims that he holds a high position or has noble lineage.

Though the motives for lying, and the damage caused, vary considerably, all of them are despised in the eyes of G-d.

In *Mesillas Yesharim*, *Ramchal* categorizes liars based on the severity of their act:

There are people who have made an art of deception,

fabricating tall tales to generate conversation or to appear wise and knowledgeable. Of such liars it is written (*Mishlei* 12:22), תּוֹעֲבַת ה׳ שִׂפְתֵי שָׁקֶר, *False lips are an abomination to Hashem.*

There are others ... who are not as creative or adept in creating false stories, but nevertheless, when they relate a true anecdote they tend to embellish and mix truth with fanciful lies. As they accustom themselves to this behavior it becomes second nature — they are the impostors, who have lost credibility; as our Sages say (*Sanhedrin* 89b), "This is the punishment of the impostor: even if he says the truth, people do not listen to him."

There are still others whose ailment is less severe. Though they do not habitually lie, they do not distance themselves from falsehood. Should the situation require it, or if it will arouse amusement, they are not loath to occasionally utter a falsehood. Many times they will say it in a joking fashion, without any evil intent. However, the wisest of all men already informed us that this defies the will of G-d ... for דְּבַר שֶׁקֶר יִשְׂנָא צַדִּיק, *A righteous person despises a false matter* (*Mishlei* 13:5).

There is an additional group of liars: those who lie to themselves, though they avoid lying to others.

Self-deceivers usually try to justify and rationalize their inappropriate actions. These people are also considered liars, even though they did not speak even one word of falsehood. A self-deceiver needs to find some "license" for his behavior, and to assuage his conscience he must convince himself that his behavior is acceptable.

The *Sfas Emes*, renowned for his pursuit of truth — as reflected in the title of his works — explains the phrase: שֹׁפְטִים וְשֹׁטְרִים תִּתֶּן לְךָ, *Judges and officers you shall appoint for yourself (Devarim* 16:18):

... this is also an assurance that every Jew has the ability to judge and police himself; as it is written, "In the way that a person wants to go, [Heavenly guidance] will lead him" (*Makkos* 10b). Should a person want to acquire the truth ... [he] will have Heavenly support. This is the meaning of, *Judges and officers you shall appoint for yourself.*

The main thing is to seek the truth, as it is written, צֶדֶק צֶדֶק תִּרְדֹּף, *Righteousness, righteousness shall you pursue* (*Devarim* 16:20); and similarly with regard to lying, מִדְּבַר שֶׁקֶר תִּרְחָק, *You shall distance yourself from a false word* (*Shemos* 23:7). I heard from my teacher, my grandfather, in the name of R' Bunim of P'shis'cha, that the [admonition to] "distance oneself" is not found at any other prohibition in the Torah except for lying ... to highlight the severity of the prohibition (*Parashas Shoftim*, 5639).

According to the *Sfas Emes* the obligation to be upright and honest, and to distance oneself from falsehood, applies even to oneself. R' Menachem Mendel of Kotzk famously quipped: "If I am I and you are you, then I am I and you are you. But, if I am you and you are I, then I am not I and you are not you!"

Once, R' Bunim of P'shis'cha went into his *beis medrash* and asked his followers, "What is a *chassid*?" One answered, "A *chassid* is a person who goes beyond the letter of the law." The Rebbe of P'shis'cha responded, "The Torah commands: וְלֹא תוֹנוּ אִישׁ אֶת עֲמִיתוֹ, *Each of you shall not aggrieve his fellow* (*Vayikra* 25:17); this is the letter of the law. Whereas going beyond the letter of the law demands that a person should not wrong himself!" (*Siach Sarfei Kodesh*). In a similar vein the Rebbe of Kotzk admonished his followers by interpreting the verse וְלֹא תוֹנוּ אִישׁ אֶת אֲמִיתוֹ, *Each of you shall not aggrieve his own truth* [by interchanging the letter *aleph* for the letter *ayin* in the word "*amito*"]. The common denominator in these Chassidic writings is an admonition not to lie to oneself — perhaps the most common and egregious transgression, and the most difficult one to correct.

◆§ The Danger in Telling Lies to Children

I once heard an excellent speech addressing the issue of "Lying, and Teaching Children to Lie." The speaker told an amazing story that aroused laughter, while some parents in the audience were noticeably embarrassed.

> Coming home after a hard day at work, Mr. Cohen stretches out on the couch, browsing through the newspaper, as he waits for dinner. Suddenly, his cellphone rings. Seeing the name of the caller on the display, he decides to ignore the call. The caller persists and the cellphone rings again. Mr. Cohen calls his nine-year-old and tells him, "Answer the phone and tell the caller that your father is not home, but he forgot his cellphone at home." The obedient child hurried to do his father's bidding.
>
> Several minutes later, the child approached his father and told him, "Father, I need you to sign the punishment sheet that I received today in school." The father asked, "Punishment? For what?!" The child responded, "I did not complete my homework." The father stood tall and angrily responded, "This morning I asked you if you did your homework, and you told me that you completed all the assignments. Now it is clear that you lied to me! Tell me my son: Who taught you to lie?" A well-mannered child, the youngster remained silent.

Lying to children is treated with a great deal of severity by our Sages (*Sotah* 46b):

> R' Zeira said, "A person should not say to a child that I will give you something, and then not give it to him, because this is likely to teach him to lie, as it is written, לִמְּדוּ לְשׁוֹנָם דַּבֶּר שֶׁקֶר, *they train their tongue to speak falsehood* (*Yirmiyahu* 9:4).

In the vignette related earlier in this chapter from *Maseches*

Yevamos (63a), R' Chiya reversed his father's instructions to ensure that his wishes would be fulfilled by his contrarian mother. Rav, his father, prohibited him from doing so; yet he alludes that he himself should have done so. How can Rav instruct his son not to lie (even in an instance in which Jewish law permits it), yet in the same breath he says to him, "I should have done this myself"? Why is the ruling different for the son than for the father?

It appears that Rav concedes that there is room to "stray" from the truth in order to increase peace between a husband and wife. However, Rav, as a mature adult, can determine to what degree he may depart from the truth, and will do his best to minimize bending the truth. At the same time, Rav understood that his young son does not yet have the discernment to make these determinations, and permitting fudging the truth, even when justified, could result in a lifelong habit. Thus, the *Rambam* in *Hilchos Shevuos* (12:8) rules:

> One needs to be very careful regarding children to teach their tongue words of truth …. This is an obligation upon fathers and teachers of children.

◆§ A Difficult Mitzvah to Fulfill

Ramchal writes in his summary on the obligation to speak the truth (*Mesillas Yesharim*):

> The Sages said, "The seal of G-d is truth" (*Shabbos* 55a). Certainly, if G-d chose truth as His seal, [imagine] how abominable is the opposite before Him!. … One of the pillars upon which the world stands is truth (see *Avos* 1:18). Thus, someone who speaks falsehood undermines the foundation of the world. And conversely: A person who is careful in telling the truth sustains the foundation of the world. Our Sages (*Sanhedrin* 97a) already indicated that wherever people were cautious in speaking only the truth, the angel of death had no dominion.

The Gerrer Rebbe, the *Pnei Menachem zt"l*, told the following story about his father, the *Imrei Emes zt"l*:

> It is written in the holy books (*Charedim, Perek* 61) that every Jew must embrace at least one positive mitzvah and one negative mitzvah, committing to fulfill them in their entirety, even if he needs to give up his life in so doing. My father told me, "I accepted upon myself the positive mitzvah of כַּבֵּד אֶת אָבִיךָ וְאֵת אִמֶּךָ, *Honor your father and your mother* (*Shemos* 20:12), and the negative mitzvah of מִדְּבַר שֶׁקֶר תִּרְחָק, *You shall distance yourself from a false word* (ibid. 23:7). When asked why he selected those, the Rebbe answered, "Because they are the hardest!" (*Rosh Golas Ariel*).

In a similar vein, the *Pnei Menachem* related that when his father, the *Imrei Emes*, escaped from the Nazis in 1940, he traveled with forged documents. As they approached the Polish border, his escorts told the Rebbe to identify himself by the false name on his passport. The Rebbe refused to lie, and providentially he was not questioned.

18

Setting Aside Fixed Times for Torah Study

In various contexts, the Talmud repeatedly stresses the importance of setting a fixed time for Torah learning. In *Maseches Berachos* (35b) the Gemara quotes Rabbah bar Bar-Chana:

> Earlier generations, who made their Torah study a fixed practice and their work secondary — were successful in both; whereas later generations, who made their work a fixed practice and their Torah study secondary — were successful in neither.

This obligation is of paramount importance, since as one will stand before the Heavenly Court upon departing this world, the first or second question he will be asked is, "Did you set aside fixed times for Torah study?" (*Shabbos* 31a). According to *Rashi*, the question of setting aside times for Torah study is even for those who must work for their livelihood:

> Since a person needs to engage in work for his livelihood — because if there is no livelihood, there is no Torah — one must set aside times for Torah study, a set amount of time, so as not to be distracted entirely with the pursuit of his livelihood.

In the same vein, Shammai said: עֲשֵׂה תוֹרָתְךָ קֶבַע, *Make your Torah study a fixed practice* (*Avos* 1:15). However, the particular words used by Shammai raise several questions:

1) Why does he use the words "**Make** your Torah" and not "**Learn** your Torah"?

2) Why does he use the language of "**your Torah**" and not "**the Torah**"?

3) Why did he prefer "a fixed practice" over the expression "Make your Torah primary" (*ikar*)?

The *Bartenura* on that Mishnah writes:

Your primary involvement day and night should be in Torah; and then, when you tire of your learning, do your work. Your primary involvement should not be mundane work, and only when you are free from work do you engage in Torah study.

According to the *Bartenura*, the meaning of the word *keva* (fixed) has both quantitative and qualitative connotations. A person is obligated to devote his best and most of his time to the study of Torah, and only when he tires from his study, should he then do the work necessary to support his family.

The *Meiri* explains that this Mishnah addresses the working man. The worker must remember that his time spent on earning a living constitutes a time of "being idle" from Torah learning:

"Make your Torah study a fixed practice" means that your work should be secondary … and your Torah should be a fixed practice, to the degree that even when you are working, your intention should be only for what you need to sustain your body and your family.

The *Rashbatz*, in *Magen Avos*, explains Shammai's words as follows:

… it means that those hours that you set aside for Torah

study will be primary, and the other work you do will support those hours.

The *Ba'al HaRoke'ach*, on the basis of a responsum by the *Rosh* (*Klal* 15:8), goes a step further:

> [Whoever] has fixed times for Torah study and never misses, and [whenever] he is free, he returns to his book and learns; and he does not wander about the marketplace except to earn a livelihood for his family, and not to increase his wealth, this is who I call a Torah sage; and anyone who embarrasses him must pay a penalty.

Calling someone a "Torah sage" is not just a titular honor, but has practical ramifications. The *Rosh* (ibid.) discusses exemptions from taxes granted to people who engage in Torah study day and night. The *Rosh* was asked whether the exemption extends to someone who "works for a minimal livelihood and spends the rest of his day learning Torah." Following is his retort:

> About whom are all of the stories and *baraisos* that discuss the exemption from taxes given to Torah sages? Do they refer to a king who has no [financial] worries? Were they said about beggars? Were they said about angels who do not eat and drink? Rather, they were said about human beings, who eat, drink, and have bodily needs.
>
> [The Sages] explicitly said (*Bava Basra* 110a), "One should even do work to which he is unaccustomed and not rely upon others for support." And, it is written (*Tehillim* 128:2), יְגִיעַ כַּפֶּיךָ כִּי תֹאכֵל אַשְׁרֶיךָ וְטוֹב לָךְ, *When you eat the labor of your hands, you will be happy, and it will be well with you.* This is the best measure of all.
>
> We learned that יָפֶה תַלְמוּד תּוֹרָה עִם דֶּרֶךְ אֶרֶץ, *Torah study is good together with an occupation* (*Avos* 2:2), and אִם אֵין קֶמַח אֵין תּוֹרָה, *If there is no flour, then there is no Torah* (ibid. 3:21). They also said, "The earlier generations, who made their

Torah study a fixed practice and their work secondary, were successful in both" (*Berachos* 35b).

From all of these statements we deduce that when the Sages exempted Torah scholars from taxes, they did not exempt them on the assumption that these individuals did not work for sustenance and livelihood for themselves and their households. But, as long as they fulfill the mitzvah of וְהָגִיתָ בּוֹ יוֹמָם וָלַיְלָה, *you should contemplate it day and night* (*Yehoshua* 1:8), each according to his strength and ability, and they are never idle from Torah study except for a mitzvah or to sustain themselves and their family, they have the status of Torah scholars, who are exempt from all of the stated taxes.

A person is obligated to dedicate a certain time every day for the study of Torah, and not to neglect his study at that time, even if it seems to result in monetary loss. According to the *Machzor Vitri*, if a person will not set aside a fixed time from which he will not waiver, he will eventually neglect all of his Torah studies. Those of us who did not merit to sit in the *beis medrash* day and night recognize too well just how true are the words of the *Machzor Vitri*, and how essential it is to devote a fixed time for the study of Torah every day, like a secured peg that cannot be removed.

Dedicating a fixed time for the study of Torah transforms that time of day into the core of one's life, around which the day's entire planned schedule revolves. For example: When an ill person requires medical treatments at certain fixed days and times, his entire daily schedule is planned around the medical appointment. So too, a person is obligated to dedicate unwavering set time for his Torah study, such that this time becomes the central activity of his entire day.

Consequently, we may understand why the Mishnah used the term "*Make* your Torah" a fixed, permanent cog around which your life revolves. The emphasis is on the need for a person to create an unwavering permanence, and to know that the time which is dedicated to the study of Torah cannot be changed or cancelled, no matter what. To establish and keep such a dedicated time requires special efforts, and a person must "make" that time "fixed."

✒️ Elevating Working for a Living to the Level of Torah

The *Sfas Emes* (*Chukas*, 5631) presents new insight into this Mishnah, and incidentally explains why Shammai uses the words "Make *your* Torah a fixed practice."

> This means that the Torah should become affixed in one's body — the knowledge of the Torah should be like a secure peg that is immovable. The Gemara states: "The earlier generations, who made their Torah study a fixed practice and their work secondary, were successful in both." It seems that even in all of the [mundane] work that they did, the paramount objective was the "learning" — for a person can learn the will of G-d from all things. One who does everything for the sake of Heaven with intensity finds the radiance of Torah [even in the mundane]. Thus, the term "their Torah" reflects the fact that toil in a physical act which is done in full accord with the Torah is called the "Torah of man."

The *Sfas Emes* teaches that a person who strives to fulfill G-d's will while working, and guides his everyday activities in accordance with the Torah, is considered as one who has made Torah learning a permanent fixture of his life. Moreover, the *Sfas Emes's* words affirm our contention that the interpersonal mitzvos are a pathway to come close to G-d. If one treats another Jew according to the will of G-d, conducts his business according to the will of G-d, and his goal in all endeavors is to gratify his Maker — he is considered as one who sets aside time for Torah and is close to G-d the entire day.

✣ The Pressing Debt of My Father, *a"h*

Growing up, I witnessed the manifestation of making Torah learning the central cog of each day. My father learned the *Daf Yomi* with his friend, R' David Zimmerman *a"h*, for nearly thirty years; they learned for about ninety minutes, starting at 4:30 a.m. — a time chosen with the encouragement of the *Beis Yisrael* of Gur.

My father encouraged me to get up early to learn at dawn, explaining that this is the best time to learn for three reasons: There are no disruptions or social obligations; one's head is clear and the quality of the learning is superb; and most importantly, the learning in the morning gives a different flavor to the entire day and influences one's conduct during the rest of the day.

During the last three years of her life, as my mother *a"h* struggled with cancer, my father did not forgo these early morning study sessions. There were sleepless nights in which he attended to my mother, yet he did not give up. His *chavrusa*, Reb David, told me that occasionally he would nod off, bent over his Gemara. "I would let him sleep for about ten minutes," Reb David added, "and then wake him up, and we would continue to learn."

This partnership was uninterrupted until both men's health deteriorated. Then another friend — knowing how important the study of the *Daf Yomi* was to my father — volunteered to come to our house, and learn with him whenever possible. One day my stepmother, a woman of sterling personality, came home and found my father sitting with his hands covering his face, sobbing. After continuous entreaties, he finally explained that he is crying because he has a debt that he will never be able to repay.

Shocked, my stepmother asked him to tell her to whom and how much he owes, promising to pay the debt immediately. He expressed appreciation for her willingness to help, but explained that unfortunately she will not be able to help in this case. Distraught, she pleaded with him. My father sighed and replied, "I owe ten pages to the *Daf Yomi*, and I fear I will not be able to pay this debt," and then he broke out in fresh tears.

❧ The Reward for Making One's Torah a Fixed Practice

The value of dedicating time for the study of Torah became even clearer when R' Moshe Zilberberg, *shlita,* showed me the words of the *Pele Yoetz* (*Os Kuf*):

> In the world of business transactions, sometimes a merchant can buy goods at a very cheap price and earn an incredible profit. Similarly, it is possible to attain a great deal in the little time set aside for Torah learning, even more than if he would study *Negaim and Ohalos* [difficult issues that require long periods of study].

The *Pele Yoetz* applies the halachic principle כָּל קָבוּעַ כְּמֶחֱצָה עַל מֶחֱצָה דָמֵי (*Kesubos* 15a), which assigns a fixed, immovable object greater weight than its absolute value. Accordingly, a person who dedicates a set hour for learning every day — and does not swerve from this routine — is considered as if he learned half a day, and is rewarded accordingly, since "Anything which is permanent creates a status of fifty-fifty ...!"

The reward for someone who makes his Torah a fixed practice and his work secondary is very great, as the *Alshich* writes in *Toras Moshe* on the verse, שֵׁשֶׁת יָמִים תַּעֲבֹד וְעָשִׂיתָ כָּל מְלַאכְתֶּךָ, *Six days shall you work and accomplish all your work* (*Shemos* 20:9):

> ... you should start from the morning to make your Torah learning a fixed practice. After you made this primary, then you will do all of your work. [G-d promises]: I will make you successful when you make your work secondary, "and you will accomplish all your work," for I will be with you to finish it, since I will help you and you will be successful in both things.

This is the same idea expressed in the commentary of the *Sforno* on the Torah (*Devarim* 28:2):

> כִּי תִשְׁמַע בְּקוֹל ה' אֱלֹקֶיךָ ..., *when you hearken to the voice of*

Hashem, your G-d ... This will be when your Torah is a affixed practice and your work is secondary, therefore all the blessings will "overcome" you without any effort.

Accordingly, the reward for someone who sets aside time for Torah study is that both his learning and his business will be successful.

19

Honor Your Wife

The value that Judaism places on marriage and family cannot be overstated. As G-d created all living things, He blessed them with the capacity for reproduction, but it was only to the human being, created in the image of G-d, and endowed with consciousness and free will, that G-d commanded, פְּרוּ וּרְבוּ וּמִלְאוּ אֶת הָאָרֶץ וְכִבְשֻׁהָ, *Be fruitful and multiply, fill the earth and subdue it ...* (*Bereishis* 1:28). Furthermore, G-d declares (*Bereishis* 2:18), לֹא טוֹב הֱיוֹת הָאָדָם לְבַדּוֹ, *It is not good that man be alone*, and thus, the purpose of the union of man and woman is not limited to procreation. Indeed, enjoined to עַל כֵּן יַעֲזָב אִישׁ אֶת אָבִיו וְאֶת אמּוֹ וְדָבַק בְּאִשְׁתּוֹ, *leave his father and his mother and cling to his wife* (2:24), man has since found comfort and completion in marriage, and in the home that he builds with his wife.

It is the home that is the cornerstone of the House of Israel, and secures its perpetuation and fulfillment through the travails of history. This chapter will focus on the Jewish view of the obligations a man has in honoring his wife, and maintaining the sanctity and strength of the Jewish home.

◆§ His Wife Is His Home

The familial cell is called *bayis*, and is identical to the second letter of the Hebraic alphabet, with a numerical value of *two*. It is customary to bless a newly married couple that they will jointly build a *bayis ne'eman b'Yisrael* — a faithful home, one that is set on a firm foundation and structured so that it will not fall. The Talmud transforms the word *bayis* into a lofty concept, as R' Yose declares (*Shabbos* 118b), "I've never called [referred to] my wife [as] my wife … but [as] my home." *Rashi* explains that this was a way to express great appreciation to the wife as the pillar of the home, as she is the primary (*ikar*) force that governs and maintains the home.

This notion lies at the heart of the requirement that the *Kohen Gadol* have a wife prior to commencing the Yom Kippur service at the Temple, for otherwise he would not be able to fulfill the Torah's command: וְכִפֶּר בַּעֲדוֹ וּבְעַד בֵּיתוֹ, *and atone for himself and for his household* (*Vayikra* 16:6); for our Sages (*Yoma* 2a) explain that "his household" is his wife.

R' Samson Raphael Hirsch (*Vayikra* 22:16) explains the metaphorical equation of the wife to the home:

> Our Sages said, "His home is his wife" (*Yoma* 2a), and the children are the "building bricks" of the home that constitute its primary purpose. We find a similar concept in the laws of *terumah*, which highlight that the wife personifies the character of the home, and that character is retained even after her husband's death — in her role as mother and grandmother of her husband's offspring [and therefore remains eligible to eat *terumah*].

Noting that the Hebraic words *banim* (children) and the verb *boneh* (build) share the same root word, R' Yaakov T. Mecklenburg *zt"l* (*HaKsav v'HaKabbalah* on *Vayikra* 21:9) notes that a couple's offspring are compared to the building blocks of a home:

> Whoever has children is called "built," whereas one who has no children is merely "ruined"; consequently [Sarah the Matriarch asks her husband to have a child with her

handmaiden], אוּלַי אִבָּנֶה מִמֶּנָּה, *perhaps I will be built up through her* (*Bereishis* 16:2).

Consequently, the fulfillment of a man's destiny is contingent on the construction and maintenance of the home, and since the home is his wife, it is vital that a man understand his obligations in honoring her.

R' Shmuel Kamenetsky *shlita* was asked to officiate at a wedding. Prior to the ceremony, Reb Shmuel asked the bridegroom if he understands the language of the *kesubah* (marriage contract) to which he was committing himself. After a moment of awkward silence, the Rabbi turned to the young man and said, "There is only one word here that you must understand, and it is *ve'okir*, which means, 'I will honor.' Honoring your wife is the only important part, the rest are just explanations and derivations of how to do so."

◆§ His Wife Is Like Himself

The affinity between a man and his wife has numerous practical halachic implications, and thus the phrase *"ishto k'gufo"* (his wife is like himself) appears throughout the Talmud. The Gemara (*Sanhedrin* 28b) derives this principle from the fact that the Torah (*Vayikra* 18:14) refers to the wife of his father's brother — his blood-related uncle (*dod*) — as an aunt (*doda*) rather than his uncle's wife. The *Rambam* (*Hilchos Eidus* 13:6) consequently rules that just as a blood relative is invalid as a witness, so is the relative's spouse, for "the wife is comparable to the husband."

The *Tiferes Yisrael* explains that any husband can cancel specific vows undertaken by his wife, such as oaths to afflict her body or that relate to their intimate relationship. However, a sage is empowered to annul the vows of others (under specific circumstances), yet he cannot annul his own wife's vows because "his wife is like himself," and he cannot annul his own vows (*Negaim* 2, *Os* 33).

The comparison of a wife to her husband is manifest in another case, regarding the ransom one is allowed to pay to redeem a captive. Our Sages (*Gittin* 45a) limited the amount paid to ransom a kidnapped captive to a set value, as a preventative measure to benefit the social order. Elsewhere (*Kesubos* 52a), the Gemara rules that a husband may pay a one-time exorbitant ransom to free his wife, for there was no limitation put on how much a man can pay to free himself from captivity. The *Tosafos* (ad loc.) reconciles these two citations by explaining that just as a man can give up all of his possessions to free himself, he may do so for his wife as well, since "his wife is like himself."

The degree to which "his wife is like himself" and vice versa is elucidated in *HaKsav v'HaKabbalah* (*Shemos* 22:21), in which R' Mecklenburg parses the Hebrew word for widow — *almanah*. He explains that it is a compound word, composed of *al* — lacking, *manah* — a part:

> For man and his wife were deemed one body, as it is written: וְהָיוּ לְבָשָׂר אֶחָד, *they shall become one flesh* (*Bereishis* 2:24), and as they [the Sages] said: "his wife is like himself." Neither one of them is complete alone, but is rather a part of the other, and therefore Scripture called the woman the portion of her man (*Koheles* 9:9): רְאֵה חַיִּים עִם אִשָּׁה ... כִּי הוּא חֶלְקֶךּ, *See life with your wife ... for she is your part*, and when one of them dies, the other is left without a part ....

Accordingly, a husband is obligated to treat his wife as himself. This, in and of itself, is quite a daunting demand, but it does not stop there, as the demand to honor one's wife is even greater.

◆§ Honoring More Than Himself

The Gemara (*Yevamos* 62b) describes the path to a peaceful home:

> Our Sages taught: He who loves his wife as himself, honors her more than himself, guides his sons and daughters on the straight path, and marries them off as they reach

maturity — of him it is written: וְיָדַעְתָּ כִּי שָׁלוֹם אָהֳלֶךָ, *You shall know that your tent is in peace* (*Iyov* 5:24).

Explaining the obligation to "honor her more than himself," *Rashi* explains that women are more sensitive to disdain, and more likely to be hurt. These words do not merely constitute good advice, but are stringent obligations, as becomes apparent in the words of the Gemara in *Chullin* (84b):

> [How are we to understand] what is written (*Tehillim* 112:5), טוֹב אִישׁ חוֹנֵן וּמַלְוֶה יְכַלְכֵּל דְּבָרָיו בְּמִשְׁפָּט, *Good is the man who is gracious and lends, who conducts his affairs with justice?* — A man should eat and drink for less than he can afford; dress and cover himself with as much as he can afford; and honor his wife and his children with more than he can [readily] afford, for they are dependent on him, and he is dependent on the One that Created the World.

Clearly, the Gemara does not define "honoring his wife" as mere lip-service, but rather on the amount of monies spent for her pleasure and benefit.

Rashi explains that one should expend less than he can readily afford on his own consumption, dress and house himself in accordance with his income, but spend more than he can readily afford on his wife. Though a person should be frugal in expending money for his own pleasure, he should be generous in expenditures for his household. The *Chida* explains that the amount spared from his food and drink should be added to the amount spent on his wife and children. However, the *Maharsha* (*Chidushei Aggados*) goes a step further:

> Honor them with beautiful clothing, with more than what he can afford; that is, if he does not have ready funds, he should borrow for their sake. However, for himself, he should conduct himself with just deliberation, that is, consuming food and drink with less than what he can

afford … and it said that your food comes before the food of your household, for it is essential; but with regard to honor, that is, beautiful garments of your wife and your children, they come before yours.

While the operational definition of "honor" is financial expenditure for clothing and jewelry that extend far beyond basic needs for sustenance, it also includes other behaviors.

The following story, exemplifying "honoring one's wife," is related in *Otzaros HaBayis HaYehudi:*

One year, the *Chofetz Chaim* visited his rebbi during Chanukah. As the hour for candle-lighting approached, Reb Nachum'ke (R' Menachem Nachum Kaplan *zt"l*) pretended not to notice. As the hours slipped by, the *Chofetz Chaim* stood astonished that his mentor did not proceed to light the candles on time. Just as he heard a knock at the door, and his wife entered the house, Reb Nachum'ke proceeded to make the *berachah* and light the candles. Unable to contain his curiosity, the *Chofetz Chaim* asked why his rebbi had delayed so long. Reb Nachum'ke answered: "The Gemara in *Maseches Shabbos* says that if one has only enough coins to pay for either Shabbos candles or Chanukah candles, he should purchase Shabbos candles for they instill peace in the home. I knew my wife would be hurt if I lit the Chanukah candles without her presence, and since peace in the home is more important than Chanukah candles, I waited for her return."

Verbal and silent gestures are no less important than the financial manifestation of honor.

The language of the Gemara, "loves his wife as himself, and honors her more than himself," reflects two aspects in the attitude toward one's wife. The obligation to relate to her "as himself" incorporates the fulfillment of all his wife's emotional and physical needs, with the same expediency and immediacy as he would fulfill his own. No normal human being needs an external stimulus to remind him of his hunger or loneliness — they are sensed directly and need no translation. A healthy person does not wait until he faints before he addresses his nutritional needs. Similarly, one should be sensitive and aware of his spouse's needs as if they were his own body's. However, with regard to her honor, one needs to be even more perceptive.

In honoring a wife through gifts or words, a man must be even more considerate of her than he would be for himself, and must understand the impact of his speech and actions on her self-esteem and on her standing among others, both within and outside of the family. In one of his guiding lectures to bridegrooms, R' Shlomo Wolbe *zt"l* cites R' Chaim Vital when he indicates that a man's evaluation in the Divine judgment is contingent on his attitude toward his wife. Surely a person's good deeds, whether through charitable gifts, visiting the poor and comforting the bereaved, etc. will stand him in good stead on the Day of Judgment, but he must recognize that in Heaven he will be scrutinized for the manner in which he treated his wife: "If he was kind to her all the days of his life, how good and joyous [his recompense]; but if he was merciless in his demands and his angry outbursts ... that will override the judgment, and all of his good deeds for others will be forgotten."

◆§ Honoring a Wife Brings Blessing

The rewards for honoring one's wife go beyond the serenity that it engenders in the home. The Gemara (*Bava Metzia* 59a) quotes R' Chelbo, who warns that one should be careful in fulfilling the obligation to honor his wife:

> For the blessing in a man's home comes only by virtue of his wife, as it is written (*Bereishis* 12:16), וּלְאַבְרָם הֵיטִיב בַּעֲבוּרָהּ, *he treated Avram well for her sake*. Consequently, Rava said to Bnei Machoza, "Honor your wives, for in that merit you will be enriched."

The *Meiri* (ad loc.) adds that it is the wife who protects and preserves the household, and that is the blessing that she brings into her husband's possessions. *Toras Chaim* on this Gemara cites the *Zohar*, saying that the wife brings the Divine Presence into the home, and that brings special blessings to the household and its possessions.

> Come and see, when a man is in his home, the mainstay of the home is his wife, because the Divine Presence does not leave the house in the merit of his wife, as we learned from the words (*Bereishis* 24:67), וַיְבִאֶהָ יִצְחָק הָאֹהֱלָה שָׂרָה אִמּוֹ, *and Yitzchak brought her [Rivkah] to the tent [of] his mother Sarah* — and the candle was relit as it was at the time of his mother Sarah, as the Divine Presence returned in the merit of his wife [Rivkah].

Consequently, our Sages said (*Yevamos* 62b), "One who lives without a wife lives without blessing, for it is written (*Yechezkel* 44:30), לְהָנִיחַ בְּרָכָה אֶל בֵּיתֶךָ, *to bring a blessing to rest upon your home.* The Gemara continues extolling the benefits that a wife brings to her husband and family:

> Any man who does not have a wife, lives without joy, without blessing, without goodness: Without joy, as it is written (*Devarim* 14:26), וְשָׂמַחְתָּ אַתָּה וּבֵיתֶךָ, *and rejoice, you and your household*; without blessing, as it is written (*Yechezkel* 44:30), לְהָנִיחַ בְּרָכָה אֶל בֵּיתֶךָ, *to bring a blessing to rest upon your home*; without goodness, as it is written (*Bereishis* 2:18), לֹא טוֹב הֱיוֹת הָאָדָם לְבַדּוֹ, *It is not good for man to be alone.* In *Maarava* [Israel] they said: without Torah, without a fortress ... Rava bar Ula said: without peace, as it is written (*Iyov* 5:24), וְיָדַעְתָּ כִּי שָׁלוֹם אָהֳלֶךָ וּפָקַדְתָּ נָוְךָ וְלֹא תֶחֱטָא, *You will know that your tent is at peace, and you will visit your home and find nothing amiss.*

A man's wife is thus the center around which the material and spiritual prosperity of the home revolves. She brings physical blessing, as well as emotional comfort and elation, while also transforming the home to a spiritual fortress in which Torah learning and living can flourish. The Gemara explains why the wife brings a man joy — for she is his home, in which he can live and thrive and find fulfillment.

Interestingly, there is a halachic debate whether an unmarried *Kohen* can bestow the Priestly Blessing (*Daf al Daf* on *Yevamos* 62b) given that the Gemara ruled that one who blesses must be in a state of joy:

> Accordingly several *Rishonim*, cited in the *Rama* (*Siman* 128, 44), indicate that a bachelor who has never married should not bestow the Priestly Blessing, for it is written that "whoever lives without a wife, lives without joy," and a mourner is not suited to bestow the blessing. The *Beis Yosef* points to the fact that *Kohanim* who are minors join their elders in bestowing the blessing even though they are unmarried, and rules that an adult bachelor can also join with others in the Priestly Blessing, but cannot bestow it alone. The *Darchei Moshe* writes that because a minor does not need a wife he is not considered to be living without joy, whereas an adult does need a wife.

In actuality the halachic ruling is that an adult unmarried *Kohen* is allowed to bestow the Priestly Blessing, but the debate indicates the value that marriage holds in Judaism.

◆§ Rises with Him, but Does Not Descend with Him

A woman's status is supposed to rise through her marriage, and not to be denigrated. This applies to various aspects of her lifestyle. Thus, if a woman had been raised in wealth and privilege, and women in her social class did not usually nurse their babies, her husband must provide a wet-nurse (*Kesubos* 61a), whether or not he comes from the same socio-economic class. If, on the other hand, she wants to nurse her babies and her husband would prefer that she not, her will prevails.

Comparably, the *Rambam* rules that a woman who has come from upper classes must be provided living quarters, food and clothing according to what she is accustomed. However, if she comes from a poor family and her husband is well-to-do, he must provide her according to the higher standards. Her rise in status is maintained even after his death (*Hilchos Ishus* 18:3).

The obligation to honor a wife continues even after her demise. The *Rambam* (*Hilchos Ishus* 14:23) rules that a man must bury his wife with appropriate eulogies and lamentations, as customary in his country, even if he is poor:

> And if he is rich, he must honor her in accord with his honor, and if her honor [social status] was greater than his, she is buried in accordance with her honor, for a wife ascends with her husband, but does not descend — even after her death.

In summation, during her life and thereafter, a husband is obligated to honor his wife. This is not a recommendation, but a duty, which brings fulfillment and blessing in its wake.

A man's wife is his anchor in a turbulent world, bringing him solace and happiness while providing the home in which he can fulfill his potential and build his legacy. The Divine Presence and much material blessing is found in a home in which a man honors his wife, sensing her needs and wishes, and striving to fulfill them as he would his own. Thus, honoring one's wife goes beyond the command of loving your fellow like yourself. It provides blanket protection, both materially and spiritually, for the husband and their children, and ensures the perpetuation of their "home" beyond their lifetimes. Seeking a wife worthy of such honor, the wisest of all men guided the young to seek the *eishes chayil*, whose virtues outshine riches, beauty and charm.

20

Shidduchim: The Perspective of Avraham and Eliezer

Over the course of recent decades, *shidduchim* (marriage matches) have become a hot topic of social discourse in the global Jewish community, emerging as a "crisis" in recent years. Much has been written on the topic, bemoaning the pervasiveness of intense (and often awkward) inquiries about a prospective match and his or her family, and the inaccurate, and often misleading, information provided by references. Rabbinical leaders and psychologists have decried the inappropriate criteria used to determine who is an appropriate match for one's son or daughter, as well as the monetary demands that have darkened the entire process.

Many have complained that the young singles and their families are too often concerned with pleasing or impressing their friends and neighbors, and in the process forget what is truly fitting in a prospective match that will result in a happy and stable new home. In the coming chapters, we will attempt to analyze the *shidduch* process as it is presented in detail in the Torah, and to learn from it concepts that have important implications for our times.

Parashas Chayei Sarah, which describes the unfolding of the *shidduch* of Yitzchak to Rivkah, is one of the most riveting stories in *Bereishis*. The Torah details Avraham's instructions to Eliezer to search for a wife for Yitzchak, the test which Eliezer devised in order to select the most appropriate spouse for Yitzchak, and the manner in which Rivkah passes the test. The narrative includes all of the events that took place in Rivkah's house and her initial meeting with Yitzchak, and concludes with her marriage to him.

Taking note of the detailed description of these events, Rav Acha said, 'The mundane conversations of our forefathers' servants is more beautiful than the Torah of their children" (*Bereishis Rabbah* 60:8). Our Sages presume that if the Torah provided such great detail, it behooves us to delve into and analyze its minutiae, so that we can derive moral values and life lessons.

◆§ Avraham Is Old and Fabulously Wealthy

The story begins by noting that Avraham was וְאַבְרָהָם זָקֵן בָּא בַּיָּמִים וַה', בֵּרַךְ אֶת אַבְרָהָם בַּכֹּל, *Avraham was old, well on in years, and Hashem blessed Avraham with everything* (*Bereishis* 24:1). Surely these facts are pertinent to understanding the unfolding tale. Old age may explain Avraham's motivation to marry off his son, and why he could not handle the matchmaking process himself and was compelled to send a proxy. However, it is unlikely that Avraham rushed to marry off his son before he reached maturity just so he could enjoy the *nachas* before he dies. Furthermore, why is it important to stress that Avraham was wealthy? The *Rashbam* explains why the Torah stresses Avraham's wealth:

> Avraham Avinu did not send his servant to take a wife from his family due to a lack of women in the land of Canaan who would want to get married to him, for Avraham was blessed with everything, and everyone wanted to marry into his family.

Thus, the Torah is implying that Avraham was inundated with *shidduch* offers for Yitzchak from local families because of his great fortune. However, for reasons which will become clear later,

Avraham refuses any of the local offers, and sends Eliezer to search for a wife for Yitzchak.

The *Kli Yakar* addresses the redundancy in mentioning Avraham's age, when the Torah already indicated that both he and Sarah were *old, well on in years* (*Bereishis* 18:11) prior to Yitzchak's birth, thirty-seven years earlier:

> Maybe we can explain based on the verse, טוֹבִים הַשְּׁנַיִם מִן הָאֶחָד ... וְהַחוּט הַמְשֻׁלָּשׁ לֹא בִמְהֵרָה יִנָּתֵק, *Two are better than one … and a three-ply cord is not easily severed* (*Koheles* 4:9-12); for a good wife adds years to her husband's life, as it is written (*Koheles* 9:9), רְאֵה חַיִּים עִם אִשָּׁה אֲשֶׁר אָהַבְתָּ, *Enjoy life with the wife you love*; and a good son also adds life to his father, since one who raises a righteous son, it is as if he does not die, even more so during his lifetime.
>
> Therefore, from the birth of Yitzchak until the death of Sarah, the cord was three-ply, because Avraham's life was animated by the presence of both his wife and son, and during that period he remained steadfast — and did not become weaker as is common among aging people — for those were days of happiness and blessing. However, prior to Yitzchak's birth, his only joy was from his wife, and after her death, his only joy was from his son, therefore these two extremes were equal — just as he was before the birth of Yitzchak, so too, was his condition after the death of Sarah. Consequently, the same language was used in both time frames, even though there much distance between them.
>
> Consequently, Avraham strove to find a wife for Yitzchak, hoping she would fill the void that Sarah had left ....

Avraham sought to fill the void left by his wife's death by marrying off his son, hoping that his daughter-in-law would — through her righteousness and kindness — revive his home and restore some happiness.

◆§ Avraham's Instructions to Eliezer

After the preamble described above, the Torah describes Eliezer's mission in acting as Avraham's agent and matchmaker (*Bereishis* 24:2-9):

וַיֹּאמֶר אַבְרָהָם אֶל עַבְדּוֹ זְקַן בֵּיתוֹ הַמּשֵׁל בְּכָל אֲשֶׁר לוֹ שִׂים נָא יָדְךָ תַּחַת יְרֵכִי, וְאַשְׁבִּיעֲךָ בַּה' אֱלֹקֵי הַשָּׁמַיִם וֵאלֹקֵי הָאָרֶץ אֲשֶׁר לֹא תִקַּח אִשָּׁה לִבְנִי מִבְּנוֹת הַכְּנַעֲנִי אֲשֶׁר אָנֹכִי יוֹשֵׁב בְּקִרְבּוֹ. כִּי אֶל אַרְצִי וְאֶל מוֹלַדְתִּי תֵּלֵךְ וְלָקַחְתָּ אִשָּׁה לִבְנִי לְיִצְחָק.

Avraham said to his servant, the elder of his household who controlled all that was his: "Place now your hand under my thigh. And I will have you swear by Hashem, G-d of heaven and G-d of earth, that you not take a wife for my son from the daughters of the Canaanites, among whom I dwell. Rather, to my land and to my kindred shall you go and take a wife for my son for Yitzchak."

וַיֹּאמֶר אֵלָיו הָעֶבֶד אוּלַי לֹא תֹאבֶה הָאִשָּׁה לָלֶכֶת אַחֲרַי אֶל הָאָרֶץ הַזֹּאת הֶהָשֵׁב אָשִׁיב אֶת בִּנְךָ אֶל הָאָרֶץ אֲשֶׁר יָצָאתָ מִשָּׁם.

The servant said to him: "Perhaps the woman shall not wish to follow me to this land; shall I take your son back to the land from which you departed?"

וַיֹּאמֶר אֵלָיו אַבְרָהָם הִשָּׁמֶר לְךָ פֶּן תָּשִׁיב אֶת בְּנִי שָׁמָּה. ה' אֱלֹקֵי הַשָּׁמַיִם אֲשֶׁר לְקָחַנִי מִבֵּית אָבִי וּמֵאֶרֶץ מוֹלַדְתִּי וַאֲשֶׁר דִּבֶּר לִי וַאֲשֶׁר נִשְׁבַּע לִי לֵאמֹר לְזַרְעֲךָ אֶתֵּן אֶת הָאָרֶץ הַזֹּאת הוּא יִשְׁלַח מַלְאָכוֹ לְפָנֶיךָ וְלָקַחְתָּ אִשָּׁה לִבְנִי מִשָּׁם. וְאִם לֹא תֹאבֶה הָאִשָּׁה לָלֶכֶת אַחֲרֶיךָ וְנִקִּיתָ מִשְּׁבֻעָתִי זֹאת רַק אֶת בְּנִי לֹא תָשֵׁב שָׁמָּה.

Avraham answered him, "Beware not to return my son to there. Hashem, G-d of heaven, Who took me from the house of my father and from the land of my birth; Who spoke concerning me, and Who swore to me saying, 'To your offspring will I give this land,' He will send His angel before you, and you will take a wife for my son from there. But if the woman will not wish to follow you, you shall then be absolved of this oath of mine. However, do not return my son to there."

וַיָּשֶׂם הָעֶבֶד אֶת יָדוֹ תַּחַת יֶרֶךְ אַבְרָהָם אֲדֹנָיו וַיִּשָּׁבַע לוֹ עַל הַדָּבָר הַזֶּה.

So the servant placed his hand under the thigh of Avraham, his master, and swore to him regarding this matter.

To summarize, Avraham ordered Eliezer the following:

1) Not to take a wife for Yitzchak from the daughters of Canaan, *among whom I dwell*. There are two commands here — not to take a Canaanite girl, and not to take a local girl.

2) To take a wife from *my land and my kindred* — referring to Avraham's kin (see *Ramban and Rashbam*).

3) Not to relocate Yitzchak to the location of the bride's family, but the bride should leave her family and live close to Avraham's residence.

4) If the bride refuses to come, then Eliezer is off the hook, and his mission is concluded.

5) *Take a wife for my son, for Yitzchak* — Avraham emphasized that the proposed woman should be fitting to be his daughter-in-law, fitting well into the "house" of Avraham. Additionally, she should be an appropriate match for Yitzchak, given his unique character and qualities.

Many of the commentaries grapple with Avraham's insistence on eliminating any consideration of a Canaanite woman. Given that all other candidates were also idol worshippers, wouldn't it have been better to opt for a local woman, thereby increasing the chance of converting her and her entire family into believers in the One G-d? The *Kli Yakar* (24:3) poses this question and offers the following answer:

> ... if he [Yitzchak] will marry a woman from the [local] daughters of Canaan, *among whom I dwell*, it is most likely that my son will reside with them, and then there is a concern lest he learn from their deeds. Similarly, if he will

marry a daughter of Lavan and Besuel, and will live among them, then there is also a concern that he learn from their deeds. However, when he marries a woman from there and lives with her here, then there is no worry: From Lavan and Besuel he will not learn, since he does not live with them; from the Canaanites he will not learn because he will not intermingle with them, and on the contrary, they will hate him because he did not want to intermarry with them.

According to the *Kli Yakar*, Avraham insisted that his son and daughter-in-law live nearby to minimize the risk that the young couple will be negatively influenced by their surroundings.

◄§ Personality and Beliefs

The *Kli Yakar* (ibid.) also deals with the question of why a Canaanite woman was deemed worse than one from Charan, since both were idol worshippers:

> Children's natural inclinations and personalities are inherited from their parents. This applies specifically [to behaviors and character traits] grounded in the flesh, like eating, licentiousness, stinginess, and jealousy, and all of the bad personality traits that are associated with physicality — these "plagues" spread from the fathers to the sons ... but beliefs are contingent upon the intellect; and G-d is the One Who imparts to each human a soul and brain — why should this transfer from the fathers to the sons? Consequently, Avraham rejected the Canaanites, who aside from engaging in idolatry were promiscuous and indulged in other sins associated with the flesh, yet he did not reject Lavan and Besuel, who only possessed the flaws of idolatry.

The words of the *Kli Yakar* are counterintuitive to common beliefs about what is primary and secondary in *shidduchim*. He suggests that bad character and personality traits pass genetically, and are therefore very difficult to change. On the other hand, belief in G-d and adherence to daily religious practices do not pass as an inheritance, and are, therefore, more amenable to change. The *Kli Yakar* (*Bereishis* 24:14) takes note of the negative character traits pervasive among the Canaanites:

> The Torah juxtaposed this *parashah* [of Yitzchak's *shidduch*] to the *parashah* of Ephron HaChiti, because he too was a descendant of Canaan [from whom Avraham purchased Sarah's burial plot for an exorbitant fee] .... Ephron was stingy and greedy, and therefore Avraham commanded [Eliezer] to reject the Canaanites, who were masters of *ayin hara* ["malicious eye"] .... The character of each person is revealed by his wallet .... To evaluate another person, scrutinize his monetary dealings and see his nature .... If he maintains his righteousness in money matters, then in all other aspects it will be revealed that he is perfect, and likewise, the opposite is true.

The Gemara affirms this judgment about Canaanites:

> Five things did Canaan charge his sons: Love one another, love robbery, love lewdness, hate your masters and do not speak the truth (*Pesachim* 113b).

Avraham reasoned that a lack of integrity and stinginess are attributes which are innate to a person's nature, and pass from father to son as an inheritance, and are very difficult to alter. Therefore, he forbade Eliezer to consider a *shidduch* for Yitzchak with a Canaanite woman.

ᥩ᷉ What Will the Neighbors Say?

We can learn another important point from Avraham's instructions to Eliezer. Avraham was very wealthy and highly respected in his locality. There is no doubt that he could have found a daughter of a local king or affluent man to marry Yitzchak. For the outside world this would have been considered a successful and smashing *shidduch*. Yet, Avraham Avinu did not want to hear of a local *shidduch*, and actually preferred to be despised by the local inhabitants, so that Yitzchak would minimize his contact with the neighbors. Avraham's only concern was: What will be best for Yitzchak — not what will the neighbors and acquaintances say!

Many times *shidduch* decisions are made based on "what would others say." Sometimes *shidduchim* are made despite indications of incompatibility; in other cases they are rejected, in spite of compatibility, only because of what others might say. Many people approach *shidduchim* with a conscious or unconscious desire to impress their friends and acquaintances, often at the expense of the happiness of the young man and woman involved. Avraham Avinu teaches us that any attention directed at motives other than the welfare of the bride and groom is invalid.

Righteousness Alone Is Not Enough

Eliezer, as Avraham Avinu's protégé and devoted servant who disseminated his master's Torah to the larger public, understood and internalized Avraham's insistence on good character. Aside from the actual test that Eliezer administered to Rivkah, which will be analyzed in the following chapter, there is one detail in the narrative that demonstrates the importance of good character, even where piety is irrefutable.

Before Eliezer approached Rivkah, asking her for a drink of water, he witnessed a miraculous occurrence. When Rivkah reached the well, the water rose to her, as described in *Midrash Rabbah* on *Parashas Chayei Sarah* (60:5):

> All the [other] women descended and filled their jugs from the spring, yet this one [Rivkah], as soon as the waters saw her they immediately ascended.

Eliezer is keenly aware that he is looking at a righteous young woman, for whom miracles happen, yet proceeds to test her character. Apparently, righteousness was insufficient for Eliezer, for piety does not guarantee good character traits.

This train of thought is quite different than the prevailing attitude in many circles today. People are very careful to verify matters of religious thinking or levels of piety. On the other hand, many just pay lip-service to the questions of comportment and character, and only rarely do they inquire about traits such as integrity and stinginess.

❦ The Importance of Good Character Traits

The importance that our Sages attributed to character traits and to interpersonal behavior that are manifestations of personality and values deeply engrained in a person, cannot be overstated. The entire tractate of *Avos* is devoted to the topic. The *Meiri*, in his introduction to *Maseches Avos*, questions why the *Tanna* chose to detail the chain of Torah transmission from generation to generation in this particular tractate. He also asks why this tractate was named *Avos* (the fathers) — a title which seems unrelated to its contents.

> What was the purpose of detailing the chain of transmission? In my opinion, it is written here to emphasize the virtue of the tractate. Many statements in this tractate do not have specific Scriptural sources … though it includes encouragement for sterling character, and admonishment for repulsive personality traits. Perhaps a person might think that praiseworthy character is not itself a mitzvah, and bad disposition is not itself a transgression, and therefore [the content] may not be taken seriously by people ….
>
> Therefore it must be made known that the content [of this tractate] is indisputable, and transmitted from our ancient Sages, and from the prophets, one prophet to another, so that a person will delve into them with a discerning eye, seeking the source of his existence, and the origin of his

being. They alluded to this in the title of the tractate — *Avos*/fathers — as if to say that these things emanated from the "fathers of the world," the pillars upon which the "House of Torah" is established; or that these are matters which are the basis, foundation, root, and fundamental precept to all wisdom and each mitzvah, and the pathway to every virtue.

According to the *Meiri*, R' Yehudah HaNasi opened *Maseches Avos* with an emphasis on the acceptance of the Torah at Sinai, and the pathway of its transmission from generation to generation, in order to stress the tremendous importance of good character traits — and to urge us to treat them as any other Divine command. *Rabbeinu HaKadosh* called this tractate *Avos*/Fathers, so that the reader will understand that everything which is stated in this tractate comes from our holy ancestral Sages, who are the pillars of Torah and the Jewish nation. Alternatively, he called good character traits *"Avos"* in order to emphasize that good character is a "father," meaning a foundation, for all of the mitzvos of the Torah.

R' Chaim Vital explains that good character is the foundation to the fulfillment of all the mitzvos. He answers the question: Why is the development of good character traits not part of the 613 mitzvos?

> Good character traits are not part of the 613 mitzvos, yet they are the primary preparation for the 613 mitzvos, either for their fulfillment or their nullification. Bad character traits are worse than the transgressions [of the mitzvos] themselves. With this one can understand what our Sages (*Zohar, Chelek 3, Amud* 179:1) wrote, "Whoever gets angry is actually an idolater!".... Likewise, they said (*Sotah* 5a), "A person who is haughty is like one who denies the fundamental existence of G-d." There are many other such statements. Since they are principles and foundations, they are not counted among the 613 mitzvos.

With this you can also understand the astonishing words which our Sages spoke about character traits; such as, "modesty and humility facilitate the attainment of Divine spirit, and the Divine Presence rests upon him."… Pay attention to these things and you will undoubtedly be successful in all your ways (*Sha'ar HaKedushah*, *Chelek* 1, *Sha'ar* 2).

Good character traits are not included in the 613 mitzvos because they are an essential precondition to the proper fulfillment of the mitzvos. It is not possible for a person to be a genuine servant of G-d without good character traits. Understandably, Avraham Avinu knew this, hence his particularism regarding good character.

When looking for the right groom or bride one should realize that propensities such as humility, forgiveness, and seeking the good in others and for others, best serve to guarantee a stable and happy home, built on the pillars of Torah and *yiras Shamayim*.

↜§ Eliezer, the Matchmaker

Eliezer, who embarked on the mission to find a suitable wife for Yitzchak, fulfilled a very important role in the house of Avraham, both in the material and spiritual realms. The dual roles of Eliezer are described in two verses in the Torah:

וַיֹּאמֶר אַבְרָם אֲדֹנָ-י ה' מַה תִּתֶּן לִי וְאָנֹכִי הוֹלֵךְ עֲרִירִי וּבֶן מֶשֶׁק בֵּיתִי הוּא דַּמֶּשֶׂק אֱלִיעֶזֶר.

Avram said, "My Lord, G-d: What can You give me seeing that I go childless, and the steward of my house is the Damascene Eliezer" (Bereishis 15:2).

וַיֹּאמֶר אַבְרָהָם אֶל עַבְדּוֹ זְקַן בֵּיתוֹ הַמֹּשֵׁל בְּכָל אֲשֶׁר לוֹ שִׂים נָא יָדְךָ תַּחַת יְרֵכִי.

Avraham said to his servant, the elder of his household who controlled all that was his: "Place now your hand under my thigh" (ibid. 24:2).

The Gemara explicates these roles (*Yoma* 28b):

> Eliezer, the servant of Avraham, was an elder who sat with the sages, as it is written … *the elder of his household who controlled all that was his.* R' Elazar said, "Who was extremely knowledgeable in his master's Torah … *who controlled all that was his.*" R' Elazar said, "Who drew from the well and gave to drink [taught] from the Torah of his master to others."

Thus, Eliezer was Avraham's exemplary student, who also served as Rosh HaYeshivah for his teacher, transmitting Avraham's teachings to others. He was a very righteous person, and came to look and behave like his master, as *Midrash Rabbah* says, "The splendor of his face was similar to Avraham's; and he controlled his evil inclination, just like Avraham did" (*Chayei Sarah* 59:8). *Rashi* explains that Eliezer was the general manager of Avraham's considerable property (*Bereishis* 24:2). Eliezer, blessed with all of these virtues, was the person closest and most loyal to Avraham.

Our Sages relate that Eliezer had a daughter, who grew up in Avraham's home, and it is likely that Avraham knew her well. All his life Eliezer was hoping that his daughter would be a bride fit to marry Yitzchak. One could only imagine how Eliezer felt when Avraham called him to go to a distant place and find a wife for Yitzchak. Eliezer looked for an opportunity to ask Avraham what is wrong with his daughter, and according to *Rashi* (*Bereishis* 24:39), he finds a chance to hint to Avraham about the matter. Avraham responded to Eliezer by saying: "My son is blessed and you are cursed. A curse does not cleave to a blessing."

Without attempting to explain Avraham's answer, such a response is likely to cause disappointment and even anger. The faithful and scholarly Eliezer, who was entrusted with all of Avraham's wealth, is "crowned" by Avraham with the title of "cursed" — whereas Yitzchak is "blessed." Though he heard his master utter words too onerous to bear, having his life's dream that

Yitzchak would be his son-in-law shattered, Eliezer goes about his mission with enthusiasm and devotion.

We learn from this that a matchmaker must not only display deftness as the negotiator of the *shidduch*, but must also remove all of his personal biases (whether positive or negative), and devote himself single-mindedly to the task of finding the most compatible match. In addition, the elaborate test that Eliezer gave to Rivkah (see Chapter 21) teaches us that a matchmaker must try to fulfill the wishes of his senders, without attempting to circumvent them or convince them to forego fundamental expectations.

Another important ingredient in every *shidduch* is prayer. Avraham Avinu, who was a prophet, prayed for the success of Eliezer's mission:

> ה׳ אֱלֹקֵי הַשָּׁמַיִם אֲשֶׁר לְקָחַנִי מִבֵּית אָבִי וּמֵאֶרֶץ מוֹלַדְתִּי וַאֲשֶׁר דִּבֶּר
> לִי וַאֲשֶׁר נִשְׁבַּע לִי לֵאמֹר לְזַרְעֲךָ אֶתֵּן אֶת הָאָרֶץ הַזֹּאת הוּא יִשְׁלַח
> מַלְאָכוֹ לְפָנֶיךָ וְלָקַחְתָּ אִשָּׁה לִבְנִי מִשָּׁם.
>
> *Hashem, G-d of heaven, Who took me from the house of my father and from the land of my birth; Who spoke concerning me, and Who swore to me saying, "To your offspring will I give this land," He will send His angel before you, and you will take a wife for my son from there (Bereishis 24:7).*

The *Ramban* explains the words, הוּא יִשְׁלַח מַלְאָכוֹ, *He will send His angel,* to mean a prayer. Eliezer also prayed from the depths of his heart for the success of his mission:

> ה׳ אֱלֹקֵי אֲדֹנִי אַבְרָהָם הַקְרֵה נָא לְפָנַי הַיּוֹם וַעֲשֵׂה חֶסֶד עִם אֲדֹנִי
> אַבְרָהָם.
>
> *Hashem, G-d of my master Avraham, may You so arrange it for me this day, and do kindness to my master Avraham (ibid. 24:12).*

Midrash Rabbah notes that Eliezer, who was heartbroken from Avraham's refusal to consider his daughter, nonetheless prays sincerely for a successful mission. G-d answers such a heartfelt plea immediately, and thus, even before he completed his prayer, וַיְהִי הוּא טֶרֶם כִּלָּה לְדַבֵּר וְהִנֵּה רִבְקָה יֹצֵאת, *it was when he had not yet finished speaking that suddenly Rivkah was coming out* (Bereishis 24:15). Aside from all human effort, one is obligated to dedicate time to prayer to the Creator of the world for the quick and easygoing success of a *shidduch*.

21

Shidduchim Part 2: Yitzchak, Rivkah, and the Gifts

Amidst the myriad details provided by the Torah's story of the search for a proper wife for Yitzchak Avinu, there is glaring silence; there is no mention — howsoever veiled — of what the bridegroom wanted in a bride. Nor does the narrative indicate that Avraham shared with his son his adamant objection to a match with a Canaanite woman. The Tolna Rebbe *shlita* (*Heima Yenachamuni, Bereishis, Chayei Sarah*) takes note of the absence of a discussion between the father and his son regarding the qualities that one should seek in a bride:

> … in the search for a wife for Yitzchak and her discovery, Avraham is the initiator and sender, Eliezer is the active agent, whereas Yitzchak himself is not a participant in all of the initial steps. Why? It is certainly possible that Yitzchak had certain expectations of the bride, who would become his wife for life?!

Even according to the *Ramban* (*Bereishis* 24:3), who posits that Avraham was confident that Yitzchak would endorse his father's preferences for a bride, it still remains unclear why Yitzchak was not approached to gauge his particular preferences.

Rashi raises an additional question as to why Eliezer rushed to present the betrothal gifts to Rivkah before inquiring about her family. After all, Avraham sent him specifically to Charan, to his kinsmen, to find a bride for Yitzchak. *Rashi* (24:23) explains that Eliezer was "confident in the merit of Avraham that G-d would make his mission successful." *Rashi's* comment, however, begs further clarification: Why would Eliezer rely upon the merit of Avraham, when he could have clarified Rivkah's lineage through a simple question, as indeed he did *after* he gave her the gifts? The Tolna Rebbe (ibid.) responds to these questions:

> It seems that by concealing the participation of Yitzchak in this narrative, the Torah intends to deliver a clear message. Yitzchak believes that only G-d מוֹשִׁיב יְחִידִים בַּיְתָה, *settles the solitary in a home* (*Tehillim* 68:7), and therefore did not act according to conventional custom by which the groom sets various conditions, etc. He [Yitzchak] relies upon his elderly and righteous father who acts according to elevated spiritual principles. In the first *shidduch* in the Torah, it was important to show … the absolute trust that one's match is from G-d!

Eliezer's rush to give Rivkah the gifts before finding out about her family was intended to deliver a similar message: After all the precautions and inquiries, one needs to have faith in G-d in order to conclude a *shidduch*. Having witnessed Rivkah's righteousness as the water rose toward her, and as she demonstrated her capacity for sensitive kindness through the test he devised, Eliezer knew that this match was made in Heaven and needed no further substantiation.

⚜ Behold, Rivkah Was Coming Out

Upon devising the test that would determine the appropriate bride for his master's son, Eliezer proceeds to pray to G-d for success in his mission, when he is struck by the sudden appearance of Rivkah:

וַיְהִי הוּא טֶרֶם כִּלָּה לְדַבֵּר וְהִנֵּה רִבְקָה יֹצֵאת אֲשֶׁר יֻלְּדָה לִבְתוּאֵל
בֶּן מִלְכָּה אֵשֶׁת נָחוֹר אֲחִי אַבְרָהָם וְכַדָּהּ עַל שִׁכְמָהּ ... וַתֵּרֶד הָעַיְנָה
וַתְּמַלֵּא כַדָּהּ וַתָּעַל.

*And it was when he had not yet finished speaking that behold
Rivkah was coming out — she who had been born to Besuel the
son of Milcah the wife of Nachor, brother of Avraham — with her
jug upon her shoulder .... She descended to the spring, filled her
jug and ascended (Bereishis 24:15-16).*

The *Malbim* among others takes note of the word הִנֵּה (*behold*)
in the phrase, וְהִנֵּה רִבְקָה יֹצֵאת, *behold, Rivkah was coming out,* which
signifies something extraordinary or unexpected. Given that Eliezer
had arrived in Charan toward evening, לְעֵת צֵאת הַשֹּׁאֲבֹת, *when the
women go out to draw water (Bereishis 24:11),* there should have been
no surprise in seeing Rivkah. The *Malbim* explains:

Rivkah had never before gone out to draw water. Her
father was rich and had many servants and maidservants
who drew water .... The word הִנֵּה indicates something
novel ... an angel encouraged her to come out, so that
Yitzchak's match would be from his kinsmen. The second
novelty was her carrying the pitcher on her shoulder. Even
though this was her first time going out to the well, and one
would expect that she takes along one of her maidservants
to carry the pitcher, as customary among the daughters of
wealthy people like Besuel, yet she carried the pitcher on
her own shoulder.

The guidance of Divine Providence was evident in every step of
this *shidduch.* Even idolatrous Lavan and Besuel could not ignore
this reality, and conceded, מֵה' יָצָא הַדָּבָר, *the matter stemmed from
Hashem!* (*Bereishis* 24:50). Indeed, the Gemara declares (*Moed Kattan*
18b):

From the Torah, from the prophets, and from the Sacred
Writings we learn that the union of a specific woman and

man comes from G-d. From the Torah, as it is written, מֵה
יָצָא הַדָּבָר, *the matter stemmed from Hashem!*

The hand of G-d is not just evident in the conclusion of a successful match, but in every step of the *shidduch* process: who is the matchmaker, who will provide references, what questions are asked, how people process the information they receive, when and how people decide to conclude the *shidduch*, and how people try to circumvent those individuals who try to frustrate the *shidduch*. Though Besuel, Rivkah's father, admitted that *the matter stemmed from Hashem*, he attempted to nullify the *shidduch* by preventing Rivkah from going with Eliezer, and an angel came and killed him that night (*Bereishis Rabbah* 60:12).

There is no doubt that people who are involved in *shidduchim* must be very diligent in collecting and verifying pertinent information. But, having fulfilled the requirements of due diligence, one must recognize that a union of a man and woman comes from G-d! While G-d directs our actions every moment of the day, the Divine intervention is most apparent in matters of *shidduchim*.

ᴥᔥ Miraculous Travel Time

The story is told of a righteous man who traveled from one end of his country to the other, for the purpose of concluding a *shidduch* for his exemplary son. He arrived in the bride's town, and shortly thereafter an engagement was announced. On his way back home, he met several acquaintances and happily told them about his son's engagement, sharing details about the bride and her family. To his amazement, one of his acquaintances vociferously responded, "It is too bad that Rebbe did not ask me before he finalized the *shidduch*! The bride's father has a horrible reputation ..." and continued to besmirch the bride's father. The groom's father interrupted him, smiled and said:

> You've just provided me with an answer to a question that
> has bothered me for many years. Avraham Avinu sends

Eliezer, his servant, to look for a *shidduch* for his son. The Torah goes to great length to describe all the miracles that happen to Eliezer. One of these miracles was the fact that on the way to fulfill his mission, his travel time was dramatically shortened, as it is written, וָאָבֹא הַיּוֹם אֶל הָעָיִן, *I came today to the spring* (*Bereishis* 24:42). *Rashi* explains that Eliezer's journey was miraculously hastened, such that he left for his mission and arrived on the same day. I always wondered why Eliezer couldn't travel like any other person, without any miracles. Furthermore, if he experienced this dramatic shortening of his trip to Charan, why did not the same occur upon his return to Avraham's house?

With a chuckle, the Rebbe continued:

But, based on my encounter with you, all my questions have been answered! If Eliezer's trip to Charan had not been shortened, he would certainly have met some "good friends" who would ask him, "Nu! Reb Eliezer, where are you going?" He would tell them, "To Charan, to finalize a *shidduch* for Yitzchak with Besuel's daughter." The friend would begin to tell Eliezer all about the horrible reputation of the future father-in-law and his son, Lavan, and the *shidduch* would be obliterated. Therefore, G-d performed a miracle for Eliezer, to speed his journey to Charan, so that the "good friends" would not have an opportunity to ruin it. On the way back from the engagement, it would not be so terrible if they would attempt to undermine what was already done ....

✑ The Bride: Rivkah

The Torah is sparse in its description of the intended bride, Rivkah — the daughter of Besuel, who was wealthy and respected by his townsmen. She is very young, beautiful, and meticulous in her modesty. Understandably, Rivkah displays outstanding character, and successfully passes the difficult test of kindness given to her by Eliezer.

Rivkah possessed another great virtue: she was decisive and consistent. After Eliezer meets her family and tells them all that had happened to him, and after they agree that, מֶה יָצָא הַדָּבָר, *The matter stemmed from Hashem*, they still attempt to delay her going with Eliezer (*Bereishis* 24:55): תֵּשֵׁב הַנַּעֲרָ אִתָּנוּ יָמִים אוֹ עָשׂוֹר אַחַר תֵּלֵךְ, *Let the maiden remain with us a year or ten [months]; then she will go.* According to *Rashi*, it indeed was the common practice to give the bride and her family time to prepare her trousseau. According to many commentaries, her family gave her assorted "logical reasons" to stay home and not to go with Eliezer:

- Her father had just died, and it would not be proper to leave immediately.
- It is inappropriate for her to go before she sees the groom, so he should come to see her.
- It is improper for her to travel with a servant (Eliezer), and they should send a dignified delegation to take her.
- The family should accompany her, but they were not ready to leave immediately.
- It is inappropriate and immodest for her to travel on a camel, and she should demand that they provide a comfortable wagon.

Rivkah listened to all of their reasoning, but decided to go with Eliezer anyway.

וַיִּקְרְאוּ לְרִבְקָה וַיֹּאמְרוּ אֵלֶיהָ הֲתֵלְכִי עִם הָאִישׁ הַזֶּה וַתֹּאמֶר אֵלֵךְ.
They called Rivkah and said to her, "Will you go with this man?" And she said, "I will go" (*Bereishis* 24:58).

Rashi explains the meaning of her statement: She meant "I will go even if you do not permit," since she stated decisively and unequivocally, *I will go*, instead of just saying, "Yes" (*Sifsei Chachamim*). Rivkah saw the guiding hand of Providence, and understood her meritorious destiny to become the wife of Yitzchak and the daughter-in-law of Avraham, and would not let anyone derail her from her holy destination.

◄§ The Gifts: An Allusion to the Essence of Marriage

Immediately after she gave water to Eliezer and his camels, Eliezer gave Rivkah the gifts that had been prepared for the bride:

וַיְהִי כַּאֲשֶׁר כִּלּוּ הַגְּמַלִּים לִשְׁתּוֹת וַיִּקַּח הָאִישׁ נֶזֶם זָהָב בֶּקַע מִשְׁקָלוֹ
וּשְׁנֵי צְמִידִים עַל יָדֶיהָ עֲשָׂרָה זָהָב מִשְׁקָלָם.

When the camels had finished drinking, the man took a golden nose ring, its weight was a beka, and two bracelets on her arms, ten gold shekels was their weight (Bereishis 24:22).

Rashi explains that all the gifts were symbolic: The golden nose ring, whose weight was a *beka*, alluded to *shekalim* which the Jewish people donated to the *Mishkan*, a *beka* for each man. The two bracelets symbolized "the two joined tablets" given to Moshe at Sinai; *ten gold shekels was their weight,* alludes to the Ten Commandments inscribed on the tablets. The Tolna Rebbe *shlita* clarifies the special meaning of those gifts:

> Every Jewish person is commanded to bring exactly a half-*shekel* and not a whole one, which alludes to interdependence and participation — a Jew cannot fulfill his ultimate purpose without his fellow Jew. Even though every person is an independent being, for this mitzvah he needs to join together with another Jew, and together they achieve a whole *shekel*. In spite of all the dissimilarities between one another, they combine together to form a complete whole.
>
> The two tablets of the covenant express a similar idea. There are specifically two tablets …. On the first were written the mitzvos between man and G-d, and on the

second tablet were written the interpersonal mitzvos. The themes are different, but they are joined together and create the completeness of the Ten Commandments — two which are united in one. This is why *Rashi* emphasizes "two joined tablets" to stress that the two things were joined together to create a whole entity (*Heima Yenachamuni*).

These gifts present a subtle message about the essence of the union between two individuals in married life. Marriage comprises a special reality, which has no comparison. There is a quintessential difference between a successful marriage and a successful business partnership. In a business partnership, the participants retain their separate — and sometimes disparate — goals, obligations and social circles. They are bound together for a specific objective during circumscribed times, because each can attain his objective more readily by working together.

The institution of marriage is absolutely different and requires self-renunciation to attain the merging of two people into one new entity. To attain such a unity, the spouses must be able to identify and empathize with one another, such that each one feels and thinks about the other, as one would about oneself. The happiness and pain of one spouse needs to be felt by the other as if it were his/her own. The legendary R' Aryeh Levin *zt"l* accompanied his wife to the doctor and told him, "My wife's foot is hurting **us**!" Indeed, in such a marriage, "his wife is like himself" (*Berachos* 24a), and her pain is truly his pain.

Marriage brings completeness to a single person, who would otherwise be just half of the whole of which he/she is capable. Therefore, our Sages indicate that on the wedding day, the past sins of the bride and groom are forgiven. The *Maharal* explains:

> The reason is that each one of them is considered a new person, and that new person did not commit the previous sins .... Before a man marries a woman, each one is called "half a person" — for a male without a female is half a

body, and now he is a whole body, a new creation (*Gur Aryeh, Parashas Vayishlach*).

Accordingly, marriage comprises a symbiosis between man and woman that leads to a new creation, one that is not merely a melding of two individuals, but a transformation of both into one entity. Marriage — according to Jewish thinking — requires humility, self-abnegation and total consideration for the spouse. Avraham Avinu wanted to ensure that Yitzchak's bride would indeed be a woman that would understand this concept, and therefore he chose the betrothal gift that would allude to the ideals which she would embrace.

◈§ The Sanctity of Marriage

The Gemara (*Kiddushin* 2b) explains why the act of marriage is called *kiddushin,* whose root literally means holiness, for in taking a woman as his wife, the groom indicated that she is no longer available to anyone else in the world except her husband. This is similar to the act of dedicating an item (*hekdesh*) exclusively for a sacred purpose, and simultaneously prohibiting its use for any other purpose. That dedication renders the item holy. Since we refer to a person as holy when he dedicates his entire life to G-d, one needs to understand, what holiness takes effect upon a woman when her husband betroths her? If the Sages intended to signify that she is prohibited upon the rest of the world, they could have chosen different words, whose meaning would more clearly connote prohibition.

There is, however, a more profound dimension to the sanctity that the act of marriage bestows. As indicated earlier, to make a marriage requires generosity, mutual understanding and empathy, an ability to rise above one's self, and humility coupled with an overwhelming desire to bring joy to one's spouse. Where such lofty character traits are developed and nurtured to form the foundation of a marital union, there is a strong probability that the "edifice" built by the newlyweds will be an eternal structure in which the Divine Presence will dwell. Therefore, our Sages chose to call this process *kiddushin*/sanctification.

Successful marriages are built upon the immutable will of both spouses to give to the other as much as possible. If, Heaven forbid, either one of the couple views marriage as a vehicle by which to receive or take from the other as much as possible, then the marriage is headed for disaster. Failure in marriage is usually a product of either or both of the couple pursuing "what's good for me" instead of "what's good for my spouse."

22

Eliezer's Test of Kindness

Avraham Avinu is called by our Sages the "pillar of kindness," such that the prophet (*Michah* 7:20) prays that G-d should bestow kindness upon His people in the merit of the kindness of Avraham. A depiction of Avraham's kindness is found in *Avos DeR' Nosson* (*Perek* 14):

> Your house should be open wide, in the same way that the house of Iyov was open on the north, south, east, and west. Iyov said … "I did not do like others — other people ate pure bread, yet fed the poor coarse bread; other people wore woolen clothing, yet provided poor people with burlap clothes. I did not do so — from whatever I ate, I also gave to the poor; from whatever I wore, I also gave to the poor … from the wool that I would shear and wear, I would make clothes for the poor."
>
> Iyov began to boast and say, "What did Avraham Avinu do, that I did not?" He was told, "Iyov, for how long will you brag? If a poor person did not come to your house, you did not have compassion upon him, but Avraham did not do like you — on the third day after his circumcision, he went and sat by the opening of his tent, as it is written,

(Bereishis 18:1), וְהוּא יֹשֵׁב פֶּתַח הָאֹהֶל כְּחֹם הַיּוֹם, *while he was
sitting at the entrance of the tent in the heat of the day.*

Both Avraham and Iyov fulfilled the mitzvah of hospitality
meticulously and to perfection. However, their approach and view
of this mitzvah were quite different. Iyov reacted with pity to the
sight of a needy person. It pained him to see a hungry person or one
dressed in tattered clothing, so he dressed and fed the needy. But
Iyov did not proactively search for the needy — he reacted to their
presence as his sympathies were aroused.

Avraham Avinu, in contrast, searched for people who needed
help. On the third day following his circumcision, at the peak of
his pain, he sends Eliezer to search for guests, even though G-d
had brought about a heat wave so that passersby would not come.
Eliezer was sent to look for guests, returned and told Avraham
that he did not find any people due to the oppressive heat. As the
Gemara (*Bava Metzia* 86a) writes, Avraham was unwilling to accept
such a response and he was about to go out and look for passersby,
at which point G-d sent the three angels.

Having witnessed the epitome of kindness, Eliezer knew
that a fitting bride for Yitzchak would need to be a woman who
personified this attribute. He devised a test that would focus on the
attribute of loving-kindness, not just mercy. The *Be'er Mayim Chaim*
writes about the fundamental difference between kindness (*chesed*)
and mercy (*rachamim*):

> The difference between one who does kindness and the
> individual who is merciful is like the distance between
> heaven and earth. [The kind person] continuously pursues
> it and goes out to find guests to bring into his home, to feed
> them and give them drink with boundless joy and good-
> heartedness. He reaches out not only to the impoverished
> person — who does not have what to eat and he gives
> him bread to sustain him; but even to the rich man, who
> is "poor" at that moment, or just an average person who

would benefit from his goodness; he bestows upon them favors with great joy, for this is his whole desire and will. This is not true about the merciful individual, who gives only to those he encounters, those who wail and complain in obvious suffering and anguish. However, when he does not see them, he never remembers them, and on the contrary, he looks the other way so that he will not see their suffering, because he claims that he cannot bear to gaze upon their pain, since his heart will be grieved and suffer great sorrow (*Bereishis* 24:14).

⋞§ Loving-Kindness, not Mercy

The difference between kindness and mercy was at the core of the test that Eliezer devised for Rivkah. He understood that the future daughter-in-law of Avraham must be a woman infused with the attribute of kindness — a woman who searches for opportunities to give to others, even when they do not request it. She must be a woman whose entire desire and spirit is to give to others.

As he embarks on his journey, Eliezer offers a prayer to G-d to send him the young woman who would successfully pass the meticulously developed test of kindness:

וַיֹּאמַר ה' אֱלֹקֵי אֲדֹנִי אַבְרָהָם הַקְרֵה נָא לְפָנַי הַיּוֹם וַעֲשֵׂה חֶסֶד עִם אֲדֹנִי אַבְרָהָם. הִנֵּה אָנֹכִי נִצָּב עַל עֵין הַמָּיִם וּבְנוֹת אַנְשֵׁי הָעִיר יֹצְאֹת לִשְׁאֹב מָיִם. וְהָיָה הַנַּעֲרָ אֲשֶׁר אֹמַר אֵלֶיהָ הַטִּי נָא כַדֵּךְ וְאֶשְׁתֶּה וְאָמְרָה שְׁתֵה וְגַם גְּמַלֶּיךָ אַשְׁקֶה אֹתָהּ הֹכַחְתָּ לְעַבְדְּךָ לְיִצְחָק וּבָהּ אֵדַע כִּי עָשִׂיתָ חֶסֶד עִם אֲדֹנִי.

And he said, "Hashem, G-d of my master Avraham, may You so arrange it for me this day that You do kindness with my master Avraham. Behold, I am standing here by the spring of water and the daughters of the townsmen come out to draw water. Let it be that the maiden to whom I shall say, 'Please tip over your jug so I may drink,' and who replies, 'Drink, and I will even water your camels,' her will You have designated for Your servant,

for Yitzchak; and may I know through her that You have done
kindness with my master" (Bereishis 24:12-14).

The Torah's description of Eliezer's initial encounter with Rivkah
can teach us a great lesson of how one is to discern the personality
traits of another individual:

וַיָּרׇץ הָעֶבֶד לִקְרָאתָהּ וַיֹּאמֶר הַגְמִיאִינִי נָא מְעַט מַיִם מִכַּדֵּךְ. וַתֹּאמֶר
שְׁתֵה אֲדֹנִי וַתְּמַהֵר וַתֹּרֶד כַּדָּהּ עַל יָדָהּ וַתַּשְׁקֵהוּ. וַתְּכַל לְהַשְׁקֹתוֹ
וַתֹּאמֶר גַּם לִגְמַלֶּיךָ אֶשְׁאָב עַד אִם כִּלּוּ לִשְׁתֹּת. וַתְּמַהֵר וַתְּעַר כַּדָּהּ אֶל
הַשֹּׁקֶת וַתָּרׇץ עוֹד אֶל הַבְּאֵר לִשְׁאֹב וַתִּשְׁאַב לְכָל גְּמַלָּיו.

The servant ran toward her and said, "Let me sip, if you please,
a little water from your jug." She said, "Drink, my lord," and
quickly she lowered her jug to her hand and gave him to drink.
When she finished giving him to drink she said, "I will draw
water even for your camels until they have finished drinking."
So she hurried and emptied her jug into the trough and kept
running to the well to draw water; and she drew for all his camels
(Bereishis 24:17-20).

In his analysis of these verses, the *Be'er Mayim Chaim* writes:

Avraham Avinu was known to all as the first "master
of kindness" in the world, and ... Eliezer desired to test
Rivkah if she too is a person who bestows kindnesses,
and is worthy of entering into the house of Avraham. As
such, if he says to her, *Let me sip ... a little water from your*
jug, and she responds, *Drink ... and I will draw water even*
for your camels, she will have proven that she possesses
the attribute of kindness, as demonstrated by not merely
fulfilling his request, but adding on to it. If she only gives
in accord with the request, it would be merely an act of
mercy. But, if she is motivated by kindness, then she must
add on to the request on her own accord, and say, *I will*
draw even for your camels; [then I will know that] *her will You*
have designated for Your servant, for Yitzchak.

Furthermore, the *Be'er Mayim Chaim* resolves the question (raised by *Rashi*) of why the verse used the double expression — *her you will have designated for your servant, for Yitzchak* — as it would suffice to say, *designated for Yitzchak*. He explained that "your servant" refers to Avraham — that she was worthy of entering into the house of Avraham, since she proved her pursuit of kindness.

When Eliezer crafted the test, his intention was to ask for a drink of water — as much as he may need. However, in actuality, all he asked of Rivkah was to sip *a little water,* as one would ask of a miser. The *Be'er Mayim Chaim* explains that Eliezer recognized that there are varying degrees even among masters of kindness. He decided to ask a little, and determine whether the young woman would merely fulfill his request, or give even more than asked. Indeed, though he begged for a sip, Rivkah told Eliezer to drink his full, and ran to refill her jug so that he would feel comfortable drinking as much as he desired. Eliezer could then see her good-heartedness; and in her volunteering to water the camels, and rushing back and forth to fill, and refill, the troughs, he could discern the joy she took in giving to others.

⇜§ Understanding the Needs of Another

The magnitude of Rivkah's generous spirit can be better appreciated when imagining the narrative through her eyes. Unaccustomed to such hard labor, Rivkah ventures for the first time to the town well to draw water. Seeing a caravan of camels and men, she is suddenly approached by one man from the group. A stranger, who clearly is surrounded by able-bodied servants, asks her, הַגְמִיאִינִי נָא מְעַט מַיִם מִכַּדֵּךְ, *Let me sip, if you please, a little water from your jug.* One could imagine the awkwardness, and perhaps even suspicion or fear, this might awaken. Here are some of the thoughts that might have entered her mind:

1) Did you go out on journey with all these camels and men without jugs of water — whether full or empty?

2) If you have jugs, why don't you or your men draw water on your own?

3) If you don't have, why not ask to borrow the jug so you could draw water for yourself and your crew?

4) If indeed you are so thirsty, what about the other men and the camels? Do you only care about yourself?

5) Perhaps you are asking for so little out of fear I will refuse.

6) Why do you ask me to lower the jug? Are you not able to take it from my shoulder, drink, and then return it?

These are surely some of the issues that could have given Rivkah pause. Yet, she did not hesitate and proceeded enthusiastically to exceed his expectations.

The *Malbim* addresses several of the obvious concerns that would have occurred to any lesser person:

> ... he asked her specifically to tip over her jug, entailing great effort ... to give him to drink. This should have piqued her anger, and prompted her to retort, "Tip it yourself and drink, so that I will not have to remove it from my shoulder." However, instead she said, *Drink, my lord*, and ... *I will draw water even for your camels*, out of her sensitivity and good-heartedness, thinking: He must surely be in pain ... or too weak to draw water for himself.

Reasoning that a man who is incapable of getting water to quench his own thirst surely cannot get water for his animals, Rivkah volunteers to do much more than she was asked.

The *Ohr HaChaim* takes note of additional details in the story, pointing to the fact that the attribute of kindness was ingrained in Rivkah:

> In response to [Eliezer's request] *Let me sip, if you please, a little water*, she said, "drink as much as you please"... *quickly she lowered her jug*, so that he would not have to

make any effort to lift the jug; and the verse relates, *and [she] gave him to drink*, meaning … she also exerted effort to bring the water close to his mouth, so that he would not even have to tilt the vessel.

The reason she did not immediately offer, *I will draw water also for your camels*, [but waited till he finished drinking] was the additional sensitivity of this righteous woman …. [so that he would not] hurry … he would think that he is Rivkah's singular concern, and so he would drink as slowly as he saw fit, and then after he drank, she immediately told him, *I will draw water for your camels (Bereishis 24:18).*

Directing our attention to another detail attesting to Rivkah's remarkable sensitivity, the *Malbim* notes that Rivkah drew water from the spring for Eliezer (verse 16), but went to the cistern to draw water for the camels (verse 20). He provides a linguistic differentiation between the two sources of water:

There is a difference between a spring and a cistern. A spring is a place from which the water flows from deep, below the ground. In front of the spring, they usually dig a large cistern, into which the waters of the spring will flow. The waters for human consumption are drawn from the spring, as that water is clear and cooler; the waters for the animals are drawn from the cistern, as they are not so clear.

Rivkah's attention to details and the special needs of those she is helping attest to her wisdom and diligence. She did not look for the easy way out to give water to all of them the same way.

Finally, Rivkah capped her demonstration of kindness by inviting Eliezer to her home. Eliezer asked her: הֲיֵשׁ בֵּית אָבִיךְ מָקוֹם לָנוּ לָלִין, *Is there room in your father's house for us to spend the night?* (*Bereishis* 24:23). Rivkah responded, גַּם תֶּבֶן גַּם מִסְפּוֹא רַב עִמָּנוּ גַּם מָקוֹם לָלוּן, *Even straw and feed is plentiful with us, as well as a place to lodge* (ibid., v. 25). *Rashi* explains that he requested to stay for one night, and her reply implied that he can stay several nights, and then she added that her household had sufficient straw and feed for the animals, something that Eliezer did not request at all.

◆§ Other Attributes that Complement the Attribute of Kindness

Rivkah's noble deeds and the manner in which she exercised kindness teach us about other benevolent traits that were hallmarks of her character:

1) **Swiftness**: Immediately upon hearing Eliezer's request for a *little water* she hurries to bring him water from the spring, as it is written, *and quickly she lowered her jug ...* Later on, when she brought water for the camels, it is written, *and kept running to the well to draw water.* All of her actions were done eagerly and swiftly, for the purpose of fulfilling the mitzvah quickly.

2) **Patience:** After Eliezer drank from the water, Rivkah tells him that now *I will draw water even for your camels until they have finished drinking.* She pledges to wait until all of the camels have finished drinking.

R' David Pinto *shlita*, in *Pachad David*, poses the following question: In light of *Bereishis Rabbah*, which explains that Eliezer ran toward Rivkah because he saw the water ascending toward her, and therefore understood that she was a righteous woman, why did Eliezer proceed with his test of character? Why did he not conclude the *shidduch* right away?

R' Pinto answers that Eliezer was not looking for a "miracle worker." He was looking for a woman who would exert herself to do deeds of kindness — which often entail a great deal of effort and patience. Indeed, as she went to draw water for Eliezer and the camels, the waters did not ascend toward Rivkah; rather, she ran and toiled in order to provide water for Eliezer and his camels. Eliezer was astonished at the effort she exerted in performing acts of kindness, and was less impressed from her great piety. *Yagdil Torah* relates in the name of R' Yechezkel of Kozmir that this story teaches that one outstanding personal attribute is better than many miracles.

❧ How Beautiful Are Their Conversations

The story of the *shidduch* of Yitzchak to Rivkah is written in great detail to teach us some important lessons. It teaches us what characteristics are truly important in the search for a compatible *shidduch*. The Torah stresses the tremendous importance of good character traits, without which a home does not stand on a solid foundation. Avraham did not look for genealogy! Avraham did not look for money. Piety alone, without good character, did not satisfy him. A prospective spouse must pass the test of good character above all.

We need to learn from the way in which Eliezer tested Rivkah how to conduct oneself when testing the mettle of another person. One should ask unanticipated questions and pay close attention to small details. It is clear that when approaching *shidduchim*, all parties will do all they can to look good. In general, the small things and the unexpected ones shed light on the character of a person and his/her essential values. Small details, like a pleasant demeanor when saying hello to a stranger, how much and with what kind of a facial expression does one tip a waiter, how one speaks about others, or a person's reaction to unexpected or even unpleasant situations — all have the power to reveal the true essence of a person! Sometimes one needs to "create" situations like these, in order to reveal the character of the individual.

23

The Essence of Compassion

Compassion is the hallmark of the Jewish people. The Gemara states:

> There are three signs that distinguish this [Jewish] nation: They are compassionate, shy, and doers of kindness .... Whoever possesses these three signs is worthy of belonging to this nation (*Yevamos* 79a)

The Gemara proceeds with a discussion of David's rejection of the *Givonim's* petition to be accepted as part of the Jewish people due to their lack of compassion. The *Rambam* writes (*Hilchos Matnos Aniyim* 10:2):

> One needs to question the genealogy of someone who is cruel and not compassionate .... All of the Jews and those who convert to Judaism are like brothers, as it is written (*Devarim* 14:1), בָּנִים אַתֶּם לַה', *You are children of Hashem.* If one will not have compassion upon his brother, who else will have compassion upon them? And, to whom do poor Jews look for help ... if not to their brothers?!

Inasmuch as compassion is a characteristic which defines the Jew, one may wonder if compassion is expressed in a class of behaviors that are independent of the actor's feelings, or perhaps compassion is defined by the person's feelings which motivate merciful behaviors? For example: One may respond to a beggar's outstretched hand by quickly depositing a few coins, without even looking at his face, let alone asking him about the nature and cause of his troubles. Having given the charity, such a person has fulfilled — at least partially — the mitzvah, though it is doubtful that such behavior can be considered compassionate.

Conversely, a person who is unable to extend a donation can, nevertheless, approach a beggar and converse with him, listen to his plight and express sympathy for his suffering, while offering to try to find some help. Would such a person not be deemed compassionate — though he could not actually provide any direct gift to the beggar? Perhaps compassion requires both the emotional response and the pragmatic deed to alleviate the suffering of another.

❧ Compassion vs. Pity

The *Malbim* differentiates between the Biblical terms for mercy or compassion and pity, often deemed synonymous in various translations. In his commentary to *Shmuel*, he explains the subtle meaning of the word חֶמְלָה (chemla), which connotes pity, but indicates a calculation of cost and benefit and the reluctance to forfeit or lose (as one would say, "It is a pity to throw out good food").

> וַיַּחְמֹל שָׁאוּל וְהָעָם עַל אֲגָג וְעַל מֵיטַב הַצֹּאן וְהַבָּקָר וְהַמִּשְׁנִים וְעַל הַכָּרִים וְעַל כָּל הַטּוֹב וְלֹא אָבוּ הַחֲרִימָם וְכָל הַמְּלָאכָה נְמִבְזָה וְנָמֵס אֹתָהּ הֶחֱרִימוּ.
>
> *Shaul … took pity on Agag, the best of the sheep, the cattle, the fatted bulls, the fatted sheep, and on all that was good; and they were not willing to destroy them; but the inferior and wretched livestock, that they did destroy (I Shmuel 15:9).*

Thus, in relating Shaul's reluctance to destroy the property of Amalek, though he had fulfilled the command to eradicate the people, the Malbim notes that Scripture uses the term חֶמְלָה (pity) in describing Shaul's sparing the livestock, as opposed to רַחֲמִים (*rachamim*), compassion for human beings:

> Compassion only applies from one human being to another, since a man's soul cannot bear to see the loss of another person or his suffering; pity (חֶמְלָה) [on the other hand] applies to all objects. G-d did not preclude Shaul from feeling compassion for Amalek even as he fulfilled G-d's command, for it is human nature to feel compassion and heartache for the killing of small children ....

According to the *Malbim*, there is an essential difference between the feeling of compassion and pity. The feeling of compassion is natural and instinctive, and does not require rational calculation. When a person encounters another human being suffering, he responds automatically and viscerally with a feeling of compassion. For example, we may feel compassion for a criminal sentenced to life imprisonment for committing a severe crime, even though we know that this sentence protects society.

◄§ Compassion of the Wicked Is Cruel

It is possible for a person to behave compassionately, and for his conduct to be considered cruel. *Mishlei* (12:10) declares, יוֹדֵעַ צַדִּיק נֶפֶשׁ בְּהֶמְתּוֹ וְרַחֲמֵי רְשָׁעִים אַכְזָרִי, *The righteous one knows the needs of his animal's soul, but the mercies of the wicked are cruel.* *Metzudas David* explains:

> The righteous individual strives to understand even the will of his animal so he can fulfill its desire, for he has mastered the quality of kindness; however, the wicked, even their compassion is cruelty, since it is only for the sake of appearance and not an expression of their heart.

One may wonder, under what circumstances may a merciful act be considered an act of cruelty? Rabbeinu Yonah in *Sha'arei Teshuvah* addresses this question (*Sha'ar* 3:36):

לֹא תְאַמֵּץ אֶת לְבָבְךָ וְלֹא תִקְפֹּץ אֶת יָדְךָ מֵאָחִיךָ הָאֶבְיוֹן, *You shall not harden your heart or close your hand against your destitute brother (Devarim 15:7)*. We are admonished to remove from our souls the attribute of cruelty, and plant in it … compassion and true kindness, as it is written (ibid., 28:9), לָלֶכֶת בִּדְרָכָיו, *you shall go in His ways*. Since it is possible that a person will not close his hand and will pity the destitute, but not in a compassionate way, as it is written (*Mishlei* 12:10), וְרַחֲמֵי רְשָׁעִים אַכְזָרִי, *the mercies of the wicked are cruel.*

According to Rabbeinu Yonah, there are two separate commands in the verse. One command is not to close one's hand: an instruction to actually help a needy person and to provide him with his necessities. In addition, there is a command to open one's heart with empathy for the suffering of the poor person. An act of giving that is merely a mechanical gesture, devoid of any feeling of compassion, is a violation of the commandment לֹא תְאַמֵּץ אֶת לְבָבְךָ, *you shall not harden your heart,* and may be categorized as cruelty.

Moreover, Rabbeinu Yonah implies that there is no neutral ground in which a person is not compassionate, but also is not cruel. If the feeling of compassion is not aroused in a situation which demands compassion, he is considered cruel even if he extended assistance. Given the *Malbim's* explanation cited above, this position is a logical deduction, since compassion is a natural response awakened by seeing the suffering of another human being. Lacking this innate feeling is an indication that one has become inhumanly cruel.

Sometimes a person acts mercifully, yet permits himself to exploit the goodwill engendered by his compassion with callous treatment of the beneficiary. R' Yehudah HaChassid in *Sefer Chassidim* (*Siman* 669) cites examples where compassionate acts can turn into cruel acts if not applied properly:

יוֹדֵעַ צַדִּיק נֶפֶשׁ בְּהֶמְתּוֹ וְרַחֲמֵי רְשָׁעִים אַכְזָרִי, *The righteous one knows the needs of his animal's soul, but the mercies of the wicked are cruel (Mishlei 12:10)*, meaning: The mercy that a cruel person shows his animal by feeding her a large amount of grain and then running her through hills and mountains the next day, thinking, "I have given her so much grain to eat!" — and therefore beats her cruelly when she can no longer run as he wishes. Consequently, the compassion that he displayed in feeding her has been transformed into cruelty. This is the meaning of, *but the mercies of the wicked are cruel.*

The excess feed given by the owner out of mercy fuels his cruelty the following day, since the well-fed animal was not able to run as he wished and was "rewarded" with lashes.

Ralbag interprets the phrase *his animal's soul* figuratively, and determines that this verse refers to the person himself. It is the obligation of a person to tend to his physical (animal) needs. However, if he will not put a limit to his material desires and will afford his body all of its cravings, he will become cruel, since both his body and soul will be destroyed by these lascivious actions:

The words, *his animal's soul*, refer to the physiological needs of man, who is also part animal, and not to the part that makes him human. Thus, as the wicked is compassionate to his body, and will not withhold from it any of its desires, he manifests compassion of cruelty which corrupts and destroys ....

Compassion also needs to be expressed judiciously, and in the proper time and place. R' Elazar said, "Whoever is compassionate upon those who are cruel will ultimately be cruel to those who deserve compassion" (*Midrash Tanchuma, Parashas Metzora, Siman* 1), warning against extending kindness to those who would misuse it or don't deserve it. Shaul, who displayed [inappropriate] mercy for Agag, eventually killed all the *Kohanim* in the city of Nov (*I Shmuel* 15:9 and 22:19).

Being strict with someone in order to change his evil ways can be considered an act of compassion. *Mishlei* (13:24) warns that חוֹשֵׂךְ שִׁבְטוֹ שׂוֹנֵא בְנוֹ וְאֹהֲבוֹ שִׁחֲרוֹ מוּסָר, *One who spares his rod hates his child, but he who loves him disciplines him in his youth*. There are times that genuine compassion demands a more "callous" approach to motivate someone who is lazy or corrupt, as long as the ultimate purpose is to better his ways. Some medical procedures cause a great deal of pain, and if they were not intended for healing they would be considered very cruel. In reality, however, inflicting some discomfort or pain can be an act of kindness, since its purpose is to benefit the patient.

To summarize, the attribute of compassion requires the following:

- Feeling the pain of the other person.
- Doing whatever possible to alleviate the pain.
- The assistance must be without any personal motives, in the proper measure, and with the perspective of the long-term benefits of the compassion.
- Misplaced compassion can lead to eventual cruelty.

❧ Compassion and Cruelty Mixed Together

To reiterate, the attribute of compassion is innate in the heart of every human being, even in the heart of a cruel person. The picture of Rudolf Hoess bending down and giving milk to a cat is one of the most bitterly ironic; the same person who cold-bloodedly and methodically masterminded the death of millions of human beings, displays touching tenderness for a thirsty cat. It is quite obvious that even the cruelest people have a natural instinct of kindness.

History has proven that people can commit horrific acts in the name of compassion. Some European countries have outlawed slaughtering of animals and circumcision as inhumane. Yet some of these "enlightened" nations did not hesitate to partner in the genocide of the Holocaust, and while speaking niceties do very little to stop the suffering and killing of millions around the globe. The Society for the Prevention of Cruelty to Animals focuses on the suffering of animals and, in the name of compassion, opposes animal testing for medical research that can save human lives.

Though compassion is inherent in the human soul of man, it is possible to transform a compassionate person to one of unspeakable cruelty. Character can be altered through behaviors; while inflicting pain and killing may be difficult for a person who is naturally kind, having engaged in such behaviors — even by force — can transform the person.

The Torah describes a city whose inhabitants conspire to join together in idolatry, and after careful investigation, meeting specific criteria, the city is declared "a city of corruption" (*Ir HaNidachas*) and is condemned to utter destruction. The Torah commands that all the inhabitants of the city be executed, and the city and its contents burned, warning:

וְלֹא יִדְבַּק בְּיָדְךָ מְאוּמָה מִן הַחֵרֶם לְמַעַן יָשׁוּב ה' מֵחֲרוֹן אַפּוֹ וְנָתַן לְךָ רַחֲמִים וְרִחַמְךָ וְהִרְבֶּךָ כַּאֲשֶׁר נִשְׁבַּע לַאֲבֹתֶיךָ.

No part of the banned property may adhere to your hand, so that Hashem will turn back from His burning wrath; and He will give you mercy and be merciful to you and multiply you, as He swore to your forefathers (Devarim 13:16-18).

The *Or HaChaim* takes note of the phrase, וְנָתַן לְךָ רַחֲמִים וְרִחַמְךָ, *and He will give you mercy and be merciful to you,* explaining:

> … the Torah commands to kill the inhabitants and destroy the entire city … including the animals. This action will engender the quality of cruelty in the hearts of these men. As the Yishmaelites who are a group of royal executioners described, they are consumed with a tremendous desire [to kill] when they execute people, since compassion has been uprooted from their hearts and they have become absolutely cruel. This same character [transformation] could become rooted in the killers of a city of corruption. For this reason, G-d promised that He would give them mercy, in spite of the natural development of cruelty; [G-d] The Source of Compassion will bestow upon them

the power of compassion anew, to eliminate the power of cruelty which resulted from their actions.

Behavior which is naturally cruel, even if done in accord with a Divine command, is likely to transform a compassionate person into a cruel one. Therefore, G-d promises that He will bestow upon them a supernatural power of renewed compassion, in order to eliminate the attribute of cruelty that was implanted by their actions. Conversely, a person who may be indifferent or callous to others can develop a feeling of compassion by engaging in merciful acts, as the *Sha'arei Teshuvah* (ibid.) writes, "We are admonished to remove from our souls the attribute of cruelty, and plant in it … compassion and true kindness."

⤳§ Degrees in the Attributes of Compassion and Cruelty

The *Rambam*, in *Mishneh Torah*, cites three different laws related to the attributes of compassion and cruelty, each applying to specific circumstances. In *Hilchos Matnos Aniyim* (10:2) he writes:

> A person will never become poor due to charity, and no evil or damage will ever result from charity …. Whoever is merciful, others will have mercy upon him, as it is written (*Devarim* 13:18), וְנָתַן לְךָ רַחֲמִים וְרִחַמְךָ וְהִרְבֶּךָ, *and He will give you mercy and be merciful to you and multiply you* …. And, whoever is cruel and does not show compassion, there is doubt about his genealogy.

Thus, encountering a person in need requires a charitable response. Indifference to a need is a manifestation of cruelty.

In *Hilchos Teshuvah* (*Perek* 2:10) the *Rambam* presents another instance in which compassion is manifest:

> It is prohibited for a person to be cruel and refuse appeasement — rather he should be easy to pacify and hard to anger. When a wrongdoer asks for forgiveness, he

should forgive willingly and wholeheartedly — even if the hurt was great, and the abuse severe; he should not be vengeful nor bear a grudge.

The *Rambam* addresses an instance in which a person who experienced grave abuse and injustice is asked by the wrongdoer for forgiveness. The *Rambam* rules that failure to respond to such requests is considered cruel. Even in this instance there is no middle ground — the lack of response to the other party is deemed cruelty.

In *Hilchos Avadim* (9:8) the *Rambam* expands the concepts of compassion and cruelty:

> [Though] it is permissible to impose hard labor on a Canaanite slave, it is an attribute of piety and the way of wisdom that a person should be compassionate and pursue justice, and he should not impose a heavy yoke upon his slave nor harass him. He should give him food and drink of all kinds and types. The earlier sages would give a slave a portion from every dish they ate, and would feed their animals and slaves first before themselves .... Likewise, he should not humiliate him with either his hands or words; they were given for servitude and not for embarrassment. He should not excessively scream or be angry, rather he should speak to him pleasantly and listen to his complaints .... the descendants of Avraham Avinu, who are the Jewish people, upon whom G-d bestowed the goodness of the Torah and commanded them righteous statutes and laws, are compassionate upon all people .... And, whoever has compassion upon others, others will have compassion upon him, as it is written (*Devarim* 13:18), וְנָתַן לְךָ רַחֲמִים וְרִחַמְךָ וְהִרְבֶּךָ, *and He will give you mercy and be merciful to you and multiply you.*

The *Rambam* rules that inconsiderate conduct, even toward pagan slaves, demonstrates cruelty, and is unbefitting a Jew who should emulate the merciful attributes of G-d.

The ruling regarding a slave is essentially different from the previous laws cited from the *Rambam*. In the preceding instances, one confronts a reality that requires an immediate response, and the lack of an appropriate response is considered cruelty. The ruling regarding a slave is not about a response to a need, but rather an attempt to avoid a reality of cruelty. Here there could be a middle ground in which the master does not treat the slave with cruelty, but he also does not demonstrate compassion, by giving him food that is unlike his own or assigning him labor that is not hard.

To manifest compassion, the master must take a proactive step to override his legal rights, and deliberately relate to the slave as an equal. The *Rambam* rules that a Jew is enjoined to treat even the lowliest members of society with honor and respect.

☙ The Punishment for Cruelty: Measure for Measure

While mercy is innate to the Jew, every Jew is expected to deliberately act with compassion because of the obligation to emulate G-d's ways (see *Shabbos* 133b), and the reward that awaits the compassionate is as great as the punishment for treating others with cruelty. The *Or HaChaim (Devarim* 13:18) writes:

> And the Torah says, *and He will give you mercy and be merciful to you,* to make us aware that as long as a person is cruel, G-d relates similarly to him, for G-d does not bestow mercy except on the merciful.

A person who treats others cruelly, even if his behavior is fulfilling G-d's commandment, will "merit" cruel treatment by the Creator, since G-d's conduct in this world is "measure for measure." The Torah therefore assures those who destroy the *Ir HaNidachas* that they will be granted renewed mercy by G-d. *Yalkut Shimoni* on the Book of *Iyov* expresses a similar idea:

When someone injures his friend, the victim needs to beseech Heaven to have mercy on the attacker .... It is written, וַיִּתְפַּלֵּל אַבְרָהָם אֶל הָאֱלֹקִים וַיִּרְפָּא אֱלֹקִים אֶת אֲבִימֶלֶךְ וְאֶת אִשְׁתּוֹ וְאַמְהֹתָיו וַיֵּלֵדוּ, *Avraham prayed to G-d, and G-d healed Avimelech, his wife, and his maids, and they were relieved* (*Bereishis* 20:17). R' Yehudah said in the name of Rabban Gamliel: "It is written, וְנָתַן לְךָ רַחֲמִים וְרִחַמְךָ, *and He will give you mercy and be merciful to you* .... Keep this [adage] in your hand: As long as you are compassionate, the Compassionate One will have compassion on you" (*Remez* 928, also in *Tosefta, Bava Kamma* 9:29).

The only way a person can secure compassion from G-d is by being compassionate himself.

৵§ A Hint and an Opportunity from Heaven

R' Eliyahu Lopian *zt"l* writes that G-d presents us with challenges that require compassionate action, so that He should be able to bestow His compassion upon us:

Our Sages (*Zohar HaKadosh, Bereishis Daf* 23) said that when G-d sees that a strict verdict is directed at a sinful individual, He sends a poor person to his house so that he should behave charitably toward him, and through this, Heaven will have compassion on him, measure for measure. This is the meaning of וְנָתַן לְךָ רַחֲמִים, *and He will give you mercy* — meaning, that He will put in your heart the will to have mercy for the poor person, and because of this, וְרִחַמְךָ, *and be merciful to you* ... (*Lev Eliyahu* I, 119).

R' Matisyahu Salomon *shlita* elaborates on this idea:

Herein another revelation of G-d's Providence: In every opportunity which requires a person to act with compassion, there is a hint that the person is threatened with strict justice from Heaven and he is in need of Heavenly mercy. However, Heaven cannot bestow mercy upon him due to his own deficiency in the attribute of compassion … (*Matnas Chaim*, a commentary on *Tomer Devorah*).

Every situation in which we can show compassion toward others should be viewed as a golden opportunity granted so that we may awaken Heavenly compassion for ourselves.

R' Solomon cites R' Dessler's interpretation on the prayer, *Machnisei Rachamim*, recited during the days of *Selichos*:

> During the days of *Selichos* we recite: "May the bearers of mercy bring our mercies before the Master of mercy." Who are these "bearers of mercy"? You should know that the beggar who knocked on your door late last night, and you refused to open for him, or the friend who approached you yesterday in the *beis medrash* and asked you to clarify a difficult passage, and you told him that you had no time — they are the ones who were sent to be your "bearers of mercy" today! …. This is the way we must perceive G-d's conduct toward us: every opportunity for compassion that happens to us, grab it immediately, for it has been sent to us from Heaven in order to remove from us severe judgment.

At times, when we hear that a friend or relative has fallen ill and is in danger, we cleave to the Book of *Tehillim* and sincerely pray for Divine mercy and healing. In light of the paragraphs above, it is likely that in addition to praying, we need to seek ways and opportunities for merciful acts. Such actions have the ability to awaken Divine compassion, and in His great kindness He will remove from us all distress and anguish, every plague and sickness, and He will send to each one the salvation and healing so desperately needed.

24

Mercy vs. Loving-Kindness

Having differentiated between compassion (or mercy) and pity, it is also instructive to distinguish between mercy and loving-kindness (*rachamim* vs. *chesed*), though both are highly praised by the Sages. *Avos DeR' Nosson (Perek 37)* states:

> There are seven attributes that serve before the Heavenly Throne: wisdom, righteousness, justice, loving-kindness, compassion, truth, and peace.

The Gemara (*Succah* 49b) writes:

> R' Elazar said: "One who acts charitably is greater than one who brings all of the sacrifices, as it is written: עֲשֹׂה צְדָקָה וּמִשְׁפָּט נִבְחָר לַה' מִזָּבַח, *Doing what is right and just is preferable to G-d than an offering*" (*Mishlei* 21:3).

The *Talmud Yerushalmi (Pe'ah* 3:1) distinguishes between charity and acts of kindness:

> Charity and acts of kindness are equivalent to all other commandments of the Torah: Charity applies to those who are alive, whereas acts of kindness apply to both the living and the dead; charity applies to the poor, whereas acts of kindness apply to the poor and the rich; and charity

involves one's money, whereas acts of kindness involve both one's money and his self. R' Yochanan bar Maria said in the name of R' Yochanan: We do not know which one of them is more beloved: charity or acts of kindness. However, the verse says: וְחֶסֶד ה׳ מֵעוֹלָם וְעַד עוֹלָם עַל יְרֵאָיו וְצִדְקָתוֹ לִבְנֵי בָנִים, *G-d's kindness is forever and ever and granted to those who fear Him, and His charity is granted to their children's children* (*Tehillim* 103:17), teaching us that acts of kindness are more beloved than charity.

These are but a few examples of the value attributed by the *Tanach* and our Sages to the concepts of charity, kindness, and compassion. Some people do not differentiate between these concepts and consider them to be synonymous. This chapter will attempt to clarify the fundamental differences, as well as similarities, between them.

⋙ Today's Charity Apparatus

The range and volume of charity prevalent in contemporary observant communities, along with the variety and number of benevolent organizations, is unprecedented in the entire history of Jewish life. A quick scan of the community phone book in Yerushalayim will uncover a list of more than three thousand *gemachim* (benevolent organizations), that encompass the entire life cycle. There is a *gemach* for every conceivable need: expensive medical equipment, party tables and chairs, diapers and pacifiers. There are thousands of foundations for no-interest loans in every corner of the world. It is doubtful that such large quantities of charity and kindness have ever been dispensed in the past.

At the same time, in spite of all these incredible acts of kindness and charity, there are still many people in vibrant Jewish communities across the world plagued by a terrible sense of isolation and misery. Many of these people are not necessarily impoverished, but may be temporarily downtrodden and longing for a little bit of warmth, a pleasant greeting, a better paying job, etc. It has been said that Jewish communities are extraordinarily attentive to the "certifiably miserable," but too often indifferent to those who do not bear the stigma of poverty or illness. Only when a person has been identified to be in deep trouble and "miserable," and in need of dramatic assistance, do the gates of compassion open wide and everyone rushes to help.

The following anecdote (with names changed), based on an actual incident, will illustrate this pervasive anomaly.

⤳ A Job Instead of Charity

A number of years ago, Reuven, an honored and esteemed individual, found himself in a perplexing and difficult situation. He had been employed by one firm for more than twenty years when the owners suddenly announced their decision to close the business. At the age of fifty-five, Reuven suddenly found himself without a job and means of support. Moreover, he had assumed extensive financial obligations due to his children's weddings. In his distress, he turned to several friends and asked for their help finding a job.

Recognizing his extensive experience, superb work ethic and devotion to his former employer, his friends set out to help him find a new job. Despite their efforts, Reuven remained unemployed with an ever-deteriorating economic situation. One morning, his friend Shimon saw a want ad with a job description that fit very well with Reuven's qualifications. Conscious of the numerous disappointments Reuven had already experienced in his job search, Shimon decided to do the ground work and inquired about the open position. To his great surprise, he discovered that the advertisement was placed by a firm owned by Levi, Reuven's childhood friend and classmate, who lived just a few blocks away from Reuven.

The next morning, Shimon called Levi and proposed that he hire Reuven. He recommended Reuven as an excellent employee, and suggested that Levi phone the former employer to inquire about Reuven. To his chagrin, Levi refused to consider this idea, and told Shimon that as a matter of principle he will not hire any acquaintances, since it would be exceedingly difficult to let them go when they do not perform as expected. Shimon suggested that Levi offer Reuven a temporary position for 3-4 months to manage a specific project so that he can gauge Levi's effectiveness as an employee. "If things do not work out, you just let him go upon completion of the project he was hired to do." However, Levi remained firm in his refusal — he does not hire friends and acquaintances.

As time passed by, a financial crisis developed in Reuven's household. His friends knew that he would refuse to accept money as charity. They secretly got together and decided that each would donate a specific amount each month, and that one of them would "hire" Reuven for a series of one-month projects. They also decided to keep the matter a secret. On the day following this meeting, Shimon bumped into Levi, who asked him whether Reuven had found a job. After a bit of hesitation, Shimon decided to tell Levi about the secret decision, hoping that it might motivate him to change his mind and employ Reuven. Instead, Levi volunteered to contribute to the monthly "stipend." He was shocked when Shimon adamantly refused his offer, saying that enough money had already been collected to satisfy Reuven's needs. Levi insisted, arguing that Shimon does not have the right to refuse his money. At that point, Shimon sternly told Levi, "Look, this whole situation arose as a result of your refusal to hire Reuven, even on a trial basis. Your desire to help may be genuine, but it comes to assuage your guilty conscience. Since we have already collected all that is needed, I refuse to afford you the opportunity to quiet your conscience, and allow you to feel that you've done what you can for Reuven."

The next day, Levi called Shimon and told him that after a sleepless night, he reconsidered and decided to hire Reuven for a specific project for the next three months. Today, five years later,

Reuven is still working for Levi, and serves as his confidant and right hand man in all his business dealings. Hiring Reuven was a noble act, but Levi's heart was awakened only after Reuven had become a "charity case."

☙ A Person that Overcame His Misfortune

Living in Yerushalayim with his family of three sons and three daughters, Yaakov and his wife were grateful for their good jobs and their circle of friends. Just before his tenth birthday, his youngest son, Yosef, started to complain about severe abdomen pain and eventually was diagnosed with an advanced cancer. While the initial treatment was performed in Israel, it was determined that he will require follow up treatment and eventually radical surgery abroad. In the ensuing months both parents missed many days of work, consumed with the medical treatment of their son. Before embarking on the trip abroad, the family needed to raise a large sum of money to schedule the expensive medical treatment required to save their son's life.

Yaakov turned to his friends for advice and one of them directed him to a prominent person, who was the director of a large free loan foundation (*gemach*). Initially, Yaakov was hesitant to approach this man, because he was associated with a different social group, and he feared that his request will be rejected. As the time drew closer to the trip abroad, Yaakov reluctantly approached the charity director. To his surprise, the man was warmly receptive to his story, and immediately approved the loan, adding hearty encouragement. In the ensuing months, both before the trip abroad and upon their return from a miraculously successful treatment abroad, the *gemach* director phoned to inquire about Yosef's progress. He would ask about Yaakov and his family whenever their paths crossed in the street.

A year passed, and with G-d's help Yosef was cured of his cursed illness, such that Yaakov and his wife returned to their respective jobs and the family's life returned to normal. After some additional time, the debt to the *gemach* was completely repaid. There was one noticeable change which bothered Yaakov greatly — the relationship with the *gemach* director cooled. The warm greeting, the hand waving from afar, the smiles — all disappeared, and quite often he was completely ignored when he encountered the director in the street.

In one of our meetings, Yaakov shared his amazement at the situation. I responded that, in my opinion, the answer is simple: The pleasant countenance and sincere interest displayed by the director of the *gemach* were expressions of mercy aroused by the plight of a family in dire circumstances. Once Yosef regained his health, the family's financial status improved, and they were no longer in need of mercy, they could be treated like other strangers. Now they yearned for some *chesed* (kindness), not mercy, and unfortunately these are two distinct attributes.

◄§ Mercy Emanates from the Desire to Take

R' Dessler in *Michtav Me'Eliyahu* (*Kuntrus HaChesed* 9) writes that though mercy is manifested by giving to others, it emanates from a desire to take rather than from a desire to give. This is because merciful action is aroused by the will to alleviate the pain felt at the sight of another human's suffering, and not from a genuine and sincere desire to give to others:

> The attribute of pity … does not originate from pure desire to bestow good upon another. Rather, the motivator of [merciful] actions is the sorrow one feels when he sees the distress of his friend ….

If a person sees his friend in great distress and in his merciful response does everything in his ability to help him, his behavior would be deemed honorable. However, according to *Michtav Me'Eliyahu*, the underlying objective is self-serenity. In contrast, if one identifies with his friend, empathizing with his friend's joys as well as his sorrows, and does whatever he can to see his friend's happiness, the behavior emanates from the desire to give.

In *Michtav Me'Eliyahu, Chelek 3,* R' Dessler adds another dimension to the understanding of the capacity of taking. He quotes the Gemara in *Maseches Pesachim* (113b):

> Canaan commanded his sons five things: love each other, love stealing, love promiscuity, hate your masters, and do not speak the truth.

R' Dessler asks, "How can we reconcile the first command of Canaan 'to love each other' with the other four commands which express utter disregard for another human being?" He answers that their love for each other emanated from egotism, and not from a genuine concern for one another:

> A band of murdering thieves must adopt for itself a strong regimen of mutual trust, and the willingness to sacrifice for the sake of each member of the group. Is this truly a mutual love emanating from kindness? Rather, their considerate treatment of one another is generated by self-love, from each one's desire to indulge his sensual desires! In order to achieve this desire, the criminals are forced to unite into a self-governing entity. It follows, then, that their cooperation and concern for one another originates from the desire to steal and murder .... As such, this "mutual agreement" is basically giving for the sake of receiving, love for another for the sake of love of oneself, as is the common practice of "takers."
>
> This is similar to flattering praise and gratitude to a donor which is motivated by the desire to induce him to continue or increase his gifts, or in order to encourage others to donate as well. This type of gratitude is fundamentally a form of taking.

Accordingly, there are many acts of giving which superficially appear to be positive, yet the impetus to do them does not come from the desire to help, but from egocentricity.

❧ Kindness vs. Mercy

The *Be'er Mayim Chaim*, on *Parashas Chayei Sarah*, writes extensively on the essential difference between the attribute of loving-kindness and the attribute of mercy:

> There are two aspects to acts of kindness and compassion. One is a person who is referred to as a "master of kindness" of whom our Sages (*Shabbos* 104a) said, "Such is the way of masters of kindness to run after the needy." Thus he runs and pursues any opportunity to perform acts of kindness and is genuinely incapable of existing without it. This is similar to a cow who nurses, that when her milk supply comes in, she runs and searches for her calf to nurse it, since the milk causes her pain. So too, the master of kindness — his heart burns within him and he searches everywhere to find a person who is in need, so that he may bestow upon him some of his goodness. In the morning he wakes up, searching and asking for the poor and unfortunate, perhaps he will be able to impart to them from his benevolence ….
>
> Then, there is one called a "master of mercy" who does not search for a poor person …. However, when he encounters a poor man and sees his suffering, and the poor man shows him a sorrowful face, then he pities him and cannot bear to see his grief, and imparts to him from his goodness. But, if he does not see a poor man his entire life, he will not remember on his own to say that perhaps there exists a poor man who needs my help ….
>
> The "master of mercy" does not give but to one who groans and sighs before him …. However, when he does not see [the poor] he does not remember them. On the contrary, he hides his face so that he does not see their suffering, claiming to do so because he is not able to see their grief since his heart will be pained and he will suffer.

Mercy is an emotional response to an external stimulus, whereas the attribute of kindness is inherent in the personality. Indeed, this was the case with Avraham Avinu, the paradigm of kindness, who — though suffering pain after his circumcision — went searching for guests to whom he could bestow his loving hospitality (cf. *Rashi, Bereishis* 18:1).

◆§ A Different Reward

The difference between kindness and mercy lie not only in the motivation for giving, but also in the rewards promised for each. The *Be'er Mayim Chaim* explains the distinct advantage of those who have mastered loving-kindness:

> It is well-known that "a person will be measured [by Heaven] by the same measure he uses for others" (*Megillah* 12b), and so for the "master of kindness" G-d pursues opportunities to bestow charity and kindness on his behalf, even though the person does not know he needs it and does not pray and petition Him at all. Sometimes, he is not even aware of the matter, and G-d performs miracles and kindnesses on his behalf. This is not so for the "master of mercy": G-d is merciful to him at times of distress as he suffers and begs mercy from his Creator. Then his Maker will have compassion on him, but He will not spare him from the stress and pain altogether.

Because of the intense desire of the "master of kindness" to give to another and bestow goodness — even when it appears that everything is in order — his reward is that G-d treats him accordingly, and gives him his needs and healing in a totally natural way, such that he does not even need to pray for himself. This is not so with the "master of mercy" who merely responds to the immense need of another person; G-d treats him in the same manner, and answers his requests and has compassion upon him, but he does not forestall misfortune.

25

Kindness Mixed with Mercy

In the previous chapter we highlighted the difference between the attributes of kindness (*chesed*) and compassion or mercy (*rachamim*). The master of kindness proactively looks for opportunities to help others, while the master of mercy reacts to a situation of pain and suffering by others, but will not pursue opportunities to help. Thus most charitable giving, particularly by individuals, is a response to an existing need, and is therefore classified with acts of mercy rather than pure loving-kindness. That is not to understate the value of charitable acts, for as R' Elazar said (*Succah* 49b): "One who performs charity is greater than one who brings all of the sacrifices."

◄§ Kindness in a Situation that Demands Compassion

It is common to encounter situations that demand compassionate reactions. Upon seeing a person in dire need of financial or emotional support, both the kind person and the merciful one will respond. One may wonder, however, if there is a discernable difference in their responses. Is it possible to perform acts of kindness which are proactive in nature while responding to a need that arouses mercy? The same R' Elazar, who praised the mitzvah of merciful charity, continues to proclaim:

The "master of kindness," on the other hand, will exert more time and effort to minimize the suffering, ensure that his help is being used to its maximum, and try to understand and empathize with the person he is assisting. He will give the impoverished person money, but will also guide him to the cheapest place to buy what he needs, will even take him there, and then will try to deal with the underlying causes of the problem and look for a long-term solution.

~§ The Provision of Emotional Needs

A genuine act of kindness must also deal with the recipient's emotional needs. The Gemara (*Bava Basra* 9b) states:

> R' Yitzchak said: Whoever gives a *prutah* (small coin) to a poor man is blessed with six blessings, and the one who appeases him with words is blessed with eleven blessings.

The *Maharsha* (ad loc.) explains that indeed the primary action of kindness with others is the attention to their emotional needs:

> If you have no money to give him, console him with words …. The reason that one who appeases a poor person is greater than one who gives him money without appeasing him is because the former deals with the person, while the other one is merely dealing with his money. For this reason acts of kindness are greater than charity ….

The *Rambam* (*Hilchos Matnos Aniyim* 10:4) adds another dimension to the Gemara's statement:

> Whoever gives charity to a poor person with a frown, or with refusal to look him in the face, even if he should give one thousand golden coins, he has lost his merit. Rather, he should give it to him with a smiling demeanor and with joy, while empathizing with his situation …. And he should express empathy and words of consolation.

Whereas the Gemara indicates that mere charity to a poor man is blessed with six blessings, and adding kind words earns the giver eleven blessings, according to the *Rambam*, it is possible that one who gives charity with an indifferent demeanor loses his merit completely. Rabbeinu Yonah, in his commentary to *Maseches Avos* (1:2), emphasizes the value of emotional support and kindly advice in transforming an act of pity to one of loving-kindness:

> Kind deeds also apply to rich people: to lend them money when they are lacking, and to give them sound advice, as Shlomo HaMelech said, שֶׁמֶן וּקְטֹרֶת יְשַׂמַּח לֵב וּמֶתֶק רֵעֵהוּ מֵעֲצַת נָפֶשׁ, *Oil and incense gladden the heart, so does the sweetness of a friend's sincere counsel* (*Mishlei* 27:9) .... This is an act of kindness which finds favor before G-d, and for this the world was created.

Often, a person in distress is consoled by the fact that someone takes an interest in his plight and wants to help him. The feeling that he is not alone and that someone cares can be as important as the practical assistance. Indeed, it is told that one of the great sages of this generation advised his followers who are matchmakers to contact the parents of older singles with suggestions for a match, even if the likelihood of success is low. The Rebbe said, "The parents desperately await phone calls from matchmakers, and the call itself, and the interest it reflects, constitutes a tremendous act of kindness, even though the chance that something will come out of the conversation is very small."

⋘ The Difficulty in Asking for Help

When R' Yechezkel Abramsky *zt"l* was a rabbi in London he worked diligently to raise money for needy members of his community. After giving him a sizable donation, a donor asked him to explain the meaning of the Sages' adage, "Greater is one who gets others to do than the doer himself" (*Bava Basra* 9b), which implies that someone who gathers money for charity is greater than the giver of the charity. "Why should the Rabbi's heavenly reward be greater than mine?" R' Abramsky answered him with a smile, "Our reward is greater because of the trepidation and embarrassment we feel standing at your door, which are more severe than your palpitations when you give us the money."

To illustrate the difficulty in asking for help, consider the following story which was related by the daughter of a pious and well-to-do man who owned a store on a busy street in Tel Aviv. A woman entered the store, waited patiently for the other customers to leave, and blushingly asked the proprietor for a loan to help pay for her daughter's wedding. The owner told her to come the next day to his store, and then, with G-d's help, he would grant her request. In the evening he came home and told his wife what had happened. Shaken, his wife said, "Is it not enough that this poor woman had to stand in the store and hesitate, and with a trembling heart approach you and ask for the money, that you force her to repeat this 'torture' tomorrow?!" Immediately, the two got into their car, traveled to the woman's house and brought her the sum she requested.

Diminishing the shame of a needy person, the radiant smile with which one greets him, the understanding of the fragile emotional state of a poor person, and the expression of encouragement and emotional support, are all part and parcel of the act of kindness.

๛ Kindness Without Intermediaries

Some people avoid the hassle of meeting with and listening to the multitudes of charity seekers by appointing an individual or organization to distribute charitable contributions on their behalf. While this may be a more efficient way of delivering charity money, it lacks the central ingredient discussed above — the personal interaction with the poor person. These people are knowingly forgoing the blessings that are bestowed on those who show a pleasant countenance, and provide emotional support, to those who need help.

The obligation to deal directly with the needy, with no intermediaries, is exemplified by our forefather Avraham Avinu, the pillar of kindness. In bringing the visiting angels to his home, Avraham busied himself in preparing food for his guests, paying attention to the smallest detail, and finally escorted them as they left. The only thing he asked his servants to do was bring water for the guests. The Gemara (*Bava Metzia* 86b) says:

> Whatever Avraham Avinu performed himself for the angels, G-d Himself performed for his descendants, and everything that Avraham did through an intermediary, G-d did for his descendants through an intermediary.

As a "measure for measure," G-d Himself provided all the needs of the Jewish people in the desert, except for the water, for which he asked Moshe to speak to the rock. Indeed, the performance of kindness by oneself, without any intermediaries, results in receiving the rewards directly from G-d, and not through a proxy.

The Gemara in *Kiddushin* (32b) describes a dialogue between *Tannaim* on this topic:

> R' Eliezer, R' Yehoshua, and R' Tzadok participated at the wedding of the son of Rabban Gamliel, and Rabban Gamliel was serving them. He gave a cup to R' Eliezer, but he would not take it; he gave it to R' Yehoshua, and he took it. R' Eliezer said to him, "What is this, Yehoshua? How can we sit and let Rabban Gamliel stand and serve us?" He responded, "We found 'someone' even greater who served — Avraham was the greatest sage of his generation, yet it is written about him (*Bereishis* 18:8), וְהוּא עֹמֵד עֲלֵיהֶם, *he stood over them!* Lest you say, perhaps they appeared to him as angels? — they appeared to him merely as Arabs! So why should Rabban Gamliel not stand and serve us?!"
>
> R' Tzadok said to them, "How long will you neglect the honor of the Omnipresent and engage in the honor of His creatures? G-d causes the winds to blow, elevates the

clouds, brings down the rain, causes the ground to sprout, and sets a table before each and every person! [Why] should not Rabban Gamliel b'Rebbi stand and serve us?!"

Of course, Rabban Gamliel had servants, yet he chose to serve his guests himself, because this is the most complete and genuine performance of kindness.

Based on all the sources cited, it appears that the following are prerequisites for a person to be classified as a "master of kindness":

1) There must be an innate and natural desire to give, which causes pain if thwarted.

2) A master of kindness can identify someone who needs help, even when it is not obvious that the person is in distress. A master of kindness can anticipate the misfortune of another person before it develops, and will offer a solution before tragedy hits.

3) Kind acts take many forms — financial assistance, physical aid and emotional support. A master of kindness will do everything in his ability to satisfy all the needs of a person, the immediate and apparent ones, as well as those that are not so immediate and are likely to emerge in the future. He also does not differentiate between poor and rich people, attempting to help every person who needs assistance.

4) A master of kindness views his assistance as a process, rather than a series of discrete acts. He provides assistance and stays in the picture to assure success. He empathizes with the other person and tries to "be in his shoes." He will also make sure that the dignity of the needy person is kept intact.

5) A master of kindness tries to provide the needed assistance himself and not through intermediaries. Direct involvement gives him the best chance to understand

the other person and his needs, assess the effectiveness of the help provided, and determine the best course of action for the long term.

ᥰᥲ A Woman of Kindness Is Her Very Essence

I was deeply affected by a genuine "master of kindness" who lived in our town. She was Rebbetzin Sarah Gluck *a"h*, who passed away in 2013 after a drawn-out period of illness and suffering. My wife and I were fortunate to partner with her in a small way in some of her manifold acts of kindness, particularly when it involved families from Israel who came to Chicago for medical treatment, and fluent Hebrew was required

My wife was very concerned about her well-being and from time to time phoned her and tried to encourage her. As her situation became critical, many women gathered to pray and say *Tehillim* on her behalf. After one such gathering, the phone rang and her number was displayed. My wife and I were very anxious, and hesitated to pick up the phone, fearful of the tragic tidings. Hesitatingly, my wife picked up the phone and heard the weak voice of Rebbetzin Gluck.

She asked us "to do her a favor" and call one of the families in Israel, to find out if they were in need of certain medical supplies that she used to ship to them once every two months from Chicago. She apologized for troubling us, but since she did not remember when the supply was last sent, she requested that we ascertain if there was a need. She followed by giving us instructions whom to contact if shipment was needed. My wife assured her that she will fulfill her request and asked her to relax and not worry, especially given her state of health.

Rebbetzin Gluck responded, "Because of my great pain, I did not have a chance to help anyone today, and I do not feel good about this. Please do me this favor and call me back to let me know what happened. This way I will be able to know that my day was not wasted and I will certainly feel better."

As the conversation ended, my wife and I tried to process what we had just heard. This woman was fighting for her very life and was in a great deal of pain, yet the absence of a chance to perform a kind act on that day pained her more than anything else. At that moment we realized that we had the great merit of knowing a truly righteous woman — a master of *chesed*.

Charity is only recompensed according to the kindness it contains, as it is written, זִרְעוּ לָכֶם לִצְדָקָה קִצְרוּ לְפִי חֶסֶד, *Sow for yourselves charity (*לִצְדָקָה*) and you will reap according to kindness (*חֶסֶד*)* (*Hoshea* 10:12).

In explaining R' Elazar's words, *Rashi* writes:

> The giving is called "charity" and the effort is "kindness," for example, [giving the beggar money is charity], while bringing the money to the beggar's home [is kindness] … as he directs his heart and mind for the benefit of the poor man.

Rashi notes that giving in a way that maximizes the benefit and dignity of the poor differentiates between merciful charity, and charity that includes loving-kindness.

The *Be'er Mayim Chaim* on *Parashas Chayei Sarah* clarifies the difference between the responses of kindness and mercy:

> When the master of kindness goes to the marketplace and finds a poor man, sighing and bemoaning his troubles with a sorrowful demeanor, he will certainly fulfill his request. However, that is not enough for him, for this is but the response of mercy and not of loving-kindness. He specifically wants to perform kindness, so what does he do? When the poor man asks for a coin or two, he increases his gift and gives him four or five coins, thereby transforming his act to one of kindness.

It is possible for two individuals to assist a needy person, yet the underlying motivations will have a great impact on the kind of help they each provide. The "master of mercy" will provide assistance for the most urgent and essential needs, as he is unable to bear the sight of a suffering being. His charity will be limited to dealing with the immediate and most pressing needs, without thinking about the long term. If tomorrow there will be a need for more help, he will deal with it at that time.

26

Gratitude

✒ A Fundamental Principle in Judaism

The first words uttered by an observant Jew as he opens his eyes in the morning are, מוֹדֶה אֲנִי לְפָנֶיךָ, מֶלֶךְ חַי וְקַיָּם, שֶׁהֶחֱזַרְתָּ בִּי נִשְׁמָתִי בְּחֶמְלָה, רַבָּה אֱמוּנָתֶךָ, *I gratefully thank You, O living and eternal King, for You have returned my soul within me with compassion.* These words express gratitude for a new day and restored life. The *Amidah*, recited three times a day, includes an elaborate section called the blessing of gratitude: מוֹדִים אֲנַחְנוּ לָךְ, *We gratefully thank you, G-d* ... which culminates with the benediction וּלְךָ נָאֶה לְהוֹדוֹת, *to You it is fitting to give thanks.* In the same vein, every Jew is expected to recite one hundred blessings daily, each of them opening with the words, בָּרוּךְ אַתָּה ה', *Blessed are You, Hashem,* which express thanks for the gifts of life, including sustenance, healthy functioning of the human body, for the beauty of the natural world, etc. Gratitude to the Creator, and awareness of His gifts, are engrained in every aspect of a Jew's daily routine.

Inherent in gratitude are awareness of goodness that has been bestowed, and a thankful acknowledgment of the Source of the good. This obligation is not limited to expressing gratitude to the Creator, but is extended to everyone and everything from which one benefits. Furthermore, being ungrateful to another human being will eventually result in being ungrateful to the Creator as well. *Rabbeinu Bachya* (*Shemos* 1:8) quotes *Midrash Tanchuma*:

> All who deny the goodness bestowed by another person, will in the end deny the goodness of Hashem, as it is written [about Pharaoh], אֲשֶׁר לֹא יָדַע אֶת יוֹסֵף, *that [he] did not know Yosef* — and eventually [he] said, לֹא יָדַעְתִּי אֶת ה', *I do not know Hashem* (*Exodus* 5:2).

According to this *Midrash*, the underlying character trait of ingratitude that allowed Pharaoh to ignore Yosef's role in saving Egypt from calamity, also led him to deny the existence of G-d. The tendency to take the good for granted is not divisible, and extends to the human and religious dimensions.

It is not possible to be an ingrate to other people and be genuinely thankful to G-d, as is explained in *Sefer HaChinuch* (*Mitzvah* 33) in the context of honoring one's parents:

> … it is appropriate for a person to recognize and reciprocate any kindness to the one that benefited him, and he should not be a vile, estranged ingrate, as this is an evil and despicable attribute before G-d and man. He should be conscious that his father and mother are the reason that he is in this world, and therefore it is indeed appropriate to bestow on them all honor and whatever good he is able to, for they brought him into the world and labored for him in his infancy. Having instilled this attribute in his soul, it will elevate him to recognize the goodness of G-d Who is the reason for his existence.

According to the *Sefer HaChinuch*, gratitude is at the heart of the commandment of honoring one's parents, and a precursor to recognizing the Divine gifts bestowed by the Creator.

◆§ Ingratitude: The Source of Sin

R' Yonason Eibeshutz (*Ya'aros Devash,* Part I, *Derush* 15) writes that the source and cause of all sin, as far back as the fall of Adam HaRishon, is ingratitude to G-d.

> Indeed, if a human were not an ingrate he would never transgress any of Hashem's mitzvos; for how could he employ evil schemes against Hashem Who beneficently bestowed upon him knowledge and understanding? How can one repay Him by using this given intelligence for evil thoughts? Hashem gave man speech ... how can one repay with scoffing, slander, lies, flattery, vulgarities, betrayal etc. Thus, one who avoids ingratitude will not easily sin.
>
> This is the meaning of the Midrash (*Shemos Rabbah* 1:8) ... [Pharaoh] was so unappreciative and pretended not to know Yosef, who had actually provided the lifeline for all of Egypt .... And it is this bad attribute that caused Pharaoh to ultimately deny Hashem ... and say, "Who is Hashem that I should obey Him?" Such is the way of those walking in crooked paths, that they eventually deny Hashem.

Ingratitude was apparent already with the first sin recorded in the Torah. Adam accuses his wife Chavah for compelling him to eat from the Tree of Knowledge, contrary to the commandment of Hashem; and in a roundabout way, he also blames the Creator of the world when he says, הָאִשָּׁה אֲשֶׁר נָתַתָּה עִמָּדִי הִוא נָתְנָה לִּי מִן הָעֵץ וָאֹכֵל, *The woman that You gave to be with me, she gave me from the Tree and I ate* (*Bereishis* 3:12). The Gemara (*Avodah Zarah* 5b) calls Adam ungrateful, and *Rashi* comments, "he blames the sin on the gift from Hashem, given to him as a helpmate."

✑§ Different Levels of Gratitude

Some mistakenly believe that the purpose of gratitude is to inform the benefactor that his good deed is indeed recognized and appreciated. The truth is that the obligation to feel and express gratitude applies even when the benefactor is unaware, and extends even to animals, plants and inanimate objects. Furthermore, one's debt of gratitude extends to anyone whose action was beneficial, even if the benefactor intended to harm.

It appears that we can categorize deeds that require gratitude as follows:

1. **When the benefactor acts with the sole intent of benefiting another.** This category includes the deeds of parents and teachers.

2. **When a benefit accrued, even if the act was not done with that intention.** One example of this is found in the Gemara (*Yevamos* 63a):

> R' Chiya's wife frequently aggravated him; nonetheless whenever he found something which she liked, he would put it in his pocket and bring it to her. Rav asked him, "but she aggravates you?" to which he answered, "It is sufficient that women raise our children and save us from sin."

Though he was constantly aggravated by his wife, R' Chiya recognized the benefits of her deeds for their children and household. In all likelihood, his wife had no intention to do it for the good of her husband R' Chiya, yet he felt a need to express his gratitude through gifts, because in reality he did derive benefit from her actions.

Similarly, *Midrash Rabbah* (*Parashah* 22, *Siman* 4) explains why Moshe Rabbeinu delegated the battle with the Midianites to Pinchas, though Hashem had commanded Moshe: וַיִּשְׁלַח אֹתָם מֹשֶׁה ... נְקֹם נִקְמַת בְּנֵי יִשְׂרָאֵל מֵאֵת הַמִּדְיָנִים אֶלֶף לַמַּטֶּה לַצָּבָא אֹתָם וְאֶת פִּינְחָס בֶּן אֶלְעָזָר הַכֹּהֵן לַצָּבָא — *Take vengeance for the Children of Israel against the Midianites .... And Moshe sent them, a thousand from each tribe, them and Pinchas, son of Elazar the Kohen, to the legion* (Bamidbar 31:2,6):

> Hashem said to Moshe, "You should take vengeance yourself, yet you send others?!" But since Moshe benefited from Midian, he thought, "It is not right

that I should persecute those who benefited me."
The parable states: Do not throw a pebble into the
well from which you have drunk.

Moshe escaped the sword of Pharaoh by fleeing to
Midian, where he married his wife and lived for many
years. He refused to go to battle against the Midianites,
even though the benefits he received from their country
were not a result of their intention to benefit him directly.

Whenever a benefit is derived, gratitude is owed to
the benefactor — even if he had no intention to cause any
benefit. The Gemara (*Bava Kamma* 92b) elaborates on this
theme:

> Rava said to Raba bar Mari: What is the source
> for the saying, "Don't throw soil into the well you
> drank from?" He answered, "It is written (*Devarim*
> 23:8), לֹא תְתַעֵב אֲדֹמִי כִּי אָחִיךָ הוּא לֹא תְתַעֵב מִצְרִי כִּי גֵר
> הָיִיתָ בְאַרְצוֹ, *You shall not detest an Edomite for he is your*
> *brother; you shall not detest an Egyptian for you lived in*
> *his land.*"

Rashi comments that even though the Egyptians killed
all the Jewish male newborn, it is forbidden to detest them
because they had allowed our forefathers to live in their
land during the great famine in Canaan. Even if the benefactor actually intended harm, but simultaneously also
provided him with some benefits, the recipient is bound
by a debt of gratitude.

**3. An action results in benefiting another person, with
neither the intent nor knowledge of the actor.**

The Torah describes Reuven rescuing Yosef from his
brothers (*Bereishis* 37:21): וַיִּשְׁמַע רְאוּבֵן וַיַּצִּלֵהוּ מִיָּדָם וַיֹּאמֶר לֹא
נַכֶּנּוּ נָפֶשׁ, *Reuven heard, and he rescued him from their hand,*
saying, "We will not strike him mortally." Bereishis Rabbah
(84:15) notes that when Reuven had been cursed by his

father for interfering in the relations with his wives, he felt that he was a pariah in the family:

> Reuven said ... "I thought that I would be banished because of that episode, yet he [Yosef] counts me among his brothers, as it says: וְאַחַד עָשָׂר כּוֹכָבִים מִשְׁתַּחֲוִים לִי, *and eleven stars were bowing down to me* (*Bereishis* 37:9), and I won't save him?!" *HaKadosh Baruch Hu* said to him: "You were the first to save people; I promise that the initial apportioning of 'cities of refuge' will be in your territory."

In *Sichos Mussar*, R' Chaim Shmulevitz elaborates on this *Midrash*:

> When the tribes judged Yosef to the death penalty, their judgment was in accordance with the law, and even Reuven agreed with the verdict. Though he did not retract from this verdict, after further contemplation, Reuven saw it as his obligation to save Yosef because of his sense of gratitude to Yosef.
>
> We have to examine Reuven's debt of gratitude to Yosef. What exactly was the good deed that Yosef did? There was nothing more than a dream, and the essence of the dream glorified Yosef, yet incidentally the dream revealed that Reuven would not be excluded because of the episode and was counted as an equal amongst his brothers.

Yosef did not intend to do anything for Reuven's benefit. Yosef was just telling a dream, and in telling the dream he made Reuven feel accepted. For this inadvertent favor Reuven felt he owes gratitude to Yosef.

4. An indirect beneficial outcome resulting from an unknown "benefactor" who did not intend to do a favor.

The Torah tells us that Moshe helped Yisro's daughters

water the sheep and defended them from the shepherds who were trying to chase them away. When they returned home earlier than usual, their father wondered why they returned early, and their response was, אִישׁ מִצְרִי הִצִּילָנוּ מִיַּד הָרֹעִים וְגַם דָּלֹה דָלָה לָנוּ וַיַּשְׁקְ אֶת הַצֹּאן, *An Egyptian man saved us from the shepherds and he even drew water for us and watered the sheep* (*Shemos* 2:19).

Midrash Rabbah (*Shemos* 1:32) offers several explanations why they referred to Moshe as an "Egyptian man" — and one of those is:

> [This can be answered with] a parable: Bitten by a wild ass, a man ran to soak his [wounded] feet in the water. As he stepped into the river, he saw a child drowning and he rescued him. The child said to him, "Were it not for you I would already be dead." He answered, "I didn't save you; the wild ass that bit me, causing me to flee, saved you." Similarly, Yisro's daughters thanked Moshe for saving them from the shepherds. Moshe replied, "That Egyptian man that I killed — he saved you." So they told their father, אִישׁ מִצְרִי הִצִּילָנוּ, *An Egyptian man saved us,* meaning, who caused him to come to us? — the Egyptian man that he had killed.

Moshe Rabbeinu tells Yisro's daughters that they should thank the wicked Egyptian that Moshe had killed and buried, because this act forced him to flee to Midian. That evil Egyptian, who had been beating the Hebrew slave when Moshe accosted him, certainly had no intention of doing anything beneficial; he did not know Yisro's daughters, yet deserved recognition because of the indirect benefit accrued through his wickedness.

5. An act done with evil intentions that results in a benefit.

R' Chaim Shmulevitz writes in *Sichos Mussar* that

Moshe was concerned about doing battle with Og, the king of Bashan, because of the "favor" he did for Avraham, informing him of his nephew Lot's capture. According to the *Midrash* (cf. *Tosafos, Niddah* 61a), Og lured Avraham into a war with the hope that he would be killed so Og could marry Sarah.

When Og and his entire nation went to wage war against Israel, it is written (*Bamidbar* 21:34), וַיֹּאמֶר ה' אֶל מֹשֶׁה אַל תִּירָא אֹתוֹ, *Hashem said to Moshe, "Do not fear him."* *Rashi* comments as follows, "For Moshe was afraid to wage war lest the merit of Avraham will protect Og."

Though Og's intention was to get Avraham killed, Moshe was fearful because of the unintended beneficial result of Og's action, namely the rescue of Lot.

6. Gratitude to inanimate objects. A person is obligated to have a sense of gratitude to inanimate objects even though it makes no difference to these objects.

We already mentioned that our Sages indicated it is forbidden to throw earth into a well that one drank from, because it is an expression of ingratitude. A similar idea is found in *Rashi,* who notes that the first round of plagues brought upon the Egyptians were orchestrated by Aharon, not Moshe:

> ... the river protected Moshe when he was cast into it, and so it was not smitten through his hand, neither for the [plague of] blood nor for the frogs (comment to *Shemos* 7:19).

In a similar vein, *Rashi* writes that the plague of lice was brought about by Aharon :

> The sand did not deserve to be stricken by Moshe because it protected him when he killed the Egyptian [taskmaster] and hid him in the sand, therefore it was stricken by Aharon (ibid. 8:12).

Although neither sand nor water comprehend or feel the pain, Moshe's sense of gratitude prevented him from "hurting" them.

R' Eliyahu Dessler in *Michtav Me'Eliyahu* (Vol. 3, p. 101) writes a fascinating explanation for the need to be thankful even to inanimate objects:

> All mental attributes are influenced and activated by the emotion and not by intellect alone. Therefore, if we do not feel a sense of gratitude to an inanimate object from which we benefited, and furthermore we treat it with disdain, our sensibilities are damaged ... and therefore the attribute of gratitude is hindered.

Defying common sense, the expression of gratitude even to an inanimate object impacts an individual's moral development and character.

The *Shitah Mekubetzes* (*Bava Kamma* 92b) writes that when R' Yosef ibn Migash was sick he used a wealthy Jew's bathhouse. Years later, when that person lost his fortune, R' Yosef refused to adjudicate the sale of the bathhouse to pay the debts, saying:

> I will not judge or comment on this bathhouse, neither with its sale nor its evaluation nor with anything that is connected with it, because I benefited from it.

The *Shitah Mekubetzes* adds, "And if this is so with an inanimate object that has no feeling, how much more so with people who feel pain and pleasure."

R' Yisrael Ze'ev Gustman *zt"l*, the Rosh Yeshivah of Netzach Yisrael, always tended and watered the bushes in the yeshivah's courtyard, explaining that he is doing it himself as an expression of gratitude. He continued to tell his students that during the Holocaust he escaped the Germans' search by hiding behind the bushes, and therefore he waters and prunes them to express his gratitude.

✎§ Kindness and Not Merit

To summarize, gratitude entails awareness that some good has been graciously derived — and is not earned. An ingrate either does not recognize the benefit he received, or thinks that he merits and deserves it. A person who feels that he is "entitled" views the benefits and kindness bestowed on him as something that is "owed." Such a person does not feel a sense of gratitude toward his parents, because everything they did for him was perfectly normal and owed to him as a son. This person is also unlikely to recognize the goodness of the Creator that is bestowed on him every moment of every day.

The fact that one wakes up every morning, can breathe and walk, are not to be taken for granted as natural occurrences "owed" to every human being. The ingrate feels no need or obligation to express any gratitude to his Creator. R' Yonason Eibeschutz in *Ya'aros Devash* (Part 1, *Derush* 15) explains that arrogance is the root cause of ingratitude:

> The truth is that the attribute of ungratefulness is also an outcome of the trait of arrogance. For the haughty cannot admit that he received some benefit from another, and must believe in his heart that he needs no one, attributing his achievements to his own wisdom and strength.

✎§ What Does a Good Guest Say?

The Gemara (*Berachos* 58a) differentiates between good and bad guests:

> What does a good guest say? "How much trouble has the host taken for me, how much meat has he brought for me, how much wine has he brought for me, how many cakes has he brought for me, and all his efforts were only for me!" But what does a bad guest say? "How little did my host exert himself?! I have eaten only one slice of bread,

one piece [of meat] have I eaten, I drank one glass of wine, all of the host's efforts are only for his wife and children."

An ingrate minimizes the benefits he receives, and will always find reasons to be unthankful. R' Avigdor HaLevi Nebenzahl *shlita* (*Sichos L'Parashas Shemos*, 5768) interprets this Gemara in an interesting way:

> These words are correct at the level of relations between man and his fellow, but are also true at the level of man and G-d. A good guest in the world of G-d is full of gratitude to Him for all creation, for the high mountains and the hills, for the seas and the rivers, for the animals and the birds, as if the entire world was not created for anyone but him …
>
> A bad guest in the world, what does he say? "G-d created the world for His own honor, not for me, and if I took something from the world for myself, did I deplete anything from G-d? I did not deprive Him of anything. If he wants He can create a thousand worlds like this one to replace what I took." He does not feel the need to thank *HaKadosh Baruch Hu* for the pleasure that he receives in this world.

R' Yisrael Salanter *zt"l* entered an inn and ordered a cup of tea. Upon receiving the hefty bill, he asked the proprietor to explain the high cost, given the fact that the cost of the ingredients — water, tea and sugar — was insignificant. The proprietor smiled and answered: "Rabbi, your logic is true for a cup of tea you drink in your own house. Here, however, you are not paying only for the ingredients, but for all the trappings that surround it — the furniture, the waiters, and all the beautiful paintings on the walls." Reb Yisrael's eyes lit up as he said, "Now I understand why the blessing for a cup of water is שֶׁהַכֹּל נִהְיֶה בִּדְבָרוֹ, *through Whose word everything* came to be. Why do we bless Him for everything, instead of blessing Him for giving us water? Now," said Reb Yisrael, "I understand it. The blessing is not just for the cup of water, but also for the 'trimmings' that surround it — the mountains and hills, the seas and rivers, the trees, grass and flowers."

The feeling of gratitude toward another person is a precondition and a precursor for true belief in the Creator and the gratitude we owe Him. Conversely, an ingrate cannot be a true believer in G-d. All a person has to do is to look around and realize that he owes a great deal of gratitude to many of the people surrounding him, as he probably benefited from them directly or indirectly, intentionally or unintentionally. Once a person realizes his great debt of gratitude, his behavior toward others will change, and his belief in G-d will be strengthened.

27

Friendship

O ne of the side effects of the ongoing revolution in technology and digital communication is the large number of "friends" that people now possess. The term "friend" had held profound emotive meaning for generations, and it has recently been emptied of most meaning. For many — especially the young — a friend may be someone they've never met, who remains essentially anonymous and amorphous. This is especially true for those using wireless communication devices which enable contact with hundreds or even thousands of virtual "friends" by the push of a button. Even for those who do not have virtual friends, the term "friend" may include any acquaintance they meet rarely or conversed with once or twice. As a result, many people do not hesitate to enumerate hundreds or even thousands as their friends.

In this chapter we will try to examine the real meaning of friendship, and its importance in Jewish thought and life.

◄§ Real Friends

I was privileged to grow up in a home where the term "friend" was not abstract, and applied to a deep and binding relationship between people. Having precious little family after the devastation of the Holocaust, we found support and community among friends, who proved their mettle and value during good times and bad.

My mother, *a"h*, a concentration camp survivor who had lost most of her family, was diagnosed with cancer when she was forty-five years old. We were two children at home; my younger brother was only three at the time and I was sixteen. For three long years my mother fought this cursed illness until she returned her pure soul to the Creator. During those three years I learned the real meaning of friendship. Ten of my mother's friends, all working women, chose to give up a day of work in a rotation of ten days to be at her bedside, enabling my father to continue working to support the family. My younger brother was cared for with unrestricted love and warmth by these families. When chemotherapy was required three times a week, a distantly related friend left his Tel Aviv business, travelled to Bnei Brak to drive her to the hospital in Tel Aviv, and following the treatment returned her home.

A month before her passing, my mother spoke to me about her friends and how grateful she was for their loyalty and steadfastness. Then she looked into my eyes and said:

> There are many people that are pleasant to talk to and a joy to be in their company, but do not be mistaken to think that all are your friends. Many of them will disappear at critical times, and will not even dip a finger into cold water for you. A person has only a few genuine friends and usually you can count them on just one hand. I have been blessed with several genuine friends that do their utmost with a full heart and a willing soul to help all of us during these difficult times.

My father was also surrounded by real friends, who proved their friendship when he fell ill many years later. During one hospital stay, the medical director approached him and remarked, "I have never seen a Holocaust survivor with so many family members." My father was astonished to hear the doctor's comments, and explained that he was the sole survivor among eleven siblings, and of his large extended family a mere three cousins escaped. Surprised, the doctor explained that seeing the stream of daily visitors and the concern they demonstrated — much beyond what he observed among friends — he assumed that they were family members.

◈§ Importance of Friendship

The value of friendship is emphasized throughout Judaic writings. Indeed, there are several synonyms for the word, each connoting a difference level or aspect of relations of trust and collaboration. In *Pirkei Avos* there are three *Mishnayos* that deal with friendship employing the term *chaver*:

יְהוֹשֻׁעַ בֶּן פְּרַחְיָה אוֹמֵר: עֲשֵׂה לְךָ רַב, וּקְנֵה לְךָ חָבֵר, וֶהֱוֵי דָן אֶת כָּל הָאָדָם לְכַף זְכוּת.

Yehoshua ben Perachya says: Make for yourself a teacher, acquire for yourself a friend, and judge every person favorably (1:6).

צְאוּ וּרְאוּ אֵיזוֹ הִיא דֶּרֶךְ טוֹבָה שֶׁיִּדְבַּק בָּהּ הָאָדָם. רַבִּי אֱלִיעֶזֶר אוֹמֵר: עַיִן טוֹבָה. רַבִּי יְהוֹשֻׁעַ אוֹמֵר: חָבֵר טוֹב.

Go and see the right way to which one should cling. R' Eliezer says: A good eye. R' Yehoshua says: A good friend (2:13).

רַבִּי אֶלְעָזָר בֶּן שַׁמּוּעַ אוֹמֵר: יְהִי כְבוֹד תַּלְמִידְךָ חָבִיב עָלֶיךָ כְּשֶׁלָּךְ, וּכְבוֹד חֲבֵרְךָ כְּמוֹרָא רַבָּךְ, וּמוֹרָא רַבָּךְ כְּמוֹרָא שָׁמָיִם.

R' Elazar ben Shammua says: Let your student's honor be as precious to you as your own; let your friend's honor be like the reverence due to your teacher; and let the reverence you have for your teacher be like the reverence due to Heaven (4:15).

Indeed, the famous episode of Hillel the Elder exemplifies the importance of friendship in Judaic thought and life. The Gemara (*Shabbos* 31a) relates that both Shammai and Hillel confronted the strange request of a non-Jew demanding to be converted as quickly as possible. While Shammai curtly rejected and ejected the non-Jew, Hillel approached him more gently, guiding him in the core principle of Torah:

That which is hateful to you do not do to your friend. That is the whole Torah and all the rest is commentary, go and learn.

The commentators explain that the source of Hillel's answer is a mitzvah in the Torah: וְאָהַבְתָּ לְרֵעֲךָ כָּמוֹךָ, *Love your fellow as yourself* (*Vayikra* 19:18). Given Hillel's answer, it appears that this is the heart of Judaism, and that it is impossible to start to even conceive of being a genuine Jew without comprehending the concept of "friend" and love of your fellow.

A careful reading of the first Mishnah cited above highlights the language used for the procurement of a friend as opposed to procuring a teacher. When referring to a teacher the Mishnah uses "*make* for yourself," but for a friend the language used is "*acquire* for yourself." The variance in language requires explanation, as does the meaning of "friend" as used in this context.

✎§ Definition of a Friend: The Good vs. the Bad

Avos DeR' Nosson (Chapter 18) describes the way friends should behave one to the other:

> And who is the friend of whom the Sages speak everywhere? One whose opinion is valued by the other; [and therefore] they eat and drink as one, and converse with each other and reveal their secrets. Of them it says, טוֹבִים הַשְּׁנַיִם מִן הָאֶחָד, *Two are better than one* (*Koheles* 4:9).

The first condition for genuine friendship is the trust and esteem that they share, such that one's opinion is appreciated by the other. As a result, there is a pronounced openness between the two, as well as shared experiences, bonding them in friendship.

Orchos Tzaddikim (*Sha'ar HaAhavah*) explains the difference between a good friend whose association one should seek, and a bad friend who should be avoided:

> Acquire for yourself a friend that chastises you when your

actions are improper and who teaches you to do good and who helps you both spiritually and financially; this is the trustworthy friend. But the friend that flatters and justifies your errors and mistakes and consoles you on improper actions, remove yourself from him. Likewise a friend that takes from you his own needs and would seriously hurt you or cause you damage for some insignificant pleasure, quickly disassociate from him.

The influence of a friend can be constructive and uplifting or, Heaven forbid, the opposite — destructive and degrading. The destructive "friend" is not a real friend, despite his wit and flattery and the fleeting pleasure of his company, and, in the words of *Orchos Tzaddikim*, "quickly disassociate from him."

When I was a yeshivah student, the Gerrer Rebbe *zt"l* frequently inquired who my friends were, and repeatedly warned me to make sure that I have good friends. The huge impact that a friend has is the core of the *Sfas Emes's* explanation of this Mishnah:

עֲשֵׂה לְךָ רַב, וּקְנֵה לְךָ חָבֵר, *Make for yourself a Rav, acquire for yourself a friend*: The simple explanation is that one needs to expend greater effort to acquire a friend than for submitting to the authority of a Rav [or teacher], because he can gain and grow much more from a friend than from a Rav.

Magen Avos by the *Rashbatz* provides an acute insight on the religious meaning of friendship:

וּקְנֵה לְךָ חָבֵר, *And acquire for yourself a friend:* The reason for this cautionary advice is because one needs friends in order to fulfill the Torah, as it says in *Pirkei De R' Nosson* (51): [If] one transgresses a commandment, and has another to warn him, then it says, טוֹבִים הַשְּׁנַיִם מִן הָאֶחָד, *Two are better than one ...* כִּי אִם יִפֹּלוּ הָאֶחָד יָקִים אֶת חֲבֵרוֹ, *for should they fall, one can lift the other* (*Koheles* 4:9,10). It also states there, שְׁנַיִם שֶׁיוֹשְׁבִין ... שְׁכִינָה שְׁרוּיָה בֵּינֵיהֶם, *Two sitting together ... the Divine Presence is between them* (*Avos* 3:3); and further in *Avodah Zarah* (16b), "Between me and from you this teaching will be clarified," and further it says in *Taanis* (23a) … "Friendship or death" …. A person needs someone who loves him, whom he can trust and take his advice and accept his rebuke should his inclination lead him astray to sin. Therefore he has to acquire him and make every effort until he obtains him (Comment to *Pirkei Avos* 1:6).

According to the *Rashbatz,* a good friend will help one in fulfilling mitzvos, by guiding and encouraging him to do the right thing, and cajoling him to avoid transgression. Furthermore, the give and take between friends learning Torah together helps both crystalize and clarify issues. Moreover, a true friend will consult and provide constructive criticism, and take risks to save his friend, even if in so doing he may incur financial or emotional costs. Such a friend, says the *Mirkeves HaMishneh,* "is difficult to find."

✑ Real Friendship: Two that Are One

Rambam, in his commentary to the Mishnah cited above, adds an interesting dimension to the term "friend":

> When you befriend someone, do not do so according to your own character but do so according to your friend's character. When both friends adhere to this instruction, each should strive to complement the will of his friend, as together they intend undoubtedly to attain the same goal. How apt is Aristotle's adage: "a friend — another who is you."

The real friend empathizes with the troubles of his fellow, senses his pain, understands his struggles, and is happy in his friend's happiness as if it were his own. While real friends are not identical, they complete and bring out the best in each other, and are thus united in their mutual reliance on each other. The *Rambam* suggests three differing types of friendship:

1. "Beneficial Friend": describes the interdependent utilitarian relationship found between two business partners, or a commander and his soldiers. Such a friendship is formed and sustained for specific objectives, and each party derives benefit from the association.

2. "Pleasant Friend": describes a relationship that provides mutual emotional satisfaction and confidence, as the *Rambam* describes:

   > A person needs a friend whom he can trust, from whom he need not conceal anything, neither in deed nor speech, and can reveal all his matters, both the pleasant and the unpleasant, without any misgiving that this may lead to any loss .... [In attaining] this level of confidence in a person, he will find much pleasure in conversing with him and in his companionship.

3. "Elevating Friend": describes a relationship based on a shared goal — bringing out the best in one another — as the *Rambam* writes:

   > Their mutual joy and intent is for one objective, namely, the good; and each one wants to help his friend in attaining the good they both aspire to. This is the friend that one is commanded to acquire, and is comparable to the mutuality between a mentor and his protégé.

The "elevating" friendship includes all the components of the "pleasant" friendship, but surpasses it because both aspire to the same exalted goal — moral improvement. It is extremely difficult for a person to perfect his character and behavior without a good friend who supports good deeds, but also provides constructive criticism. Such a friendship provides a safety net for both parties and imparts emotional and spiritual security. This type of friendship provides a high-level bond between people and is difficult to attain.

ৰ্হ Iyov and His Friends

The Book of *Iyov* provides a description of a profound bond of friendship of the kind praised by the *Rambam*. Having heard of all of his troubles and sufferings, Iyov's friends come to console and commiserate with him:

וַיִּשְׁמְעוּ שְׁלֹשֶׁת רֵעֵי אִיּוֹב אֵת כָּל הָרָעָה הַזֹּאת הַבָּאָה עָלָיו וַיָּבֹאוּ
אִישׁ מִמְּקֹמוֹ אֱלִיפַז הַתֵּימָנִי וּבִלְדַּד הַשּׁוּחִי וְצוֹפַר הַנַּעֲמָתִי וַיִּוָּעֲדוּ יַחְדָּו
לָבוֹא לָנוּד לוֹ וּלְנַחֲמוֹ.

Iyov's three friends heard about this catastrophe that came upon him and each came from his own place: Eliphaz the Temenite, Bildad the Shuchite and Zophar the Na'amatite; for they gathered together to mourn with him and comfort him (Iyov 2:11).

Yalkut Shimoni (*Iyov* 893) explains how these men, who lived so far from one another, and lacked any means of communicating with each other, all heard of Iyov's calamity, and assembled at the same time to visit their suffering friend:

It is known that between each was a distance of 300 *parsos*, from where did they know of Job's troubles? Some say that they had a garland made from flowers, and others say they had trees — and because these wilted they knew. Rava said, "This is why people say: '[Give me] a friend like the friends of Iyov, or [give me] death.'"

Iyov's three friends lived a great distance from Iyov's home and from one another. As each commenced on his journey, he had no inkling that the others were coming too, yet they all assembled at the same time, entering the town through the same gate. They all came with one objective — to support their friend Iyov. Their friendship was so deep and meaningful, that each one felt Iyov's pain and came to help him. They understood from the wilting of the flowers or the trees that a tragedy occurred, and they intended single-mindedly to come to his assistance. This was the kind of friendship that aroused the Sages' envy.

It is told that the revered *tzaddik*, R' Moshe Leib of Sassov, once encountered two drunks at an inn imbibing copious amounts of liquor:

Warmed by his drink, one said to his comrade, "Know that you have no better friend than I!"

The second drunk responded, "How can you say that you are my best friend if you don't know what I am missing?"

Reb Moshe Leib said, "They taught me a great secret: a real friend knows what his counterpart is missing and concerns himself to fulfill it for him."

To summarize, friendship is a complex construct, and true friends are rare. To be a friend requires complete identification with one's fellow and a readiness to make sacrifices on his behalf. A true friend anticipates needs, is sensitive to his friend's difficulties, and rejoices in his friend's success as if it were his own. True friends do not take each other for granted.

It is clear that in order to obtain a true and worthy friend, and to be a worthy friend, one has to invest a great deal of time and effort. It is a long process and there are no shortcuts. Words alone do not create true friendships: empathy and genuine concern, willingness to sacrifice, desire for mutual growth and true love of the other person are all basic ingredients in establishing a true and meaningful friendship. The basis for true friendship is not compassion or mercy, but comes from the ability to identify with another in various situations over an extended period of time.

◄§ Acquiring a Friend

The language of the Mishnah, עֲשֵׂה לְךָ רַב, וּקְנֵה לְךָ חָבֵר, *Make for yourself a teacher (Rav), acquire for yourself a friend*, begs an explanation. The first phrase is a demand to designate a Rabbi who can answer halachic questions and provide guidance in making life's choices in accordance with Torah values. *Chazal* warn us (*Eruvin* 6b) that a person cannot "shop" among various Rabbis for a desired response, but needs to consistently follow his one spiritual teacher.

The second phrase, however, needs clarification, as the term "acquire" implies that one can buy a true friend. The *Rambam* in his commentary to the Mishnah indicates that the verb connotes that genuine friendship entails costs of time and effort:

> This is expressed in the language of *acquire* and not "make" for yourself a friend, or join a group of friends, etc. to express the intention that one should acquire at any cost a friend who will correct him in all matters, as it says, "either a friend or death"; and if he did not find one easily, he must make the necessary efforts to procure one, even by accommodating himself to the other person until this is achieved.

According to the *Rambam* the word "acquire" indicates that one should do whatever it takes, even if this demands a financial or mental effort, and even if it necessitates undertaking actions to please the other person and draw him near to you. Hence, to acquire a good friend, one must also be a good friend.

In the second Mishnah (*Avos* 2:13) cited earlier, R' Yochanan ben Zakai gathered his students and asked them to look for the most important attribute which encompasses most other positive character traits. R' Yehoshua's response — "a good friend" — won the praise of his teacher for it encompasses all of the other fine attributes that are hallmarks of good character. However, this response begs further explanation since choosing a good friend is not an inherent personality trait like the others cited in the Mishnah, such as a "good heart" or a "good eye," and is dependent on others.

Several commentators resolve this difficulty by explaining that the intent of the Mishnah is to teach a person to be a good friend, rather than to seek a good friend. Such is the position of the *Sfas Emes* and also of the *Mirkeves HaMishneh*, who explains that "acquiring a friend" is actually a directive "that he himself should be a friend to others and guide them on the straight path, and this is the meaning of וְאָהַבְתָּ לְרֵעֲךָ כָּמוֹךָ, *you shall love your fellow as yourself* (*Vayikra* 19:18)." That is also the position of *Pirkei Moshe*:

> The best path is that a person should be a good friend to all, for one who has a good temperament and disposition, with which he can obtain virtuous good characteristics, will be a good friend to all people .... Therefore it says a "good friend" to indicate that the best path [in life] that a person should cling to is to be a good friend to another.

Accordingly, R' Yehoshua chose "good friend" as the penultimate virtuous path in life for it entails the manifestation of many other attributes, such as a good eye and good heart.

⏤§ The Respect of a Friend and the Respect of Heaven

The third Mishnah in *Avos* that refers to friendship deals with the respect that a person is obliged to accord to his friend: וּכְבוֹד חֲבֵרְךָ כְּמוֹרָא רַבָּךְ, וּמוֹרָא רַבָּךְ כְּמוֹרָא שָׁמָיִם, *Let your friend's honor be like the reverence due to your teacher, and let the reverence you have for your teacher be like the reverence due to Heaven* (*Avos* 4:15). This equation is stunning! The implication of this Mishnah is that honoring one's friend is either a prerequisite to becoming G-d-fearing, or is comparable to the awe due to the Almighty. While the comparison of a good friend to a teacher is understandable in light of the *Sfas Emes's* assertion that a friend's influence can override that of a teacher's, the comparison of the obligation to respect a human being to the respect accorded to the Almighty is not nearly so understandable.

Real friendship is compared to reverence for G-d, in that both require humility and the willingness to submit one's ego and selfish needs for a higher purpose. A real friend is prepared to relinquish his rights for the benefit of his friend, and is prepared to understand that there are others who should be at the center of his universe. These are equivalent to the foundations of genuine faith in the Creator of the world. A faithful relationship with the Almighty requires submission and abnegation of independence for the higher power. It follows then that a person who is capable of being a true friend also has the capability of being a genuine believer in the Creator of the world, to recognize all the good He bestows, while submitting to His Will.

◆§ Manifestation of Friendship

The following story from *Otzer HaMidrashim* provides an apt conclusion and example of the manifestation of real friendship.

There were two people who abundantly loved each other such that their souls were bound to each other, though — due to war — they had become separated and lived in different kingdoms. When one traveled to visit his friend, he was suspected of being a spy for the rival country, and was brought before the king, who condemned him to death. Unable to persuade the king of his innocence, he fell at his feet and pleaded with him for one last favor.

The king asked, "What may that be?" He told him, "Your majesty, I was a great merchant and I gave most of my merchandise to people on trust and did not write any promissory notes. My wife and sons do not know about this, and if I die without informing them and write proper notes of the debt, they will remain complete indigents. Please let me go to do this and I promise to return." The king said, "And who can believe that you will return?!" He replied, "My lord, my friend who resides in this town will be my guarantor."

The king said to the friend, "Will you guarantee that if your friend does not return before the appointed time you will die instead?" He said, "Yes, my lord, I will guarantee for him — my soul for his soul." The king said, "Upon my life, I wish to see this great thing," and he released the prisoner on condition he return in one month.

On the last day of the month the king awaited the return of the prisoner all day long, and as the sun set he commanded that the friend, who was held as ransom in the prison, be executed. As they took the friend to the town square, and prepared to behead him, a commotion ensued and someone yelled, "Here is the right man!" Seeing his friend prepared to die for him, he rushed toward him, lifted him from the block, and placed his neck under the sword. But his friend did the same, crying, "I will die in your place."

Marveling at the sight of such mutual dedication, the king commanded that they remove both from the execution platform. He pardoned them and gave them great treasures, saying, "Since you displayed such strong love between you, please make me your third friend."

28

Verbal Oppression

The Torah prohibits behaviors that aggrieve others, whether through business deception or through verbal abuse. In *Vayikra* the Torah warns against fraudulent behavior in monetary transactions: וְכִי תִמְכְּרוּ מִמְכָּר לַעֲמִיתֶךָ אוֹ קָנֹה מִיַּד עֲמִיתֶךָ אַל תּוֹנוּ אִישׁ אֶת אָחִיו, *When you make a sale to your fellow or make a purchase from the hand of your fellow, do not aggrieve* (תּוֹנוּ) *one another* (25:14). Immediately thereafter, the Torah uses the same verb: וְלֹא תּוֹנוּ אִישׁ אֶת עֲמִיתוֹ וְיָרֵאתָ מֵאֱלֹקֶיךָ כִּי אֲנִי ה' אֱלֹקֵיכֶם, *Do not aggrieve one another, and you shall have fear of your G-d, for I am Hashem your G-d* (ibid., v. 17), referring to other forms of verbal abuse.

Malbim and R' S. R. Hirsch explain that the root of the verb תּוֹנוּ signifies the exploitation of naiveté or ignorance of another for personal gain or amusement, and has no equivalent in English. In this chapter we will examine the prohibition of verbal abuse, and the elements common to it and monetary fraud.

Rashi (*Vayikra* 25:17) explains the prohibition of aggrieving one another through verbal abuse:

> The Torah warns us about verbal fraud, [which entails]
> that one should not verbally aggravate his fellow, nor give
> him advice that is not appropriate for him .... And if you
> will say, "Who knows if I had bad intentions when I gave

the advice?" That is why it says, וְיָרֵאתָ מֵאֱלֹקֶיךָ, *you shall have fear of your G-d,* for the One Who knows thoughts, He knows your intentions.

The Gemara (*Bava Metzia* 58b) details a number of behaviors that are defined as verbal abuse.

> If he was a repentant (*ba'al teshuvah*), do not say to him "Remember your previous deeds"; if he was descended of converts, do not say to him, "Remember the deeds of your fathers"; if he is a convert and comes to learn Torah, do not say to him, "The mouth that ate prohibited and non-kosher animals, vermin and insects, comes to learn the Torah pronounced by the mouth of the Almighty?!"

The Gemara proceeds to describe the various manifestations of this prohibition, which include malicious teasing, expression of hurtful words, and providing misleading directions to a stranger, as well as examining and bargaining for goods that one has no intention of buying.

The *Torah Temimah* (*Vayikra* 25 note 105) explains that the thread common to the multiple examples cited in the Gemara is that the behavior misleads or hurts someone while feigning concern for his benefit. Disguising the real intent is at the core of the prohibition of verbal abuse:

> It is written in the *Korban Aharon* that all of these apply only when said as "constructive criticism"; if not, then it is not verbal abuse, but rather blasphemy and defamation.

Direct insults and harsh words are considered "blasphemy and defamation" and not verbal abuse. Hurting, mocking or degrading someone intentionally under the guise of reprimand, guidance, flattery or friendship is considered אוֹנָאַת דְּבָרִים, verbal abuse, particularly when the victim is helpless.

The examples that the Gemara presents for "verbal aggrieving" include various behaviors which can be classified as follows:

1. **Indirectly humiliating someone.** In this instance, the purpose of the speech is to degrade another human being, under the pretext that he has his best interest at heart. For example, a person who for no apparent reason says to a repentant (*ba'al teshuvah*), "I thank G-d for giving you the wisdom to repent." While pretending to care about the other, the real purpose is to belittle him by reminding him of his past. This category also includes humiliating someone by asking him a question when it is clear that the person being asked cannot answer the question.

2. **One who justifies another's suffering.** This includes false comfort offered to someone who is suffering greatly (such as, grieving at the loss of a loved one, or through a severe disease), by telling the sufferer that his pain is a consequence of his sins. Such statements, disguised as pious platitudes, may reflect a desire to hurt and shame.

3. **One who leads his friend astray under the guise of helping him.** This category includes giving a stranger wrong directions, or directing someone to buy an item at a shop that does not carry such an item. The *Shulchan Aruch* includes in this category going into a store and giving the shopkeeper the false impression that one is seriously considering making a purchase, with no real intention of doing so (*Choshen Mishpat* 228).

The *Maharal* explains that: "The one who is disgraced [through verbal abuse] is viewed by the abuser as 'nothing'" (*Chidushei Aggados, Bava Metzia*, III:22). Underlying verbal abuse and fraud is absolute contempt for the other person, and a complete lack of consideration for the pain and shame caused by words.

The *Sefer HaChinuch* adds that the prohibition does not lie in the intention but in the result of verbal abuse (*Mitzvah* 338). He explains that it is forbidden to say anything unhelpful that can cause another human being pain and distress:

And it is proper to be careful that there should not be even a hint of defamation in his words … it is impossible to detail all the things that can cause distress to people, but everyone has to be careful as much as possible because G-d knows every step and every hint.

The Torah forbids even truthful speech that can shame or mislead. Accordingly, it is quite possible that a seemingly friendly discussion can become a transgression of the prohibition of verbal fraud and abuse. If one of the participants tries to "sweet talk" the other, or provides insincere advice, there is a good chance that his talk will be classified as verbal abuse.

⨋ A Conversation Between Educators

A few years ago, I became aware of a rivalry between two teachers assigned to the same class. They taught the same group of children, though each was assigned a different subject. One was a veteran teacher who was known as a competent, though uninspiring educator. The second one was younger and very charismatic, and soon proved to be extremely popular. The problem for the elder teacher was that he was always compared to the new "star" — and that comparison made him look worse.

One day in the teachers' lounge, as the two were discussing some educational issues impacting the classroom, the elder teacher suggested to his colleague that "for his own good" he should transfer to teach a lower grade, providing various "good reasons" for doing so. The younger teacher refuted all the reasons, claiming that his talents are not suited for lower grades. After more argumentation, the elder teacher declared that he plans to discuss the matter with the principal of the school.

Hearing this exchange, I approached the veteran teacher, who held some influence on programming at the school, to express my dismay. It had become clear to me that the real reason for his argument was the desire to remove the other teacher from his class to avoid the constant comparison between the two of them. When I pointed out that his words may be a transgression of a serious Torah prohibition of "verbal deception," he raised his eyebrows incredulously and dismissed my suggestion, even after I cited several sources detailing the essence of this prohibition.

◆§ Verbal Abuse and Monetary Fraud: The Common Denominator

The Hebrew word for both verbal and monetary fraud is "ona'ah." The Mishnah (*Bava Metzia* 58b) states, "Just as there is fraud in monetary matters so there is fraud in verbal matters." The common denominator between the two is in the resulting pain and damage; the underlying motivations, however, are significantly different: The purpose of monetary fraud is monetary gain, whereas the purpose of verbal abuse and fraud is more subtle: to mislead or cause anguish to another person. We need to understand, therefore, why both actions are given an identical name.

Rabbeinu Yonah in *Iggeres HaTeshuvah* (1:19) and in *Sha'arei Teshuvah* (3) says that the root meaning of the word *ona'ah* is "anguish":

> It is forbidden to cause anguish to any Jew whether verbally or commercially, as it says, אַל תּוֹנוּ אִישׁ אֶת אָחִיו, *do not aggrieve one another* (*Vayikra* 25:14), and our Rabbis have stated that this refers to verbal abuse and oppression .... When the term is not used in the context of monetary transactions, it refers to verbal oppression.

According to Rabbeinu Yonah, the common thread between these two types of fraud is the fact that they cause anguish. R' Samson Raphael Hirsh in his commentary on the Torah (*Vayikra* 25) explains the connection as follows:

> The term *ona'ah* can be defined as exploitation of a weakness of another person for the purpose of hurting him. There is a common factor between monetary deceit and verbal fraud.

In both of them, the perpetrator exploits the weakness of his fellow-man to his detriment, [the weakness is in] his lack of knowing the quality of the merchandise or in his emotional sensitivity ....

The Gemara (*Bava Metzia* 58b) compares the severity of verbal and monetary transgressions:

Verbal fraud is a greater sin than monetary deceit, for it says, וְיָרֵאתָ מֵאֱלֹקֶיךָ, *you shall have fear of your G-d* (*Vayikra* 25:17), whereas concerning this [monetary deceit] it does not say, וְיָרֵאתָ מֵאֱלֹקֶיךָ, *you shall have fear of your G-d*. R' Elazar says: This [verbal abuse] affects his soul and this [monetary deceit] affects only his money. R' Shmuel bar Nachmani said: This [monetary deceit] can be restituted and that cannot be restituted.

The *Gemara* also cites Rebbi's explanation of why the Torah stresses וְיָרֵאתָ מֵאֱלֹקֶיךָ, *you shall have fear of your G-d,* right after forbidding verbal oppression and abuse. Given that the transgression lies in the intent, and can easily be disguised as innocent words intended to help, the Torah reminds us that G-d cannot be deceived and knows the underlying intentions of all verbal expressions. The *Rambam* explains that the Torah warns of Divine retribution particularly in those situations where the violation cannot be adjudicated in a human court.

The evaluation of verbal fraud as a moral abrogation more severe than monetary fraud underscores its corrosive effect on the victim's mind. Moreover, it subtly destroys the social fabric which relies on mutual trust. When someone has been cheated in a business deal, he has legal recourse, and he can present objective evidence to substantiate his claim of damage. The damage done through verbal oppression and fraud is much more elusive and far more enduring. It is better for one to know who loves him and who despises him; and when abuse is disguised as concern and kindness, the victim often loses self-confidence and trust in others.

◈§ Retribution for Verbal Abuse

Our Sages (*Bava Metzia* 59a) warned that G-d is always receptive to the pleas of those victimized by verbal fraud and abuse: "R' Eliezer said: All punishments are delivered through a messenger, except the punishment for oppression …" *Rashi* explains that the Gemara refers here to verbal abuse, and that G-d always listens to these victims and punishes the offenders. The *Sefer HaChinuch* (*Mitzvah* 338) writes, "There are many lashes without a leather strap in the hand of the One Who commands this," to stress that G-d has multiple means of retribution to those who verbally abuse and hurt others.

The *Maharal* explains that G-d Himself exacts retribution for verbal fraud, as its victims have no one to rely on, other than their Father in heaven:

> And more so, because the offender of "verbal fraud" is not "G-d fearing" for if he feared G-d he would think: Though his fellow is lowly, there is a Judge Who executes justice for the exploited and oppressed, because the weak rely on G-d … (*Chidushei Aggados*, ibid.).

The prohibition of verbal oppression extends even when relating to young children, as the *Sefer HaChinuch* writes:

> This commandment applies everywhere and at all times, to males and females and even with minor children. It is appropriate to be careful not to hurt them with words, except as needed to correct them; [this applies] even for his sons, daughters and all his household members. And the one who is lenient with them, avoiding hurting them, will find life, blessing and honor.

It is interesting to note that according to *Sefer HaChinuch* a person is rewarded handsomely with "life, blessing and honor" for not committing a sin, though one usually does not receive reward for refraining from sin. Apparently, extra restraint is required in guarding one's speech with members of one's household.

Special attention is given by our Sages to verbal oppression of one's wife: "Rav said a person must always be careful of oppressing his wife, as her tears flow easily, so retribution is quick" (*Bava Metzia* 59a). *Rashi* explains that this refers to verbal abuse. The *Maharal* in *Chidushei Aggados* (III: 24) writes:

> [The husband] should be especially careful with his wife, because as he rules over her, tears come easily. Verbal abuse of a stranger does not have such an impact ... but the wife who is under the rule of her husband, and yet remains important in her own right, if she suffers anguish from her husband, the impact on her is more pronounced and therefore her tears are more common.

The words of the *Maharal* imply that the greater the dependency of a person upon his fellow man, the greater the obligation to avoid causing distress and pain, since the dependency intensifies the impact of even a small insult.

29

Anger and Forbearance

It is impossible to find a trait that is so berated in the writings of our Sages as the trait of anger. Following are some pointed examples:

> Anyone who becomes angry, all types of *Gehinnom* overtake him .... He who is angry forgets his learning and increases his stupidity (*Nedarim* 22a-b).
>
> He who tears his clothes in fury, breaks vessels in fury, or scatters coins in fury, should be regarded as an idolater (*Shabbos* 105b).

Anger warps logical thinking and leads to judgment errors. Therefore the *Maggid Mesharim* (*Bereishis*) guides R' Yosef Karo as follows:

> Be careful to distance yourself greatly from anger and your words should be said calmly and without a trace of anger, even if some will speak or do things that are befitting anger.

In the same vein, R' Chaim Vital writes that his teacher the *Arizal* avoided anger, including righteous indignation:

> His reasoning was that any other sin blemishes only one limb, while the trait of anger blemishes the entire soul and completely alters it ....

From this we can conclude that the easily-angered person has no remedy … and he cannot attain any [lasting] achievement, even if he be a righteous person in all other ways, because it [anger] destroys whatever he built each time he gets angry (*Shemonah She'arim, Sha'ar Ruach HaKodesh*).

The *Menoras HaMaor* takes it a step further and writes that an angry person causes others to sin:

He who is quick to anger, is responsible for his own sins and the sins of others; his iniquity is great and his punishment is also great, as it says, אִישׁ אַף יְגָרֶה מָדוֹן וּבַעַל חֵמָה רַב פָּשַׁע, *A man of anger will incite strife and a man of wrath is full of offense* (*Mishlei* 29:22). Whoever is easily angered causes contention and causes souls of Israel to be killed …. And anger is one of twenty-four things that prevent repentance (Chapter 15).

The *Orchos Tzaddikim* (*Sha'ar* 12) succinctly summarizes the damage anger causes to himself and others:

Whosoever's anger and fury are pronounced is not far from insanity; and whoever is accustomed to anger, his life is no life and he is never happy. And because he is never happy, he does not accept events in his life with love and happiness … and cannot serve Hashem with happiness.

The consequences of unbridled anger, and the madness that it engenders, have plagued mankind since the beginning of history.

☙ Cain and Hevel: The First Murder

The story of the first murder in history, when Cain killed his brother Hevel, opens with a curious verse that hides more than it reveals: וַיֹּאמֶר קַיִן אֶל הֶבֶל אָחִיו וַיְהִי בִּהְיוֹתָם בַּשָּׂדֶה וַיָּקָם קַיִן אֶל הֶבֶל אָחִיו וַיַּהַרְגֵהוּ, *Cain spoke with his brother Hevel, and it happened when they were in the field that Cain rose up against his brother and killed him* (*Bereishis*

4:8). Our Sages struggled to explain the unwritten contents of the conversation between the brothers that ultimately led to murder (*Bereishis Rabbah* 22:7):

> They said, "Let's divide the world." One took the land and one took all the movable objects. One said, "The ground that you are standing upon is mine," and one said, "That which you are wearing is mine." One said, "Remove your clothes," and one said, "Fly off my ground." Out of this [argument], וַיָּקָם קַיִן אֶל הֶבֶל אָחִיו וַיַּהַרְגֵהוּ, *And Cain rose up against his brother Hevel and killed him* (*Bereishis* 4:8).
>
> R' Yehoshua of Sachnin said in the name of R' Levi: This one said, "The Temple will be built in my portion,"and this one said, "The Temple will be built in my portion"…. Out of this [argument] — וַיָּקָם קַיִן אֶל הֶבֶל, *and Cain rose up against Hevel.*

One may wonder why the Torah relates that Cain spoke to Hevel, without detailing the nature of the conversation that ultimately led to the murder. R' Baruch Mordechai Ezrachi *shlita* writes, that the Torah teaches that the contents of the conversation are unimportant, but the fact that there were words between brothers is critical. Once the argument began — regardless of why — the inevitable quarrel ensued, and tempers flared, and each side became ever more vociferous:

> … as these matters naturally develop, nothing can stop the argument … each insists that he cannot depart from his stance, only his judgment is correct; he is right, and he won't relent …. Such is the beginning of every feud … (*Bircas Mordechai, Bereishis*).

R' Ezrachi explains that it is not the substance of the quarrel, but rather the refusal to back down or remain silent, that allows even a minor dispute to snowball into a major war. The Gemara says: "The world would not exist but for the one who restrains himself at the moment of contention" (*Chullin* 89a).

✑ Is There "Justified" Anger?

Generally the *Rambam* advocates the "golden mean" as the ideal ethic. However, with regard to anger, the *Rambam* does not abide any middle road, and advises that one should "distance himself from it [anger] until the furthest extremity" (*Hilchos Dei'os* 2:2). Even in cases where anger can be rationalized, one should avoid it, "and train himself to become indifferent," to avoid provocation by insults or wrongdoing.

As alluded earlier, anger is forbidden even when it is intended to spur someone to do a mitzvah or to prevent someone from sinning. The *Midrash* (*Vayikra Rabbah, Shemini, 13:1*) counts three instances in which Moshe became angry and as a result forgot the law. In one incident, Moshe was enraged when some Israelites collected too much manna — violating G-d's explicit directive — and as a result Moshe forgot to relay G-d's command to collect a double portion of manna on Fridays. R' Chaim Shmulevitz writes:

> … his wisdom departed from him, not as a punishment for the sin of anger, but rather as a natural occurrence, in that anger "consumes" a person's wisdom; and it matters not that the anger is justified (*Sichos Mussar* 87).

Moshe's fury was "justified," yet wisdom and anger cannot coexist, regardless of the cause of the anger.

✑ Control vs. Prevention of Anger

The American Psychological Association (APA) defines the attribute of anger as follows:

> Anger is a normal human emotion and even healthy. However, when the emotion becomes uncontrollable it becomes a destructive element leading to problems at work, personal relationships and the quality of life.

According to this definition, anger is natural and unavoidable and, at best, needs to be managed. Therapeutic efforts should be directed to "anger management" and not to its prevention.

While Judaic thought may concur with modern psychology on the need to control anger once it is aroused, it differs sharply in the evaluation of anger as an unavoidable, and even healthy, human emotion. On the contrary, as indicated earlier, the *Rambam* insists that anger must be avoided as much as possible, and should not be "managed." *Orchos Tzaddikim* writes that "Anger is an evil trait and just as eczema is a disease of the body so is anger a disease of the soul" (*Sha'ar* 12). One must try to prevent anger just as one would try to prevent physical disease (though it is natural). He continues to explain that for most, anger cannot be modulated:

> Whoever gets angry quickly is better off ignoring and dismissing. He should avoid reacting and remain calm rather than [controlling his anger] by getting "only slightly" angry. It is impossible for such a person to do that — once he gets slightly angry he cannot refrain from developing a great anger.

Anger prevention, not anger management, is therefore the goal.

The *Chofetz Chaim* was very careful to avoid anger and to speak softly and calmly. He was walking in the streets of Radin with one of his students, when a passerby accosted the student. A loud quarrel ensued with that man, with whom the student had had some dispute. Voices were raised, and the passerby insulted and cursed the student in front of his rebbi. Unable to withstand the insults, the student finally gave way to his temper and responded with harsh words.

As they continued on their walk and resumed their conversation, they encountered a large dog barking furiously at them. The student ignored it and continued speaking with his rebbi. The *Chofetz Chaim* turned toward his student and asked, "Why don't you answer the dog?" Surprised, the student replied, "The dog is barking at anyone on the street, and does not mean me at all." The *Chofetz Chaim* told him gently, "Look, my son, why did you respond when the passerby insulted you? If you would have treated his insults like the barking of the dog, you would not have sinned by being angry."

✍️ Humility and Faith Prevent Anger

The *Orchos Tzaddikim* (ibid.) suggests that anger is rooted in arrogance, and a measure of humility can avoid anger. Most anger is a response to an affront to one's ego. Otherwise, what difference does it make if someone spoke to one in an objectionable fashion?! Anger stems from the feeling of personal insult or a degradation of one's honor. The more confident we are in ourselves, the more humble we are, and the less likely we are to become angry.

R' Godel Eisner *zt"l* made an analogy to a feather and lead that are thrown to the floor. The feather flutters and gently and calmly lands, whereas the heavy lead falls quickly and breaks the floor upon reaching it. Similarly, a person who is calm and pleasant to others will be able to withstand a challenge and move along, like the light feather. The heavy and uncompromising person, who is easily insulted and quick to get angry, will in explosive rage break relations with those around him.

Humility and faith in Hashem will prevent anger. A person who believes that whatever happens is from Hashem (good or bad) would not rage at an insult, but would view the insulter as a temporary messenger of Hashem. Obviously, such faith does not absolve the "messenger" from moral responsibility for his behavior; but the believer leaves retribution to G-d. Instead of getting angry, a faithful and humble person should try to understand the message that Hashem sends him, so he can become a better person. Such an approach can avoid anger.

✍️ Slowness to Anger — Master of Emotions

It is written (*Mishlei* 16:32), טוֹב אֶרֶךְ אַפַּיִם מִגִּבּוֹר וּמֹשֵׁל בְּרוּחוֹ מִלֹּכֵד עִיר, *He who is slow to anger is better than the warrior, and a master of* his passions is better than a city's conqueror. Metzudas David explains that "master of his passion" is someone who can conquer his anger. The Malbim and the Rashbatz differentiate between the two parts of the verse: while the first half refers to the strength of one who can control anger once it is aroused, refraining from reaction, the latter half refers to someone who refrains completely from feeling angry, and thus has imposed his will on his passions. In the words of the Malbim:

> טוֹב אֶרֶךְ אַפַּיִם מִגִּבּוֹר, Slow to anger is better than a warrior. The warrior lacks any patience and takes revenge upon his enemies, displays his strength by overpowering his enemy...
>
> But he who is also a master of his passions to subdue his [internal] enemies, avoiding any images of vengeance in his heart, he is better than a conqueror of a city, because the spirit is equivalent to a fortified city full of many soldiers of the old and foolish inclination.

R' Chaim Shmulevitz writes (Sichos Mussar 47) that a person should view a situation that may cause anger as an opportunity to exercise restraint and calm, and thank Hashem for giving him the opportunity to do so.

The Gemara (Eruvin 54b) relates a story of R' Preida, who had a student who was a very slow learner and needed to be taught the same material four hundred times before he grasped it. On one occasion the student lost his concentration, and R' Preida needed to repeat the material eight hundred times before the student grasped it. For this dedication R' Preida was rewarded from heaven — he lived an extra 400 years, and merited the World to Come for himself and his entire generation.

From whence did R' Preida derive his patience? How did R' Preida, a great scholar, sacrifice his own advancement for one student? R' Shmulevitz suggests that R' Preida viewed teaching a slow student as an opportunity to hone his skills of patience and forbearance, so highly valued and rewarded by G-d.

◂§ Self-Control is Wisdom

King Solomon writes, אֶרֶךְ אַפַּיִם רַב תְּבוּנָה וּקְצַר רוּחַ מֵרִים אִוֶּלֶת, *Slowness to anger shows great wisdom but a short-tempered person increases foolishness (Mishlei 14:29). Ibn Ezra* explains that the anger of a short-tempered person transforms small and foolish issues into major ones, while forbearance helps minimize tension and anger. The Gemara (*Gittin* 36b) says:

> Those insulted who refrain from insulting, hear their abuse and do not answer ... about them it is written, וְאֹהֲבָיו כְּצֵאת הַשֶּׁמֶשׁ בִּגְבֻרָתוֹ, *those that love Him are like the rising sun in its might (Shoftim* 5:31).

The *Meiri* (*Beis HaBechirah*) explains the resemblance of one who exhibits such restraint to the rising sun, on the basis of a parable in *Chullin* (60b). Being an equal to the sun as a source of light, the moon complained to the Creator that two kings cannot share a crown. G-d therefore diminished the moon. The sun heard how the moon attempted to undermine, but did not respond. Therefore, the sun was rewarded for its silence and became the primary source of light and warmth. So is the reward of the one who is insulted but refrains from responding in kind, as he is beloved by Hashem and in his silence illuminates the world.

The wisdom of silence is the message that my friend, R' Moshe Wolf, conveys in his role as chaplain of the Chicago Police Force. In his voluntary role, R' Wolf has won the hearts of countless policemen of all faiths and ethnic groups, as a walking *kiddush Hashem*. One of his most memorable lectures at the police academy is entitled, "Not Everything Requires a Response." Many officers recall that lecture, and credit it with saving them in many tense and dangerous situations.

Often, when a policeman stops a driver for a traffic violation, he is subject to verbal abuse and even threats. R' Wolf guides the officers to turn a deaf ear to the insults and curses, telling them, "Write the ticket and say 'Thank you, have a good day' and move on." This is a lesson that should be internalized by everyone.

Many are obsessed with the need to retort immediately to every provocation and insult, feeling that a response is needed in self-protection. Actually, a response — howsoever clever — merely escalates a dispute. We often raise our voices when arguing with someone, unconsciously presuming that we can out-shout a debate or that the disagreement is a result of hearing impairment. In so doing, we actually turn small disagreements into larger quarrels.

◄§ Silence Is Not Always an Admission

When a person is being verbally abused, especially in front of others, the natural tendency is to respond in "self-defense." Remaining silent in the face of defamation or insult may be wrongly interpreted as admission of guilt. After all, the Gemara rules that in monetary disputes "silence is admission." Therefore, *Sefer HaChinuch* (*Mitzvah* 338) writes that under such circumstances one may respond, but only in a calm manner. He notes that there are righteous people who fear that any response (particularly to a false accusation) will arouse their anger, and therefore they opt to refrain from any response; and these are the people compared to כְּצֵאת הַשֶּׁמֶשׁ בִּגְבֻרָתוֹ, *the rising sun in its might*.

The *Chofetz Chaim* warns against drawing conclusions about the innocence or guilt of those who remain silent in the face of verbal abuse:

> There is no permission to believe *lashon hara* even if it is said to the face of the subject of the gossip. Even if he [the victim of the gossip] remains silent, it is not an indication that whatever is said is true. Even if that person is not usually silent in similar situations, his present silence may

be a result of his desire to overcome his natural tendencies and avoid a quarrel ... (*Hilchos Lashon Hara,* Ch. 7, 2).

Restraint in the face of insults, particularly those hurled in public, is not easily attained. But this type of restraint prevents quarrels and quells anger — all of which cause destruction of civilization. Thus, the Gemara (*Chullin* 89a) declares:

> The world would not exist but for he who restrains himself at the moment of contention.

Mesillas Yesharim (Ch. 11) explains that this adage refers to one who has been humiliated, his anger aroused, and yet he finds the strength to remain silent and to refrain from response; but he adds that a person should aspire to even more:

> However, the virtues of Hillel the Elder surpassed all of the above, as he was oblivious to any insults, and even arousal of anger never transpired with him (*Shabbos* 31a).

⮠§ Controlling Anger

While the ultimate goal is avoidance of anger, it is not always attainable — at least in the short term. If overcome by anger, one must control it, avoid inappropriate behavior, and eventually eliminate the anger. *Orchos Tzaddikim* suggests the following steps to control anger:

1. "Silence abolishes anger." If and when anger is aroused, the best a person can do is to not respond. Silence not only prevents inappropriate behavior, but eventually weakens and even terminates the anger.
2. When a response is necessary, use calm talk. "When ... anger is aroused, one should remain silent or speak calmly without raising his voice ... raising the voice at the moment of anger further arouses the anger, but a soft voice and silence quell the anger."

The *Ramban* concurs and advises his son: "Always speak calmly, to every person and at all times, and this will save you from anger that is an evil trait causing people to sin" (*Iggeres HaRamban*).

It is interesting to note that modern psychology has come to similar conclusions. In an article about anger management published by Mayo Clinic, the following suggestions are given:

1. Take a time out — take a deep breath, even a short one, to enable you to calm down.

2. Keep a distance from those who annoy you.

3. Exercise — physical activities can help you relax and calm down.

4. Practice relaxation skills, such as deep breathing, repeating calming words, and imagining relaxing scenes.

5. Think well before you speak, and try to identify solutions to your current situation before speaking.

6. Explain your anger only when you are relaxed and calmed down.

7. Use your sense of humor, which tends to calm and prevents anger.

8. Don't harbor a grudge toward the one who wronged you. It is always good to be forgiving.

✎§ Be Deliberate in Judgment

Among the outcomes of exercising patience and forbearance is the enhancement of decision-making. The ability to withstand external pressure and master one's passions leads to logical and analytical thought, and more accurate judgment. The Gemara (*Eruvin* 13b) says:

> For what reason did Beis Hillel merit that the law followed their method? Because they were calm and humble, and they carefully considered their views as well as those of

Beis Shammai, and even preferred to study Beis Shammai's opinions before their own.

Quoting this Gemara, the *Maharal* concludes:

> A calm person never strays from straight thinking and always remains balanced. It is the opposite for a person who is not calm, and consequently strays from being balanced. For that reason Beis Hillel merited that the law was fixed according to them because they were calm … as he who is impatient because of his great anger, loses his balanced thinking.

The benefits for forbearance are immense. Beyond the Divine reward in both worlds, exercising patience and forbearance allows for clear thinking and good decisions. The quality of our decisions, and their consequences, has a great impact on the quality of a person's life both in the short and long terms.

30

Congenial Speech and a Smiling Face

ffective communication between people involves more than the exchange of words. The meaning of words is affected by various factors including tone, accentuation, facial expressions and hand gestures. Thus, the phrase "give me money" can be modulated to mean a request, a demand or even a threat. Aware of the impact that tone can make, the *Ramban* advised his son to "Make it a habit to always speak calmly, to everyone and at all times. This will rescue you from anger ..." (*Iggeres HaRamban*).

Speaking "calmly" entails many elements, including not raising one's voice, using a pleasant tone while articulating words in a steady pace, maintaining a placid facial expression, and gentle hand movements appropriate to the message. Shlomo HaMelech says: דִּבְרֵי חֲכָמִים בְּנַחַת נִשְׁמָעִים מִזַּעֲקַת מוֹשֵׁל בַּכְּסִילִים, *The gentle words of the wise are heard above the shouts of a ruler over fools* (*Koheles* 9:17). In explaining this verse, the *Alshich* notes that words that are spoken calmly and softly are more likely to be listened to. The *Ramchal* in *Mesillas Yesharim* (Ch. 29) concurs:

> Our Sages said (*Yoma* 86a) that a person's speech should always be congenial with other people .... His words must

be words of respect and not words of disdain, and so it says (*Mishlei* 11:12), בָּז לְרֵעֵהוּ חֲסַר לֵב, *He who derides his friend lacks a heart.*

According to the *Ramchal*, the term "congenial speech" refers to the content of the spoken words. Quite obviously, if the content of the words is degrading, saying them softly and smilingly will not take the sting out of the insult.

The Gemara (*Taanis* 6a) writes that the first rain of the season is called *"Yoreh"* (יוֹרֶה) because it falls gently and not "furiously." *Rashi* notes that the root of the word יוֹרֶה is similar to the Hebrew words "teacher" and "shooting":

> It descends gently, like a person teaching his students gently, as it is written (*Koheles* 9:17), דִּבְרֵי חֲכָמִים בְּנַחַת נִשְׁמָעִים, *The gentle words of the wise are heard.* Another interpretation, it implies a shot arrow which travels straight and does not veer from side to side. Another implication [to the word *yoreh*] is that it is directed to the earth and does not descend with ferocity.

According to *Rashi*, the phrase "gentle words" has three implications, and all are pertinent to effective interpersonal communication:

1) The soft-spoken manner in which the message is delivered.

2) Speech should be delivered with kindly facial expressions, and not with those indicating anger and fury — like the rain that "does not descend with ferocity."

3) Messages should be brief and to the point, like a "shot arrow that travels straight and does not veer from side to side."

Midrash Koheles Rabbah (9:24) adds a fascinating dimension to the verse, דִּבְרֵי חֲכָמִים בְּנַחַת נִשְׁמָעִים, *The gentle words of the wise are heard.* The *Midrash* explains that "gentle speech" was exemplified by Amram and his colleagues among the elders of the Hebrews in Egypt. Upon hearing Pharaoh's decree that all male babies born to the Israelite slaves would be killed, the elders decided in secret consultation to separate from their wives, to foil Pharaoh's evil design. Many of the Israelites adhered to this decision because it was accepted discretely "behind the fence and behind the shutters."

This *Midrash* highlights that it is not only what and how something is said, but also when and where. Advice or critique given gently and privately is more likely to be accepted. Furthermore, the Gemara (*Yoma* 86a) implies that congenial speech is an obligation, not just good advice:

> Abaye said: It is written (*Devarim* 6:5), וְאָהַבְתָּ אֵת ה' אֱלֹקֶיךָ, *You shall love Hashem, your G-d*, implying that the name of Heaven will be endeared by you … that one should be congenial in his dealings with people. What do people say about him? Fortunate is his father who taught him Torah, fortunate is his teacher who taught him Torah …. This person that learned Torah, look how pleasant his ways are, how perfected are his deeds ….

The way a person communicates with others can cause either an endearment or desecration of Hashem's Name.

⋅⋙ Feeding His Father Pheasant

The Gemara (*Kiddushin* 31a-31b) provides wonderful examples of how the context and mode of delivery of a message can change not only the meaning of the spoken word, but the meaning of an action:

> There is a person who feeds his father fattened pheasant, yet will be punished with a hastened death; and there is a person who makes him grind with a millstone, and is rewarded with a share in the World to Come.

Rashi and *Tosafos* explain how an act that seems to dishonor a father is so richly rewarded, while an act that seems like an extravagant honor of one's parent reaps punishment. *Tosafos* cite the *Talmud Yerushalmi* (*Pe'ah* 1) that describes more fully the case at hand:

> There was one who fed his father fattened pheasant. When his father once asked him, "From where do you have all this?" he responded, "Old man, why do you care? Just chew and eat!" .... This [rude answer] revealed how burdensome he is to his son. There was another case of a miller who had an elderly father who was ordered to come and work for the king. The son told him, "You shall grind, and I will go in your place to work for the king."

The son who provides his father with expensive delicacies turns a noble act into an insulting and embarrassing one by his arrogant and humiliating response to his father's question; and therefore, he is swiftly and harshly punished. On the other hand, the son who puts his father to work at the millstone appears to show lack of respect to his father, yet given the circumstances and the explanation, turns this into a noble act which fulfills the commandment to honor one's father; and the son merits eternal life in the World to Come.

✎ A Cheerful Face and an Encouraging Word

Apart from the obligation to speak pleasantly, there is an obligation to relate to every person "with a cheerful face" as directed in *Avos* (1:15):

שַׁמַּאי אוֹמֵר: עֲשֵׂה תוֹרָתְךָ קֶבַע, אֱמוֹר מְעַט וַעֲשֵׂה הַרְבֵּה, וֶהֱוֵי מְקַבֵּל אֶת כָּל הָאָדָם בְּסֵבֶר פָּנִים יָפוֹת.

Shammai says: Make your Torah study a fixed practice, say little and do much, and receive every person with a cheerful face.

The *Rambam* explains the words "cheerful face" to mean "willingness and pleasantness." Facial expression impacts how messages are understood: an angry or dismissive demeanor can radically alter the meaning of sweet words. Conversely, a smile and cheerful look transmits warmth and willingness to accommodate, and can soften the harshest message.

The *Bartenura,* in his commentary on that Mishnah, writes that when receiving a guest, the host should not avoid eye contact, as this will negate whatever good he is doing for that person. This idea is echoed in *Avos DeR' Nosson* (Ch. 23):

> You should receive everybody with a cheerful face. For example, if a person gives his friend a large sum of money and he does not look directly at him, it is as if he gave him nothing.

Unlike the case of a son who speaks to his father in a humiliating way, this case deals with displaying inappropriate facial expressions while doing a charitable deed. Though one has not uttered a word, the facial expression can — regardless of intent — reflect disdain or impatience, and thereby negates the charitable act and the rewards associated with it. Furthermore, a congenial facial expression, particularly when accompanied by a kind and encouraging word, can outweigh a good deed. *Avos DeR' Nosson* (ibid.) writes:

> Even if he gave his friend nothing, but he looked at him, it is as if he gives a large sum of money; and therefore it says, וֶהֱוֵי מְקַבֵּל אֶת כָּל הָאָדָם בְּסֵבֶר פָּנִים יָפוֹת, *receive everybody with a cheerful face."*

The *Rambam* (*Hilchos Matnos Aniyim* 10:4) writes:

> He should give with a benevolent countenance and with joy, and empathize with him over his troubles … and he should speak to him words of compassion and comfort, as it says (*Iyov* 29:13), וְלֵב אַלְמָנָה אַרְנִן, *I would bring joyous song to a widow's heart.*

This ruling of the *Rambam* is based on the Gemara (*Bava Basra* 9b):

> Whoever gives a *prutah* to a pauper is blessed with six

blessings, and the one who calms him with words, is blessed with eleven blessings.

Positive and encouraging words almost double the rewards given for an act of charity.

Such words are further enhanced by the warmth of a smile, the value of which is stressed in the Gemara (*Kesubos* 111b): "R' Yochanan said: Better he that whitens his teeth toward his friend than one who gives him milk to drink." *Rashi* explains that this idiom refers to a smile which reveals one's teeth, and that the Gemara prefers causing someone to smile than any tangible gift. The emotional satisfaction and uplift elicited by a kind word and a warm smile is sometimes more beneficial than providing material satisfaction. Furthermore, this is a gift that should be given to everyone, not just the despondent and the poor. Every person derives pleasure from a bright and warm smile.

The obligation to welcome people with a smile, a cheerful face and encouraging words should not be taken lightly. Obviously, our Sages did not mean an artificial smile or platitudes, as those are not genuine and their falsehood can be detected intuitively. Our Sages intended to foster love and sensitivity among people, and to encourage each person to try to genuinely understand the feelings of the other person and help him as much as possible.

Indeed, elaborating on the Mishnah (*Avos* 1:15), עֲשֵׂה תוֹרָתְךָ קֶבַע, אֱמוֹר מְעַט וַעֲשֵׂה הַרְבֵּה, וֶהֱוֵי מְקַבֵּל אֶת כָּל הָאָדָם בְּסֵבֶר פָּנִים יָפוֹת, *Make your Torah study a fixed practice, say little and do much, and receive every person with a cheerful face*, the *Bartenura* writes:

> The three teachings that Shammai advises correspond to three attributes that Jeremiah lauds: the wise, the strong and the rich. To the wise he says, "Make your Torah study a fixed practice"; to the rich he says, "say little and do much"; and in reference to the strong — "receive everyone with a cheerful face," so that he should conquer his evil inclination and fight against his evil heart. As we learned,

אֵיזֶהוּ גִבּוֹר? הַכּוֹבֵשׁ אֶת יִצְרוֹ, *Who is the strong? The one who conquers his inclination* (*Avos* 4:1).

Accordingly, receiving everyone with a benevolent countenance requires overcoming the evil inclination. Clearly, this battle against the evil inclination does not exist among friends and relatives who truly love each other. One is all too happy to welcome their beloved with a cheerful face and a bright smile. The battle with one's natural inclinations only arises when meeting strangers and — even more so — adversaries.

The Mishnah directs us to "receive everyone" with a congenial face, including those whom we prefer not to encounter, even if doing so requires an inner battle.

⊷§ Deafening Silence

A young newlywed arrived home in the evenings after a long day of Torah study in the kollel. He would exchange very few words with his wife as he ate dinner, and would return promptly to his studies until the late hours of the night. Feeling extremely lonely and despondent, the young wife went to the saintly R' Yosef Chaim Sonnenfeld *zt"l* of Jerusalem, and told him of her distress, complaining that her husband hardly talked to her. The Rabbi promised that he will speak to her husband and hopefully will be able to rectify the situation.

The following morning the Rabbi sent someone to the young husband, requesting that he come to his home that afternoon. Very excited and honored by this invitation, the young man was overcome with anticipation, and counted the minutes until the appointed time. As he arrived at the Rabbi's home, and was escorted to his study, he stood in exalted awe in front of the Rabbi waiting to hear why he had been summoned. The Rabbi sat and continued his study without uttering a single word to this young scholar.

As the endless moments passed in silence, the young man's anxiety increased, until he could no longer restrain himself. After more than half an hour of waiting, the young scholar summoned all of his courage, and with a trembling voice he asked the Rabbi what and how he can help. The Rabbi responded softly, "I just wanted you to experience what your wife feels when you come home and do not talk to her."

◆§ The Smiling Face of Hashem

The value of a smiling face is emphasized in the priestly blessing, יָאֵר ה׳ פָּנָיו אֵלֶיךָ, *May Hashem illuminate His countenance toward you* (*Bamidbar* 6:25). *Rashi* interprets this verse as, "May He show you a smiling face," implying that the ineffable and invisible G-d can show us a smiling face or, heaven forbid, an angry face, and the *Kohanim* bless us that He will show us a smiling face.

The smiling face of the Creator ensures the survival of the world, and is manifest in the timely gift of dew and rain, as *Rashi* explains the term in *Tehillim* (67:2), יָאֵר פָּנָיו אִתָּנוּ, *May He illuminate His countenance with us.* The smiling face of the Almighty manifests itself in rain that arrives in the right season, in the required amounts and without damaging storms, all of which ensure that there will be no drought and famine.

As indicated earlier, the way of Hashem is "measure for measure" and He deals with us as we deal with our fellow man. Therefore, to merit the benevolent countenance of the Creator of the world, it is incumbent upon us to do so with our fellow man. Apart from all the goodness that flows to other human beings from a bright countenance and a cheerful face, the whole world will enjoy the benefits of blessed rain elicited by greeting every person with a shining countenance and a kindly word.

Afterword

⊷ Yes, We Can ... Yes, We Should

As the reader may have surmised, the unifying thesis that runs through all the chapters of this book is that the Divine Presence is to be found in all aspects of our lives. G-d permeates every nook and cranny of our space, so we must be conscious of His Presence and serve Him in every act of our daily lives: in the sacred and the mundane, in the synagogue and the workplace, in our prayer and in our family routines.

As we awake with *Modeh Ani,* aware of a restored soul and the gift of a new day, as we bid "good morning" to our children, and nod a greeting to the neighbor — as we recite the morning prayers, and later eat breakfast — in each minor act of our daily routine at home and at work, and with every face we see, we can walk hand in hand with G-d.

The division of mitzvos into categories — differentiating those that bind us to our Creator from those that connect us to other human beings — may be useful intellectually, but such distinctions can be dangerous when used to prioritize. The Torah insists that dividing between commandments that appear religious and ritualistic and those that seem to be social and ethical is tantamount to dissecting an organism whose very life depends on the harmonious unity of its parts. Both categories of mitzvos were given at Sinai, and both are compelling by virtue of their Divine origin. Consequently, honoring one's parents and keeping the Sabbath day holy must both be observed in accordance with halachah, and whether or not they make equal sense to our limited minds.

The purpose of this book is to highlight the inseparability between our interpersonal behavior and our relationship with the Divine. David HaMelech (*Tehillim* 16:8) guides the Jew to see G-d's Presence at all times, and to understand that love and reverence of G-d must find expression in every aspect of his life: שִׁוִּיתִי ה׳ לְנֶגְדִּי תָמִיד. A believing Jew perceives G-d's Presence before him at all times and in all places, and recognizes that the warmth of a smile to a neighbor pleases his Creator no less than intentional prayer; eating kosher food is not more important than honest business dealings and congenial deference to the needs of others. Proper interactions with others provide us with the opportunity to please and serve the Creator every minute of the day.

Finally, the purpose of this book is not to admonish but to awaken, in firm belief that human beings have the capacity to master and refine their behavior, polishing and uplifting their characters — and in so doing, they can transform themselves and the world.